Sensation, Perception, and the Aging Process
Part II

Professor Francis B. Colavita

THE TEACHING COMPANY ®

PUBLISHED BY:

THE TEACHING COMPANY
4840 Westfields Boulevard, Suite 500
Chantilly, Virginia 20151-2299
1-800-TEACH-12
Fax—703-378-3819
www.teach12.com

ISBN 1-59803-230-5

Francis B. Colavita, Ph.D.

Emeritus Associate Professor of Psychology, University of Pittsburgh

Francis B. Colavita is an Emeritus Associate Professor of Psychology at the University of Pittsburgh, having recently retired after 39 years as a faculty member. Dr. Colavita served as Psychology Department Chairman from 1980 to 1988. He has received five awards for teaching excellence, including the Chancellor's Distinguished Teaching Award in 1997. This is the highest award for teaching excellence bestowed by the University of Pittsburgh. Dr. Colavita was selected to participate as a faculty member on the fall 2000 voyage of the Semester at Sea Program and was chosen to serve as academic dean on the summer 2003 Semester at Sea voyage.

Dr. Colavita attended the University of Maryland on an athletic scholarship, graduating with a B.A. in Experimental Psychology in 1961. He received his Ph.D. in Physiological Psychology from the University of Indiana in 1964. He then completed a two-year U.S. Public Health Service Postdoctoral Research Fellowship at the Center for Neural Sciences before accepting an assistant professorship at the University of Pittsburgh in 1966. In addition to his affiliation with the University of Pittsburgh, Dr. Colavita also holds an adjunct faculty position at Florida Atlantic University.

Dr. Colavita's 30 published scholarly articles are in the areas of sensory processes, perception, and recovery of function following brain damage. His book, *Sensory Changes in the Elderly*, was published in 1978. In addition to his academic pursuits, Dr. Colavita is a licensed psychologist who has maintained a small clinical practice in neuropsychology for the past 20 years, specializing in the assessment of perceptual and cognitive deficits in individuals with head injuries and/or learning disabilities.

Table of Contents
Sensation, Perception, and the Aging Process
Part II

Sensation, Perception, and the Aging Process

Scope:

The 24 lectures in this course are taught from the perspective of academic psychology. Thus, a recurring concern throughout the course is the understanding of human behavior. Behavior does not occur randomly or haphazardly. Behavior has reasons. It happens in response to some detectable stimulus event that has taken place in our internal environment (for example, a thought or memory) or our external environment (for example, a sight or sound). A complete understanding of some behavior requires that we identify the stimulus that elicited that behavior. For instance, we cannot understand the behavior of a sleeping house cat that suddenly wakes up and runs to the back door unless we somehow discover that mice on the back porch are vocalizing in the ultrasonic range, which is well beyond the frequency range of the human ear but not that of the feline ear. Once we identify the stimulus, we understand the cat's behavior.

As alluded to above, one of the primary goals of psychology is understanding behavior. Accordingly, since its inception around 1910, behavioristic psychology has had a strong interest in the study of sensory processes. A major determinant of behavior is the information from the environment sent to our brain by our various sensory systems. Because the sensory systems of different animal species have different sensitivity characteristics, different species may live in the same physical space, but they live in very different "sensory worlds." We may define the sensory world as that part of the physical world accessible to our sensory receptors. The honeybee can see ultraviolet light; humans cannot. Humans can see the colors of the rainbow; cats cannot. Cats can hear ultrasonic frequencies; humans cannot. It is clear that some of the behavioral differences between different species can be better understood by having knowledge of the sensory capacities of these different species. You can fool your spouse with a good Halloween costume, but you cannot fool the family dog once it gets downwind of you. This is because the olfactory sensitivity of the dog is many times greater than that of the human.

It is true, as far as it goes, to say that behavior occurs in response to some detectable stimulus. However, it is more precise to say that behavior is the result, not just of one's sensations, but of one's perceptions. Simply put, a perception is a sensory event along with the meaning that the sensory event has acquired because of a particular organism's previous experience with that or a similar sensory event. As an example of the difference between a sensation, which may be relatively devoid of meaning, and a perception, which may be charged with meaning, consider the following: Two dogs hear a short, 1,000-cycle-per-second tone. One dog orients toward the tone briefly, then quickly loses interest. The second dog begins to wag its tail and salivate at the sound of the tone, showing obvious excitement. The behavioral differences between these dogs make more sense if we are told that the year is 1900 and that the latter animal has spent time as a subject in the classical conditioning laboratory of Dr. Ivan P. Pavlov. The meaning that the tone has acquired for this animal, namely, that dried meat powder is about to be blown into its mouth, is an example of a perception. To employ a human example of the difference between a sensation and a perception, imagine the following hypothetical situation: Two people are standing in a crowd in Vatican Square, one a devout Catholic who lives in Rome and the other an Asian tourist who knows nothing of Catholicism or its rituals. Suddenly a puff of white smoke is emitted from the upper level of the Sistine Chapel. The meaning that this visual stimulus will have for these two individuals is the difference between a sensation and a perception. We see that for different dogs or humans or what have you, the same sensory events can and do acquire different meanings, leading to different perceptions. Thus, it is not simply our sensory world that determines our behavior but our "perceptual world," which is determined by our unique life experiences.

This course describes how our sensory systems respond to the energy from our physical environment and how, based upon our past experience with a particular sensory event, the brain creates the perceptions that determine our behavior. Another important component of the course is a consideration of the way the aging process influences both our sensations and our perceptions. Unavoidable changes occur in the sensitivity and acuity of our sensory systems as we age, resulting in young people and older people actually living in different sensory worlds. It is also the case that young people and old people have generally had different life experiences, which is how stimuli acquire meaning and result in our perceptions. The aging process has implications for one's sensory world and one's perceptual world. The first 12 lectures in this course will expand on the difference between a sensation and a perception and elaborate on the concept of the perceptual world. The functioning of the visual, auditory, and cutaneous systems, and the changes in functioning associated with the aging process, will also be discussed in these 12 lectures. The last 12 lectures will deal with the senses of pain, taste, smell, vestibulation, and kinesthesis. Special categories of human perception, such as speech perception, face recognition, and person perception, will also be addressed. As in the initial 12 lectures, attention will be paid to the role of the aging process. All lectures are presented at a level that does not presume previous coursework in sensory processes.

Lecture Thirteen
Pain—Early History

Scope:

Until the early 1900s, there was some question as to whether pain existed as a separate sense or whether it was simply the result of overstimulation of one of the other senses. The confusion arose because the receptors for pain, free nerve endings, are the most primitive receptors in the body. They are equally responsive to a wide array of energy forms, rather than having specialized in the detection of a single energy form, as have the receptors of all our other sensory systems. Pain is frequently thought of as simple, direct (that is, proportional to the amount of tissue damage), and necessary. It may be necessary (as a warning system), but it is neither simple nor proportional to tissue damage.

Although we learn more about pain year by year, many aspects remain a puzzle. For instance, what is the difference between "good pain" and "bad pain"? Also, pain perception can be influenced by cultural conditioning, attentional factors, expectation, and the meaning we attach to the stimulus. Questions remain regarding the phenomenon of the placebo effect, whereby an inert substance can significantly reduce pain magnitude if one believes that it can. Another pain-related issue suggesting that pain is not so simple is the phenomenon of acupuncture. Acupuncture has been used in China as a component of traditional Chinese medicine (TCM) for at least 5,000 years, yet Western science has acknowledged its existence only in the last 35 years. Does acupuncture alleviate pain, and if it does, what is the mechanism? These questions and others are raised in this lecture. The answers will be provided in Lecture Fourteen.

Outline

I. As recently as 100 years ago, some scientists questioned whether pain was actually a separate sense or whether it was simply overstimulation of one of the other senses.

    A. The confusion arose because free nerve endings, which serve as pain receptors, are the most primitive of the body's receptors.

1. Most receptors have evolved with a sensitivity to a single form of energy, such as light, sound, taste, or smell.
2. Free nerve endings have no "preferred" mode of stimulation, being equally responsive to chemicals, pressure, extremes of temperature, tissue damage, electricity, or radiant energy.
3. Free nerve endings also respond to the standard categories of cutaneous stimuli, although with less precision than the encapsulated end organs.

B. Pain also differs from the other senses in that pain has both sensory and drive-like qualities.
1. It is not possible to concentrate on anything else when, for instance, you are experiencing a severe toothache, a migraine headache, or kidney stones.
2. Some pain medications and surgical procedures do not abolish pain but provide relief by reducing pain's drive-like properties.

II. Even after pain was identified as being more than overstimulation of some other sense, scientists continued to erroneously view pain as simple, direct, and necessary. This characterization turned out to be inaccurate.

A. Pain is unquestionably necessary. People with no pain sensitivity exist, and they are at great risk of injury. Pain provides us with important warning signals that permit us to avoid injuries.
1. Such individuals tend to die young because they do not suffer the effects of pain and, therefore, are often risk-takers.
2. Such children have bitten off their tongues or one of their fingers with no feeling of pain.
3. Another such individual developed infected blisters on his feet from wearing improperly sized shoes with no discomfort.
4. Barefoot individuals with a congenital indifference to pain have inadvertently walked through broken glass or live campfire embers.

B. Pain has a signaling function, but problems arise when the pain continues after we get the signal. That is considered "bad pain."

1. Endurance athletes make the distinction between "good pain" and "bad pain."
2. The "good pain" might provide them with information about their level of performance.

C. Although pain may be necessary, it is certainly not simple and direct.
  1. The degree of attention we pay to a stimulus contributes significantly to whether or not we experience it as painful.
  2. The meaning we attribute to a stimulus contributes significantly to how painful we perceive that stimulus to be.
  3. If we expect something to be painful, it is more likely to be experienced as painful.

III. The existence of the *placebo effect* (the situation in which an inert substance can have analgesic properties if one believes it is a true analgesic) indicates that pain is far from simple.

A. A placebo treatment can be expected to be effective in approximately 35 percent of people treated with it. This is why clinical trials with new drugs include a placebo group.

B. Some physicians believe that the use of a placebo treatment is appropriate to help relieve the discomfort of a patient with hypochondriacal tendencies. Other physicians believe there is an ethical issue here, in that some deception of the patient is involved.

IV. Cultural factors influence pain.

A. An experience perceived as painful in one culture may have no such connotation in another.

B. Examples of such experiences include intentional decorative scarring of the face, childbirth, or boxing.

V. Another puzzle about pain involves the efficacy of acupuncture anesthesia.

A. Does acupuncture reduce or eliminate pain?

B. If acupuncture works, what is the mechanism by which it produces analgesia?

C. Acupuncture has existed for at least 5,000 years. Why has Western science paid attention to this phenomenon only for the past few decades?

Suggested Reading:

Goldstein, *Sensation and Perception* (6th ed.), pp. 460–466.

Questions to Consider:

1. If a medical procedure existed to eliminate pain but left the other cutaneous sensations intact, would you opt for it? If so, why? If not, why not?

2. People frequently speak of "emotional pain." Do you feel that this is an appropriate use of the word *pain*?

Lecture Thirteen—Transcript
Pain—Early History

Hi. In our last lecture, Lecture Twelve, we talked about some of the aspects of the aging process and changes in cutaneous sensitivity. We talked about the concerns of some cultural anthropologists that Americans are a non-tactile society. We talked about the distinction between active touch and passive touch, and we are now ready to begin our discussion of the sense of pain.

In this lecture I will be talking about some of the historical aspects of research into pain, and we will continue into more modern findings in a lecture to come. First of all, let me warn you that there are subjective elements involved in talking about pain or studying pain. In other words, you cannot feel somebody else's pain, and it's not the kind of thing that we can have group consensus on. If I hold up a red square, and I say, "What color is that?" everybody says, "Red," and we can all agree on a 1,000 cycle-per-second tone, but how can we agree on pain when each person's pain is unique and individual to them?

I remember once—I was single at the time—having a romantic relationship relationship with this woman that involved a candlelight dinner, and as she was reaching across the table to take my hand, she jogged the candle. Some melting candle wax fell on her hand, and she started screaming and moaning, and she ran to the ladies' room to wash her hand. I felt very bad, and I wanted to be able to empathize with her, so I reached over and I took a candle and dripped some hot candle wax on my hand. I hardly felt it. Now, I came to the conclusion that we cannot judge another person's pain. She was serious, and she was sincere in feeling that that was very painful.

So we need to keep that in mind. When we talk about pain, it may mean different things to different people. Different people may have different pain thresholds or different definitions of pain or different tolerance for pain.

Okay, with that caveat, let's begin talking about pain. The first thing I will share with you is that up until about 100 years ago, people weren't even sure that there was such a thing as pain. Now, that may sound bizarre, but what I mean by that is researchers were not convinced that there was a separate pain sense. They thought that possibly pain represented over-stimulation of one of the other sensory systems, so that when light gets too bright, it becomes painful. When sound gets too loud, it becomes painful. When touch gets too intense, it becomes painful. When heat gets too hot, it becomes painful. This was proposed as an alternative to pain being a separate sense with its own receptors and pathways.

More recently, we have discovered that, indeed, pain does represent an entity unto itself, that it's not simply over-stimulation of the existing sensory systems. What caused this confusion? The confusion came about because pain receptors are the most primitive receptors in the body. People couldn't conceive of a receptor that could respond equally to bee venom or a knife cut or hot water or being stuck with a pin or having acetic acid spilled on your hand, because no other receptors in any other sensory system are so broad-spectrum in the things they will respond to.

The visual receptors respond to 400–700 nm of electromagnetic radiation; the auditory receptors to 20–20,000 vibrations; smell to gaseous, odorous molecules; taste to things that go into solution in saliva; but pain? Pain receptors will respond to virtually anything, and it took a while for people to realize that these primitive receptors were, in fact, involved in a separate sense modality—the modality of pain. Okay, so yes, pain is a separate sense and it does have its own receptors, primitive though they may be, and actually the nerve fibers that carry pain messages to the brain are also primitive, and we'll talk more about that in a bit.

Let's talk about some of the characteristics of pain. Another difference between pain and the other sense modalities is that pain has both sensory qualities and drive-like qualities. In other words, if you have a toothache, you can point exactly to which tooth aches. You can localize where the sensory sensations are coming from. Or if you have a blister that's hurting, you can point right to the blister—you can localize it—but pain also has the property of being able to distract us from doing anything else until we deal with the pain.

If you have a migraine headache, it's silly to try and get some work done. If you have kidney stones, you can't even conceive of getting on with daily life. And if you have a toothache, it's pretty hard to concentrate on the daily tasks at hand. This drive-like quality of pain propels you to focus on the pain and deal with it. Now, why does pain have this drive-like quality? It's because pain pathways go to the midbrain, which is concerned with, remember, level of arousal, so pain has direct pathways to the centers of the brain that cause us to be aroused, and pain pathways also go to the limbic system, which has motivational significance.

None of the other senses is able, as efficiently, to arouse us and motivate us. You can't feel that way over a red color or a tone or a smell or a taste. Pain has special connections with—I guess you would call them—more primitive parts of the brain that can just activate us and cause us grief until we deal with the pain.

It has been demonstrated, in fact, well—let me share with you a story I heard from a clinical colleague of mine who is now deceased. He was about 25 years older than I. As a young clinician, part of his training involved interviewing cancer patients who had developed such a tolerance to morphine that they were in chronic pain and had opted to undergo a lobotomy, because it seemed that people who underwent a lobotomy stopped feeling pain.

So sometimes a patient in desperation would agree to undergo a frontal lobotomy, and my clinical colleague used to go around and interview these people and collect what data he could get from them. He shared with me the story about talking to a terminal cancer patient who had been in intense pain and developed a tolerance to morphine who, in desperation, agreed to undergo a frontal lobotomy. My clinical friend said, "It must be better for you now that the pain has gone away." The patient said, "What are you talking about?" And my clinical friend said, "Well, the pain, the pain that you used to have, and now it's gone." The patient responded, "The pain isn't gone." My clinical friend was puzzled, and he said, "Well, you used to moan and groan all the time, and now you seem to be perfectly relaxed and content." And the man said, "The pain is still there as bad as ever. I just don't care any more." Somehow the lobotomy had taken away that drive-like quality of the pain, but the sensory aspects were still intact. Some drugs, some pain medications, operate not on the pain directly, but on the motivational aspects of pain.

People typically think of pain as being simple and direct and necessary. Now, what do they mean by "simple and direct"? Well, by "simple and direct" they mean that pain is usually the result of tissue damage, and the amount of pain is directly proportional to the amount of tissue damage. We'll deal with that belief about pain shortly.

Let me deal with the other belief that pain is "necessary," because we can answer that one in the affirmative. Yes, pain is necessary. On what basis do we say that, that "pain is necessary"? Pain seems to cause so much misery, how can we say it's necessary? Well, for one thing, we have had the opportunity to investigate and to study and follow the lives of people who are born with a congenital indifference to pain. There are people who feel no pain. Is that a blessing? Not necessarily; for one thing, people born with no ability to perceive pain tend to die young. Why is this? Well, there are probably several different reasons for this. For one thing, these people tend to develop a kind of personality that increases the likelihood that they will take dares and challenges and do crazy things that you really shouldn't do, because if they mess up, it doesn't hurt them. So they develop a personality where they actually view other people as being kind of sissified and not very bold and daring. That probably contributes to the fact that people with no pain sensitivity die young.

It's also the case that pain, whether we like it or not, is providing us with information, important information, and these people are lacking that information. As a result of lacking pain information these people put themselves in harm's way in a number of different circumstances. For instance, there was a woman who actually died of a spinal infection. She had no pain sensitivity, and it turned out that she was unable to feel the muscle and joint aches that propel most of us to change our posture when we're asleep at night. We shift our position in bed over the course of a night many times. Time-lapse photography has documented this. This woman never changed her position, and so these internal issues that should have signaled to her that something was wrong never became conscious to her, and she actually died from this.

There are instances of children born with no sense of pain, who have chewed their tongues off because they felt no pain; who have chewed their fingers off, because they felt no pain. This seems too bizarre to be true, but it is, indeed, true. There was another case of a fellow who had serious gangrene that was threatening to require amputation of his leg. What happened was, he was wearing ill-fitting shoes, and he had developed blisters on his feet, but because he couldn't feel the pain from the blisters, he never bothered to buy shoes that fit properly, and these blisters became infected and, in fact, turned into a gangrenous condition.

Here are just a couple of other examples that involve situations where people might be walking barefoot, at the beach for example. People with a congenital indifference to pain have been known to—now they wouldn't do this on purpose, of course, but they're not paying attention—walk through broken glass and badly cut their feet, or end up with an incredibly severe sunburn, and feel no discomfort, so they don't take any action to protect themselves. In one case, a young man actually walked barefoot through the live embers of a little campfire that somebody had built on the beach, severely burned his feet, and never even noticed it. Somebody said, "Hey, what's that cooking?" It happened that it was his feet that were cooking from walking through these burning embers.

So, is pain necessary? It certainly appears to be necessary. Now, the problem is, as I said, pain has a signaling function. Where we run into problems is sometimes even after you have received the message, the pain continues. This is what we might call bad pain. I mean, how often do you need to be reminded by pain, that, "Yes, I've severely burned my arm," and yet the pain keeps coming. Or, "Yes, I have cancer, and it hurts," yet the pain keeps coming. Or, "Yes I have shingles," or whatever. So when we're dealing with a situation where the message has been delivered and we know we have a problem, it would be nice if we could turn the pain off, and have it go away.

It doesn't work that way, however, and in those cases, people need to seek medical help, either drugs or meditational techniques, or whatever works for them, because, yes, we need pain, but we don't need that much pain after the message has been delivered.

On the other hand, some pain might actually be labeled as good pain. Good pain is pain that we actively seek, because it's providing us important information. Let me give you just a few examples. Weightlifters and bodybuilders use the expression "no pain, no gain." They are actually seeking a level of pain. They are attempting to use that level of pain to tell them that they have worked out sufficiently hard that they have broken down the individual muscle fibers. When those muscle fibers reconstitute, they will be bigger and thicker and bulkier, which is what the weightlifters are looking for.

Endurance athletes, marathon runners, long-distance swimmers, and bicyclists seek—they actively seek—a level of pain that's telling them they are performing at an optimal level. So when you're doing it right, it hurts—if you're running a marathon or biking or swimming or even mountain climbing. So, what they do is they attempt to maintain that level of physical discomfort—which would probably be perceived as very, very painful by most of us—because it's providing them important information about their level of performance.

Okay, so I'm going to summarize the above by saying, "Yes, pain seems to be necessary," and it's also the case that if you choose to do so, you may label some pain "good pain" and some pain "bad pain."

Now, let's deal with the other belief that people have about pain—that it is simple and direct. Here I share with you an unequivocal "no." It is far from simple and direct. Pain is highly complicated, and we're still beginning to unravel what some people call, "the puzzle of pain." How can something be simple if it can be modified by the degree of attention you're paying to a stimulus, and in fact, that's quite true. If you're not paying attention to something, it doesn't hurt anywhere near as much as if you're looking at it. Why should that be the case if it is the degree of tissue damage that determines pain rather than whether you're paying attention to it or not?

Let me give you some examples. Basketball players have been known to badly sprain an ankle and not even be aware of it until the first time-out is called, and "Hey, that really hurts." When they're not paying attention to it, they're not aware of it.

I'll share another childhood story with you. I wasn't really that bad of a kid. I did sneak under the hootchy-kootchy tent, and I did go on a pineapple-stealing foray with a friend of mine. We lived close to a pineapple farm, and one day we thought it would be fun to go steal a pineapple. So we sneaked over and we didn't see the farmer and we grabbed a pineapple and off we ran. The farmer spotted us and began chasing us, and we ran and we ran and we ran. We were beginning to outrun the farmer and we jumped off a little hill. My friend landed on a big metal stake in the ground that gashed his calf to the muscle, but we don't know it at the time, because we were running. When we finally outran the farmer, we were elated, and we were going to sit down and eat our pineapples, then the kid looked at his leg, and he fell down in pain. He wasn't even aware of this massive gash while we were evading the farmer. So the degree of attention that you pay to a stimulus is an obvious factor in whether you'll perceive that pain or not.

One more example—in my laboratory, in my early days as an animal researcher, we would perform surgery on experimental animals. We didn't want them to become infected, so we treated them with antibiotics. I used to use penicillin in an oil base. It's thicker than in a water base, but it is absorbed more slowly, so you can give the animal one shot every few days instead of a shot a day. It used to take three of us to give a cat an injection because, of course, they don't like injections. So one would hold the cat by the back of the neck, and one would pull its feet down, and the other one would find the right quadrant in the flank and administer the injection.

I was in the laboratory one day when the university vet came to check on the sanitary conditions and the care of the animals, and he said, "What's going on?" I said, "Well, I'm waiting for two people to come in so we can give this cat an injection." He said, "It takes three of you to give a cat an injection?" I said, "Yes, it does." He said, "Watch this." He took the syringe with the oil-based penicillin in it and he said, "Which cat?" I said, "That one." He went over and he grabbed the cat by the scruff of the neck. He eyeballed the flank to see where he wanted to administer the shot and he looked right in the cat's face, He had the needle all set and he blew in the cat's face, "Ffffft!" While the cat did that—"Ffffft!"—he gave the cat the shot, pulled the needle out, and after the fact, the cat looked around as if to say, "Hey, what's going on?" While he was having his face blown into and his attention was directed there, the cat didn't seem to pay any attention to the shot.

So, yes, attention is a factor. Does that sound like a system that is simple and direct—that the meaning that attribute to a painful stimulus will determine how painful? An anesthesiologist by the name of Beecher wrote a book about his experiences on the battlefield in World War II. He reported that sometimes a soldier would be shot in the arm or the leg or the foot or something like that, and when he went to administer an anesthetic, the soldier would actually be elated and actually complain that the needle hurt when he had a big hole in his leg. They viewed this wound, which was a non-life-threatening wound, as a ticket out of the war. The meaning of that wound for them was, "Hey, I'm probably not going to get killed because I'm getting out of here now."

So the meaning we attribute to a stimulus will significantly determine the degree to which we perceive it as painful or not painful or even notice it at all. The fact is that Ivan Pavlov knew that a hundred and something years ago. Pavlov is well known for conditioning dogs to salivate when they heard a tone, but he also conditioned them to salivate and wag their tails when they were touched on the flank. So Pavlov would touch the dog and give it meat powder, touch the dog and give it meat powder. Pretty soon it was salivating when he touched it on the flank. Then Pavlov would up the ante. He would poke the dog with his finger and give it meat powder. Poke, meat powder. Then he would poke it with a dull pencil—poke, meat powder; poke, meat powder. Eventually Pavlov, through this slow process of successive approximations, he could poke the dog with a hatpin deep enough to draw blood, and the dog would salivate and wag its tail. Through classical conditioning, he had changed the meaning of that poke from "ouch, pain, hurt," to "Hey, meat powder is about to be given to me," and the dogs wagged their tails and salivated.

Your expectation in a situation will also determine whether you perceive it as painful or not. Dentists know this. When they're about to give you a Novocain shot or whatever, dentists now say, "You're going to feel a little pinch." Now, they're putting the thought in your mind that you're going to feel a little pinch, not a massive pain, when they poke you with this big needle. In fact, the dentist who tells you, "You're going to feel a little pinch," is less likely to elicit a major startle reaction than one who says nothing. And in fact, the dentist who tells you, "You're going to feel a little pinch," is less likely to get a major startle reaction than somebody who is told nothing, because then you are free to interpret this as a painful stimulus.

Another piece of evidence suggesting that pain is neither simple nor direct is the phenomenon known as the placebo effect. Most people have heard of this, but let me give you a quick and simple definition. The placebo effect is demonstrated when "an inert substance seems to have the ability to reduce pain." The first historical documented instance of a placebo effect on a large scale took place back in 1941 in Boston when a nightclub fire broke out—the very well known Coconut Grove Fire. There was a big, wooden building that was overcrowded, and some of the exits were blocked. The building went up and many people were burned and some died, and the ones who didn't die suffered from painful burns. All of the available medical personnel in the city converged on the Coconut Grove scene, and they started administering morphine to the burn victims. Some of these health professionals ran out of morphine, and they leveled with the patient, and they said, "Listen, I'm sorry, we're out of morphine, but more is on the way. Just try and take it easy and take deep breaths." Others of them deceived the burn victims, and gave them injections of distilled water, and told them it was morphine. Thirty-five percent of the people who had shots of distilled water felt their pain alleviated. "Ah, thank you, that feels much better." Okay. That's an example of the placebo effect.

Now, the thing about the placebo effect is that it only works if you believe it's going to work. Let me share with you an example of what turned out to be the placebo effect that didn't work. In the late 1950s, a belief had somehow sprung up in the dental profession that if you have a patient listen to white noise over earphones, you could do dental procedures without needing an anesthetic—you could drill, you could perform extractions, and minor oral surgery. What you did was to put headphones on the patient and gave the patient access to a knob and say to the patient, "This is going to prevent pain. If you start feeling anything, simply make the noise louder."

Some people who avoided the dentist because of a fear of injections thought this was wonderful; they tried it, and it seemed to work. Then people that weren't so sure tried it, and it didn't work, and pretty soon it stopped working for anybody. Now, I know about audioanalgesia because when I was started my laboratory, I needed electronic equipment, and I bought it from a company called Novasonics Corporation, which built dental consoles—with microphones, with earphones, a white-noise generator and what have you. They went out of business when audio analgesics stopped working for anybody, and I was able to buy some very nice equipment to stock my laboratory. So, yes, the placebo effect works if you believe it's going to work.

One more, quick thing about the placebo effect—it was a point of controversy in the medical profession. At an APA Conference some time ago, doctors apparently disagreed significantly about whether the placebo effect should be used in medicine or not, with some doctors saying, "You know, my job is to make my patient feel better. If I know this person is a hypochondriac, what's the harm in saying, 'Here's a pill that's going to make you feel better,' and they feel better?" Other doctors would say, "That's unethical because it's deceiving the patient." The fact is that this issue was never resolved. There are still situations where a doctor might resort to a little deception if he or she knows the patient very well, and knows that this is likely to improve his or her quality of life. That's an issue that I guess is still unresolved.

All right—back to this notion of pain not being simple and direct. Let me share with you some data provided by cultural anthropologists about different responses to pain in different societies. Different cultures would appear to have different levels of tolerance for pain. By the way, that's not true. If you take people from any culture in the world into a laboratory and measure their pain sensitivity, it's the same. So there's something else going on here.

I was first made aware of cultural differences in the reactions to pain when I was a graduate student. I met a foreign graduate student from Africa, who I came to know well enough to ask him about his tribal scars. I made some inane remark about "How many people did it take to hold you down while they…" And he was puzzled, because those tribal scars didn't mean pain to him at all. To him it meant full acceptance and responsibility in the society and manhood and things of that nature. He didn't think of it as pain at all.

In some cultures there is absolutely no connotation of pain regarding childbirth. In some societies, such as our own, we think of childbirth in the context of being some really painful thing, and in other societies, they would shake their heads. They would be puzzled by this attitude.

Perhaps the most dramatic cultural difference in pain sensitivity or reactions to what should be a painful stimulus was something I heard about in a visit to India in the year 2000. I heard about a ceremony that takes place in rural farming villages, not all over India. One man in the society is chosen—and apparently, it's somewhat of an honor to be chosen—to be the representative of the gods. What they do is, with no anesthetic, they take big, sharp steel hooks, and they embed them in this fellow's back under the skin and under the back muscles, such that when these hooks are tied to ropes, he can actually be lifted off the ground by these hooks embedded in his back. Then the top of the ropes are tied to a frame over a horse-drawn cart, and this fellow is taken from village to village suspended by these hooks in his back. When he comes to a village, he blesses the children and he blesses the crops, and then he's taken on to another village. This goes on all day; and at the end of the day, the hooks are taken out, with apparently no ill effects on the part of the gentleman who was suspended that way all day. The wounds are treated with wood ash, and they apparently heal quickly, with very little in the way of scarring.

The business of cultural differences in sensitivity to pain and what have you has an analogue with a subculture in our own country—that is, professional boxers. These people—and I've seen 100s of interviews with boxers—never refer to pain. They never talk about it, and you have the impression that the idea of associating pain with what they do for a living is foreign to them. What seems to be in all the cases—the man with the hooks or the tribal scars or the boxers or whatever—is attitude and acceptance. In all cases, these people have agreed to put themselves in this situation so they have a positive attitude toward it, and they are accepting of the fact that things are going to happen to them that might not be the most pleasant, but you never hear them talk about boxing or this hook ceremony or the tribal scars in the context of it being a painful stimulus.

I will mention one more phenomenon that again demonstrates that pain is not simple and direct, but indeed incredibly puzzling, and that phenomenon is acupuncture, acupuncture anesthesia. Now, most people have several predictable questions about acupuncture. Does acupuncture really work to reduce pain? If it does reduce pain, how does it do this? Does acupuncture work for animals? If acupuncture has actually been around for 5,000 years, why have we only recently heard about it in the United States? Another question that might be asked is, does acupuncture only work in treating pain, or will it cure diseases?

Now, I will tell you right now that my discussion with you of acupuncture is going to be restricted to the anesthetic properties of acupuncture, because at the present time, Western science and Western medicine are willing to acknowledge—although it took quite a while for them to do that—that acupuncture does have merit as an anesthetic agent. Western science, at the present time, has no official opinion on whether or not acupuncture has curative properties because some of the claims of acupuncture practitioners are that it can cure impotence and blindness and it can cure memory ailments and these kinds of things. Western science is unwilling to express an opinion on those claims.

So in our next lecture I will answer some of those questions. Does acupuncture work? Why do we think it works? Does it work in animals, and why have we just begun to hear about acupuncture when it's been around for over five centuries? Thank you.

Lecture Fourteen
Pain—Acupuncture, Endorphins, and Aging

Scope:

Western medicine was unable to acknowledge the existence, let alone the effectiveness, of acupuncture anesthesia because the Chinese explanation for acupuncture involved the balance and flow of an invisible, unmeasurable life force, *Qi* (pronounced "chee"), and Western science was used to dealing with phenomena that are public and measurable. The gate-control theory of pain proposed by Canadian researchers Ronald Melzack and Patrick Wall in 1965 suggested a mechanism for the effectiveness of acupuncture that was visible and measurable, thereby permitting Western science to talk about and study acupuncture. This set the stage for Western medicine to eventually accept acupuncture as effective.

An interesting scientific event that relates to pain and to acupuncture was the discovery of the endorphins in the mid-1970s. Endorphins are morphine-like substances produced in the brain and released in response to pain. There is some evidence that at least some of the analgesic effects of acupuncture are due to the fact that stimulation of some acupuncture sites causes the release of endorphins. Further, the release of endorphins has been implicated in the effectiveness of the placebo effect. Pretreatment of human subjects with naloxone, an opiate antagonist, reduces or abolishes the placebo effect for pain.

The question of the aging process and pain perception turns out to be somewhat complicated. We must first differentiate between superficial (*bright*) pain and deep (*dull*) pain. Data suggest that as we age, we become less sensitive to superficial pain and more sensitive to deep pain.

Outline

I.   Acupuncture has been a part of TCM for more than 5,000 years, yet most Westerners had never heard of it until the early 1970s.

    A.   James Reston, an American journalist in China in connection with President Nixon's 1972 visit, was treated with acupuncture in a Chinese hospital. This event marked the beginning of interest in alternative medicine in the United States.

B. Western science continued to ignore acupuncture because the Chinese explanation did not meet the criteria for Western science.

    1. Acupuncture was thought by Chinese practitioners to unblock the flow of an invisible, unmeasurable life force known as *Qi*.

    2. Qi was supposed to flow through 12 meridians in the human body, but those meridians could not be found by Western anatomists.

II. Shortly before this time, a theory of pain had been proposed by two Western scientists, Ronald Melzack and Patrick Wall. Although not directly addressing acupuncture, this theory, the *gate-control theory*, suggested a possible mechanism for the efficacy of acupuncture anesthesia that was compatible with known anatomical facts.

A. Events on the surface of the skin reach the nervous system by way of *A-delta nerve fibers*, which come from encapsulated end organs, and *C fibers*, which come from free nerve endings. Both fibers go into the spine on the way up to the brain.

B. On the way to the brain, these two types of nerve fibers send off branches to the *substantia gelatinosa*, which acts as a gate.

C. More A-delta fibers are stimulated by touch, warm, and cold stimuli, while more free nerve endings are activated by stimuli that are typically thought of as painful.

D. The gate-control theory of pain proposed that anything that increases excitation in the substantia gelatinosa causes the gate to close, thus closing the door to pain. Anything that inhibits electrical activity in the substantia gelatinosa causes the gate to open, thus opening the door to pain.

E. C fibers, when they send collaterals to the substantia gelatinosa, produce an inhibitory effect in it, whereas A-delta fibers produce an excitatory effect in it.

F. The theory predicted that increasing activity in A-delta fibers should reduce pain. The ratio of A-delta to C fibers that a given stimulus activated would determine whether that stimulus would be perceived as warmth, cold, or touch as opposed to pain.

1. So-called counter-irritants, such as ice packs, heating pads, massages, whirlpool baths, and alcohol rubs, increase activity in A-delta fibers and reduce pain.
2. Insertion of acupuncture needles, as done by a trained practitioner, can also increase activity in A-delta fibers. Those needles may also be rotated, tapped, heated, or hooked up to a battery to increase effectiveness.
3. Acupuncture may also make use of what are called *trigger zones*, which are neurological links between parts of the body.

III. The discovery was made in the early 1970s that the body produces its own opiates, substances known as *endorphins*. The word *endorphin* is a composite of the words *endogenous* and *morphine*.

    A. Endorphins have the capacity to reduce the severity of (not eliminate) pain.

    B. Endorphins have been implicated in some of the analgesic effects of acupuncture.

    C. There are two categories of endorphins:
        1. *True endorphins* are pituitary hormones.
        2. *Enkephalins* are peptide neurotransmitters that function in certain parts of the brain.
        3. Pituitary hormones can enter the bloodstream, possibly explaining why a needle inserted at one site in the body can reduce pain sensitivity at some other site in the body.
        4. Inserting needles in some standard acupuncture sites has been shown to cause the release of endorphins in the body.
        5. Pretreatment with naloxone (an opiate antagonist) reduces the effectiveness of acupuncture anesthesia.

IV. Endorphins are released in the body when we experience pain. In addition to pain, there are some other experiences that can cause endorphin release.

    A. Effort can result in endorphin release; some people feel that the so-called "runner's high" may be due to endorphins.

    B. Certain pleasant stimuli, such as music, cause endorphin release.

C. A pleasant event that results in a tingling in your spine is most likely releasing endorphins.

D. The discovery in the early 1980s of *Substance P,* a pain neuro-transmitter, has added to our understanding of pain and ways to alleviate it.

V. Normal aging (even in the absence of neuropathology) has been shown to influence pain sensitivity.

A. There are differences of opinion as to how pain sensitivity changes with age.

    1. The elderly are sometimes portrayed as spending a good deal of time talking about their aches and pains. This suggests the possibility of greater pain sensitivity with age.

    2. Some physicians feel that the elderly become less sensitive to pain in that they seem to experience less discomfort in receiving shots, can undergo minor surgical procedures without anesthetic, and may be unaware of accidental cuts and scratches until they see blood. This suggests less pain sensitivity with age.

B. The confusion may be the result of the fact that there are two broad categories of pain, superficial pain and deep pain.

    1. Superficial pain, also called *bright pain*, involves the surface of the body and typically results from cuts or puncture wounds.

    2. Deep pain, also called *dull pain*, is more associated with muscles, joints, ligaments, and tendons and yields a throbbing, aching sensation.

C. Pain sensitivity was studied in human subjects ranging in age from 18 to 80.

    1. Superficial pain sensitivity appeared to decrease with age.

    2. Deep pain sensitivity appeared to increase with age.

Suggested Reading:

Colavita, *Sensory Changes in the Elderly*, chapter 8.

Filshie and White, *Medical Acupuncture: A Western Approach.*

Questions to Consider:

1. Does the expression "no pain, no gain" sound philosophical or silly to you? Why?

2. Does your health insurance cover acupuncture? How do you feel about this?

Lecture Fourteen—Transcript
Pain—Acupuncture, Endorphins, and Aging

Welcome to Lecture Fourteen. In Lecture Thirteen, we talked about what might be generally referred to as "the puzzle of pain," ending up with some questions about acupuncture. In Lecture Fourteen we will deal with some of those questions and extend them a bit farther.

Acupuncture is one of the main tools of a health delivery system called Traditional Chinese Medicine, TCM, and TCM is an example of a holistic health system. It has been in use in China in virtually the same form for over 5,000 years. TCM was a little slow in being recognized and adopted in the West because in the West we tend to compartmentalize our illnesses. In other words, if you have a medical illness, you see a doctor. If you have an emotional illness, you see a clinical psychologist. If you have a spiritual illness, you see a clergy person, and if you have a mental illness, you see a psychiatrist.

In the holistic system you would see the same person for all of those ills because their belief is that all illness—spiritual, mental, emotional, whatever—comes from imbalances of vital life forces, and acupuncture was developed to rebalance those vital life forces. So you can see why it would take awhile for Americans, especially those with a scientific bent, to warm up to acupuncture. In fact, most of us had never even heard of acupuncture until the 1970s, and then it was brought to our attention in such a way that we couldn't ignore it.

I guess the story starts with President Richard Nixon's visit to China in 1972. This was the first visit to China by a sitting American president, and it, of course, was very newsworthy. One of the journalists who was in China as part of the group to chronicle Nixon's visit was a gentleman by the name of James Reston. While in China, Reston experienced an acute attack of appendicitis and had to be medically treated by the Chinese health facilities. He was treated with acupuncture to relieve his pain. He underwent surgery with acupuncture anesthesia.

It was played up in the press, and everybody read about it, some of us with varying degrees of disbelief and what have you. But then a team of journalists, scientists, and physicians from Western Europe were invited to China to actually witness surgical procedures done under acupuncture anesthesia, and they made movies of these things. In one operation, a patient had a thyroidectomy with the anesthetic being a needle in the back of the wrist and a needle in the back of the neck.

In another surgical procedure, the patient had a partial lung resection, and the anesthetic was four needles in each ear hooked up together by wires and attached to a DC battery. In a third operation, a patient had surgery for a bleeding ulcer, and in that case the acupuncture anesthetic was a two-inch needle in the right bicep's muscle. This was documented on film. You could see that the patients were not in a trance, they were not unconscious, they appeared to be awake and alert, they were able to converse with the surgeon, and they experienced no apparent discomfort.

The general public, through magazine articles and newspaper articles, became aware of the existence of acupuncture. The medical community and the scientific community had no alternative but to continue to ignore it. You couldn't even say "acupuncture" if you were a teaching professor in a medical school, for example. Why is this? It's because of the theory underlying acupuncture. The only theory was the Chinese theory, and that was that there is this universal life force, known as *Qi*—it's pronounced "chee," but it's spelled *Q-I*—and that this universal life force flows through 12 meridians in the body.

Western science could find no evidence for the existence of Qi, or for the existence of these 12 meridians in the body. Now, remember, Western science feels that we can only deal with things that are public, repeatable, and measurable, and neither Qi nor' the meridians fit those criteria. So scientists and teachers had no alternative but to ignore it. But we were desperate for a Western theory that would permit us to recognize and study and talk about acupuncture. This theory appeared in the late 1960s with the publication of the so-called gate control theory of pain, by Drs. Ronald Melzack and Patrick Wall. The name Melzack you may remember from an earlier lecture. He's the gentleman who raised puppies in isolation and found that their responses to pain were very weird when they grew up.

Anyway, Melzack and Wall had a theory of pain that was based on known anatomical facts. Now, let me try and give you a quick overview of the gate control theory of pain. Recall that we have two populations of receptors in the skin: we have the encapsulated end organs, and we have the free nerve endings. Also recall that these two populations of receptors have different nerve fibers, and they take different pathways through the brain, with the free nerve endings having thinner, more primitive nerve fibers, and they go to the midbrain and then to limbic system. On the other hand, the encapsulated end organs travel to the brain by way of the medial meniscus—rapidly conducting, thick diameter fibers—and they end up in the somatosensory cortex and the anterior portion of the parietal lobe. On their way to their respective projection sites in the brain, these two categories of nerve fibers make a detour.

First let me give you some vocabulary. The larger diameter fibers that carry information from the encapsulated end organs are called A-delta fibers. The smaller diameter, more primitive fibers that carry information from free nerve endings are known as C fibers. Both A-delta and C fibers go into the spinal cord in order to ascend up to the brain. What they do, according to the gate control theory—and anatomical evidence suggests that it's in fact what happen—is they send off branches or collaterals to an interesting area of the spinal cord known as the substantia gelatinosa. Now, the substantia gelatinosa is the gate in the gate control theory of pain. Anything that increases excitation in the substantia gelatinosa closes the door on pain. Anything that inhibits electrical activity in the substantia gelatinosa permits the gate to stay open and pain impulses to go up to the brain.

I will tell you—even though in their original proposal of the theory Melzack and Wall didn't mention this: probably whether the gate— the substantia gelatinosa—opens and closes has to do with whether or not it permits fiber messages to ascend in the spinothalamic tract. Now, C fibers, when they send off collaterals to the substantia gelatinosa, produce an inhibitory effect in it, whereas A-delta fibers produce an excitatory effect in it.

Now, we probably know enough to understand some of what I'm going to share with you. Suppose that you're minding your own business and a bee stings you. Now you have bee venom in your skin, and it hurts. What receptors could possibly be responding to bee venom? Certainly not the encapsulated end organs, they are too specialized. They respond to warmth and cold and touch and pressure, but certainly not bee venom. The receptors that are responding to bee venom would be those old primitive free nerve endings that will respond to anything. So the free nerve endings are signaling the C fibers, and the C fibers are sending inhibitory messages to the substantia gelatinosa, opening the gate, and permitting pain messages to ascend to the brain.

Now, according to the gate control theory, the way to reduce the feelings of pain is to increase some activity in A-delta fibers. The gate control theory of pain proposes that what determines whether a stimulus will be perceived as touch or warmth or cold or pressure or pain is the ratio of A-delta fibers to C fibers that are stimulating the substantia gelatinosa. If the ratio favors the A-delta fibers, the gate is closed, and you don't experience pain. If the ratio favors the C fibers, the gate is open, and we experience pain.

Let's go back to our hypothetical situation. You have all this bee venom, and the C fibers are just having a ball, and they're opening the gate on pain. How do we change that? We do something that will increase activity in the encapsulated end organs, and increase activity in the A-delta fibers to increase stimulation in the substantia gelatinosa and shut the gate on pain. So what do we do? We rub it. We put ice on it. We massage it. Now, rubbing, ice, massage, and things of that nature do, in fact, stimulate encapsulated end organs. The pressure receptors and the vibration receptors and the temperature receptors, and we're increasing activity in the A-delta fibers, and we're experiencing pain relief.

As a matter of fact, the gate control theory of pain explains why the counterirritants work, and what are the counterirritants? For hundreds of years medical people have known that if you have a pain, if you have an ache, put a heating pad on it, put an ice pack on it, massage it, put it in a whirlpool bath, give it an alcohol rub—all of those counterirritants have the function of increasing activity in encapsulated end organs, thereby increasing activity in the A-delta fibers. So the counterirritants, which medicine has used for hundreds of years—even though they didn't have a clue why they worked— now make sense in the context of the Melzack and Wall gate control theory.

Now, how does this theory give the West an "excuse," if you will, to start paying attention to acupuncture? Well, you need to assume that somehow insertion of those needles is increasing activity in A-delta fibers, and it's possible to make such an assumption. What I haven't told you yet is that practitioners don't just stick the needles in and forget about them, and this was demonstrated in those three surgeries that were witnessed and filmed by Western scientists and journalists.

You stick the needles in and you rotate them for 15 seconds every minute or two. You tap on the end of the end of them periodically at regular intervals. Or the way the so-called barefoot doctors—these are the practitioners out in the rural areas of China; they're called the barefoot doctors—when they stick acupuncture needles in a patient, they will burn an herb at the end of the needle so it has this smoking incense coming off it. What's probably happening is heat is traveling down the barrel of the needle, and perhaps stimulating Ruffini's cylinders. Or sometimes they will hook these needles up with a common wire and hook it up to a DC battery, which may in fact somehow be electrically short-circuiting the encapsulated end organs, and causing them to activate A-delta fibers.

In other words, it is possible to make a case that somehow these needles that are being tapped or twisted or vibrated or heated or having current passed through them are stimulating A-delta fibers. At least that gave the West an opportunity to acknowledge the existence of acupuncture.

Then, another problem arises. How can you perform a thyroid operation, and stick a needle in somebody's wrist? I mean if you're going to increase activity in the A-delta fibers, shouldn't it be in the vicinity of where the damage has been done? Or how can you operate on the stomach and put needles in the ear, or what have you? It didn't make sense.

The way the West attempted to deal with that—and I admit, this is stretching things a bit—is to suggest that maybe there have been neurological links between different parts of the body all along, and we just never bothered to look for them. As evidence for this, people would point to the existence of so-called trigger zones. For example, when you are experiencing cardiac disease, where do you feel the pain—in your heart? No. You feel it in your shoulder and upper arm. Okay. As a matter of fact, massaging the shoulder and upper arm can actually reduce the severity of cardiac pain.

So the West started looking around for neurological links between parts of the body that nobody had ever thought to look for before, and they found some interesting things. For example, applying ice to the shin of the leg reduces the sensitivity of the tooth pulp to pain stimulation. Who would have ever thought to try that? In any event, it was stretching things.

Luckily, another discovery was made that helped make the case for why acupuncture could, in fact, be explainable, even when you stick the needle in a site remote from where the pain actually is. In 1972, one of the NIH Laboratories in Bethesda discovered the endorphins. That's over 30 years ago, so most people have heard of them. The word endorphin is a composite of endogenous and morphine. The endogenous opiates—the endorphins, the body's own morphine— were discovered in the mouse, in the brain of the mouse, in 1972. Endorphins. It was really a remarkable discovery. This caused the researchers to begin to look in the brains of other animals. Is this just some weird thing that only happens in the mouse? No. Endorphins were found in the brains of every animal that was investigated, and they were also found in human cerebral spinal fluid. We have endorphins, too. We produce endorphins, too.

So now, if you could show that somehow certain acupuncture sites lead to the release of endorphins then you could make a case that wouldn't require looking for neurological links between widely disparate parts of the body. In fact, there does appear to be evidence that certain acupuncture sites do lead to the release of endorphins.

Let me tell you a couple of things about endorphins. There are actually two categories of endorphins. One is true endorphins, and true endorphins are actually pituitary hormones. The other category of endorphins is actually called enkephalins, and these are peptide neurotransmitters that probably function in a specific region of the brain. But hormones, when they are released, enter the bloodstream and can circulate all through the body. So if certain acupuncture sites are actually able to stimulate the release of these true endorphins, the pituitary hormones, which are dumped into the blood, then it could cause a general anesthetic effect all over the body.

There is some evidence that this is, indeed, the case. Acupuncture has been used in animal surgery, and what this tells you, among other things, is that it's not suggestibility, because animals don't believe in the placebo effect, or know about things like suggestibility. So here's some animal that's been needled, then it can have surgery, and apparently not feel any pain. What researchers did was they inserted the needles in one animal, and then they gave another animal a transfusion of the first animal's blood, and operated on the second animal. The implication here is that needling the first animal brought about some chemical change in its blood that had an anesthetic effect, and then you give the second animal a transfusion, and it can undergo the surgery with apparently no appearance of experiencing pain.

Another piece of evidence suggesting a connection between certain acupuncture sites and the release of the endorphins was seen in the following: If you pre-treat an animal with naloxone—naloxone is an opiate antagonist. Now an antagonist is a drug that blocks all the receptor sites so that when you then put the drug of interest in, it doesn't work, it doesn't have any effect, because the receptor sites are already taken up with the antagonist. So if you pre-treat an animal with naloxone, it should gain no benefit, even from real morphine. Well, when you pre-treat animals with naloxone and then use acupuncture anesthesia, it doesn't seem to work, suggesting that at least part of the efficacy of acupuncture anesthesia is due to the fact that it causes the release of endorphins.

So now we have two ways that needling could, in fact, bring about an anesthetic effect that are acceptable to the West. One, sticking in those needles, and tapping, twisting, and heating, and so on could directly stimulate encapsulated end organs, and increase activity in A-delta fibers à la the gate control theory; or two, it could lead to the release of endorphins and produce a chemically mediated desensitization to pain.

Actually, the endorphins are interesting enough that I'd like to elaborate on them just a little bit. It turns out that there are three different situations that we might find ourselves in that could lead to the release of endorphins. One, of course, is pain. Pain leads to the release of endorphins, and we should feel the pain diminish in intensity. It may never be totally abolished, but when you hurt yourself, the initial hurt is always worse than the hurt is in the immediately following period. So pain leads to the release of endorphins.

You can demonstrate this in an animal experiment quite easily. You give an animal a mild painful stimulus, and then give it a severe painful stimulus, and in this case, the response to the severe stimulus is much muted compared to if you just give the animal the painful stimulus to begin with. So the mild pain apparently causes the release of endorphins, so the animal is desensitized when you give it the extreme pain.

Another situation that has been shown to lead to the release of endorphins is effort. Apparently, engaging in effortful behavior—at least some aspects of effortful behavior—can lead to the release of endorphins. Some people point to the so-called "runner's high" as an example of how effort can lead to the release of endorphins, because when endorphins are released, it does give us a heady feeling. Some people report having experienced the runner's high; other people who have been running all their lives have never experienced the runner's high. I don't know what else to do except share with you that some people believe that the runner's high, in people for whom it has made itself apparent, is due to the release of endorphins.

Another stimulus that has been shown to release endorphins is what the researchers called thrilling music. Now, how do you define thrilling music? Well, they defined thrilling music as music that gives you a tingling in your spine, and it turns out that this initial statement about thrilling music may indicate other situations that give you a tingling in your spine and may also cause a release of the endorphins. For example, well I can remember the first time I saw one of my daughters in a high school play. I was sitting there, and all of a sudden I had this tingling in my spine; I was just so thrilled so see her up there doing a good job, and the chances are I was experiencing the result of the release of endorphins.

Let me tell me about an experiment that was done in October of 2005—not that long ago—by physicians at the Yale New Haven Hospital. These physicians had 90 patients scheduled for elective outpatient surgery. This is where they would do the surgery, the patients would recover in a recovery area, and then, probably that same day, they would be permitted to go home. Okay now—90 patients—they decided they could divide them into three groups, and give each of them a different postoperative treatment. All of the patients underwent their surgery, and then they were put in the recovery area. They were given access to an IV drip of a sedative, with which they could control the amount of sedative that they were given. They were in control of the IV drip, and if the pain became too bad, they were to increase the drip and increase the sedation effect.

One group of 30 people listened to thrilling music. One group of 30 people listened to white noise—now white noise is the auditory equivalent of white light; it's random contributions of all of the audible frequencies, and it sounds like what you have when you have your radio tuned between stations. The third group heard standard operating room sounds. The results were clear and unequivocal. The group that listened to the thrilling music—first of all—79% of them didn't use the drip at all; they needed no medication. Of the remaining people in the music group, they used approximately one-half the dosage of medication that the people in the white noise group and the operating room noise group used.

Now, the thing is, you can't point to that as a consequence of distraction, because white noise is a distractor, and so is all the operating room noise. So the conclusion that these physicians reached was that the music group was, in fact, experiencing the benefit of endorphin release.

While we are talking about some of the chemistry of pain, let me share with you another discovery. This one was made in 1981. Researchers discovered a substance called substance P, and of course P in "substance P" stands for pain. This was a neurotransmitter that was known to be involved in conduction of activity, of information from one part of the brain to another in areas of the brain where pain messages were received—substance P. It turns out that in parts of the brain where substance P is the neurotransmitter, it is in those parts of the brain where we find the enkephalins. Now, enkephalins are the peptide neurotransmitters that work in specific parts of the brain rather than all over, the way hormones do. So we have here a situation where the enkephalins are in a position to block or inhibit the activity of substance P.

The discovery of substance P as a pain neurotransmitter also gave us insight into another interesting aspect of pain. There is a substance called capsaicin that is a component of jalapeno peppers and other hot spicy peppers and what have you. Many local application products for arthritis actually contain capsaicin, and some people report getting great relief by rubbing capsaicin on their aching joints when bouts of arthritis kick up.

What does capsaicin do? Well, it turns out that capsaicin has the ability to release substance P from the synaptic vesicles in the neurons where it is stored. Now, you would think that releasing substance P would cause pain, not alleviate pain, but it's a paradoxical effect. You see, capsaicin causes a slow, gradual release of substance P, so that what you have instead of pain is a sensation of warmth. So you rub this stuff on your aching joints and you experience warmth, because substance P is being released in a controlled fashion.

The other thing capsaicin does is that it prevents the regeneration of substance P, so that, in fact, you may rub that stuff on, and you may remain pain free for hours, or in some fortunate cases, for days, because it stops the re-buildup of substance P after it causes this slow release of the stuff. So we are learning more and more about the chemistry of pain year by year, and it makes sense of things that were previously puzzling to us.

In the time remaining, let me say a few things about the aging process, and what it does to pain. Now, historically there have been two points of view. I remember being in a tennis league where after we played tennis, we would sit around and drink beer together, and some of the guys were complaining bitterly about their aging parents and relatives, about how much they complained about their aches and pains. One guy said, "You know, I hate to ask my mother how she's feeling, because she says, 'Oh, my shoulder hurts and my ankle hurts and my hip hurts, and this and that hurts,' I don't even want to ask any more." And other people were saying, "Yeah, you're right. They must really increase their pain sensitivity when they grow old."

On the other hand, I have talked to physicians who have exactly the opposite perspective. They say, "You know, older people can sure stand pain better than younger people." I say, "Why do you say that?" He says, "Well, when you give them an injection they don't complain. If you do a needle biopsy they don't show any discomfort. You can actually do minor incisions with either very little or no anesthetic, and they don't seem to complain at all."

So here we have two opposing points of view, one saying old people feel pain more, and the other saying old people feel pain less. Which is true? Well, I did a little research, and I discovered that both are true. This confusion comes about because we fail to recognize that there are two categories of pain. There is "bright" superficial pain, and there is dull, deep pain. I came across one experiment in the literature that not only looked at pain sensitivity across a broad range of ages, but also made the distinction between bright pain and dull pain—or superficial pain and deep pain.

Here is what this experiment did. By the way the subjects in this experiment ranged in age from 18 to 80. They produced the sensation of bright pain by using a condensing lens and a light bulb. They would focus the beam of light at a precise point on the subject's forehead, and they would increase the intensity of the light—make it brighter and brighter, and hotter and hotter—the sensation that it produced was like being poked in the head with a needle—until the subject said, "Ouch, that hurts." This is producing what you might call superficial, or surface pain, like being stuck in the forehead with a needle. In this case, the young people said, "Ouch, that hurts," first.

The other pain was a little more complicated. What they did was to put two wooden rods on either side of the Achilles tendon, and then they would exert pressure on the Achilles tendon. Now, you can demonstrate for yourself by squeezing your Achilles tendon that it produces a dull, but painful sensory experience when you squeeze the Achilles tendon. They would increase the pressure on these two wooden rods until the subjects said, "Ouch, that hurts." Now the older people said, "Ouch, that hurts," first.

So what this experiment demonstrated was that whether young people feel more pain, or old people feel more pain, or vice versa, depends upon whether you're talking about bright, superficial pain or deep, dull pain. Apparently, the superficial pain is less of a problem for the elderly maybe because they have lost more skin receptors, and maybe the internal pain receptors, the internal free nerve endings, are more protected from age-related loss. In any event, the elderly seem to be more sensitive to deep pain, which is why they would feel pain in their joints and muscles and what have you, and they're less sensitive to surface pain, which is just the opposite for young people.

This lecture ends our treatment of the sense of pain. In our next lecture we will begin to talk about the first of our two chemical senses, the chemical senses being taste and smell. In our next lecture we will talk about taste, and we will start out by describing the stimuli, the nature of stimuli that we can taste, and we'll talk about the supporting structures and the receptors in the sense of taste. Thank you.

Lecture Fifteen
Taste—Stimulus, Structures, and Receptors

Scope:

When most people think of the taste of a favorite food, they unconsciously include its aroma, color, texture, and temperature. Hot, spicy foods also owe their characteristic taste to mild pain components. However, to a taste researcher, the sense of taste is composed of the four taste primaries, which are sweet, salty, sour, and bitter.

A misconception held by many people is that the raised spots visible on the tongue are taste buds or taste receptors. They are not. The visible spots are taste papillae, each spot marking the location of a tiny crater in the tongue. The taste buds are goblet shaped clusters of cells down in the craters, and the taste receptors are also located—one receptor per taste bud—in the craters. Neither taste buds nor taste receptors can be seen with the naked eye. The middle of the tongue has no taste buds or receptors and is, in fact, taste blind.

Humans, along with rats, dogs, horses, and monkeys to name a few other species, are born with a "sweet tooth" (an unlearned preference for the taste of sweet). Although it is not as strong, we also have an unlearned preference for salt, but bitter and sour are acquired tastes. We actually start life with an aversion to these two flavors.

Another interesting taste-related phenomenon is *wisdom of the body*, which refers to the ability of animals to actively seek out substances they need to maintain adequate nutrition. This is why deer travel long distances in the dead of winter to lick salt blocks put out for them by forest rangers. In the laboratory, rats have been deprived of different vitamins. When presented with a cafeteria-style feeding situation, the deprived animals select foods high in whichever vitamin they need. If the sense of taste is destroyed, the animals no longer choose the needed food. There is evidence that humans also seek out foods that compensate for a nutritional deficit.

Outline

I. To a scientist working in the area of sensory processes, the word *taste* refers only to the four taste primaries: sweet, salty, sour, and bitter.

©2006 The Teaching Company.

A. Japanese taste researchers have suggested a fifth taste primary, which they call *umami*. This translates approximately to "savory."

B. Most people use the word *taste* when they really mean *flavor*. Whereas *taste* refers to sweet, sour, salty, and bitter, *flavor* includes the smell, temperature, texture, and color of a food.

C. The exemplar for sweet is sugar; for salty, sodium chloride; for sour, dilute acetic acid; for bitter, quinine powder; and for umami, MSG.

II. The structures on the tongue that are involved in the sense of taste are the taste papillae, the taste buds, and the taste receptors. (Figure 15a)

A. The visible bumps on the surface of the tongue are the taste papillae. The papillae mark the locations on the tongue of small moat-like depressions that surround the papilla (singular), much as a castle is surrounded by a moat.

B. Molecules of the taste substance mix with saliva and flow into the moat, where they encounter taste buds that are located in the walls of the moat.

C. A taste bud is composed of a goblet-cluster of 20–24 cells, the middle cell being the actual taste receptor.

D. On the tip of the tongue, we have the *fungiform papillae*; on the edge of the tongue, we have the *foliate papillae*; and on the back of the tongue, we have the *circumvallate papillae*.

E. The middle of the tongue has no taste buds or receptors and is, in fact, taste blind.

F. Taste receptors die every 7–10 days and are replaced by another cell in the taste bud, which becomes the new receptor.

G. Taste receptors completely adapt to the taste of a substance in from 1½ to 3 minutes. If you were to hold a substance in your mouth for this length of time, it would lose its taste. Some very strong tastes might take slightly longer to adapt.

III. Most people have heard of the "sweet-tooth" phenomenon, an expression that refers to the preference most of us have for a sweet taste over a salty, sour, or bitter taste.

A. The sweet-tooth phenomenon is almost universal in the mammalian species, although cats are an exception.

B. Experiments indicate that the preference for a sweet taste is innate, rather than the result of learning and experience.

    1. Neural connections have been identified between taste nerves and parts of the brain involved in feelings of pleasure.

    2. In the wild, sweet-tasting substances are not usually poisonous and typically contain sugar, a good source of energy.

    3. Animals born with an innate preference for sweet are more likely to survive.

    4. Although less well developed than our preference for sweet, our preference for salty foods stems from our need for sodium chloride.

IV. There is evidence that animals somehow sense when they have a nutritional deficit and will actively seek out a diet that corrects this deficiency.

A. This ability to detect and correct a dietary deficiency has been called *wisdom of the body*.

B. Examples of wisdom of the body include deer traveling long distances in winter to lick blocks of salt put out by game wardens and cows seeking out salt blocks strategically placed by dairy farmers.

C. Wisdom of the body also occurs in humans. Children or adults with adrenal insufficiency (a medical condition requiring increased salt intake) develop a craving for salt, although they are unaware of the increased need for salt.

D. Laboratory experiments with animals indicate that such cravings can also be established for different vitamins.

V. Experiments with human subjects have revealed where on our tongues we experience various tastes.

A. The tip of the tongue is maximally sensitive to sweet.

B. The sides of the tongue are best at discriminating sour and bitter.

C. The back of the tongue plays more of a role in foods for which hot, spicy, and mild pain components are an aspect.

Suggested Reading:

Carlson, *Physiology of Behavior* (8th ed.), pp. 233–238.

Goldstein, *Sensation and Perception* (6th ed.), pp. 487–499.

Questions to Consider:

1. What is flavor?

2. Why are most people unaware that the middle of the tongue is taste blind?

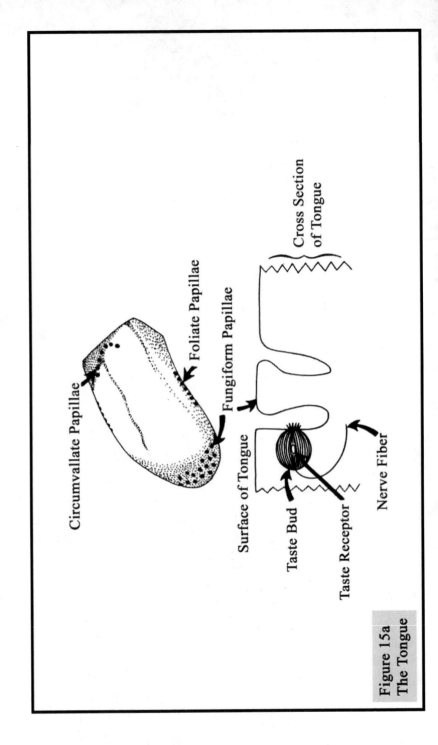

Figure 15a
The Tongue

Lecture Fifteen—Transcript
Taste—Stimulus, Structures, and Receptors

Hello, and welcome to Lecture Fifteen. For continuity, let me remind you that in Lecture Fourteen we talked about various aspects of pain, including acupuncture, the endorphins, and the aging process. Lecture Fifteen represents our introduction to a new sensory system. Actually, it represents an introduction to the sense of taste, which is one of our two chemical senses. We will have a total of four lectures on the chemical senses—taste and smell. I'd just like to mention that, phylogenetically speaking, taste and smell are far more important than hearing and seeing. That is, if you're a lower animal, you're bound to have some chemical sensitivity, but not necessarily to have auditory or visual sensitivity.

First, let's start with some definitional issues. What do we mean when we use the word taste? Well, most people in their everyday usage of the term taste are actually referring to far more than taste. They're also referring to the aroma of the substance they're talking about, the texture of the substance they're talking about, the temperature of the substance they're talking about, and even whether or not that substance has pain components associated with it. Color also plays a role in the broad definition of taste. Let me give you some examples. If you can't smell your food you say, "Gosh, I can't taste it." Well, actually you really can. Even holding your nose, take a lick of some salt, and a lick of some sugar, and tell me you can't tell the difference. So smell is not technically a part of taste. How about texture? People say, "Lumpy mashed potatoes don't taste as good as smooth mashed potatoes." Well, they really do, it's just the texture. People say, "Cold soup doesn't taste as good as hot soup." The taste is the same; it is the temperature that's different.

People say—well, let me give you an experiment that was done at a smorgasbord, a roast beef place, some years ago in Pittsburgh. When you go to these places where they carve the roast beef right in front of you, it's always under a nice red lamp, and it gives it this red, rosy appearance. Some researchers paid the establishment to substitute a green bulb for the red bulb, and very few people chose the green roast beef, and those who did choose it, reported that it didn't taste as good as it usually did. Then they changed the taste again by simply taking out the green bulb and putting the red one back in, then it tasted good again.

Now, how about pain components? Well it turns out that flat Coca-Cola™, people say it doesn't taste as good as fresh Coca-Cola™, and the only difference is those bubbles of carbonation that are producing mild pain sensations on the back of the throat. So when we use the word taste in our everyday colloquial usage, we're talking about all of those components.

When a taste researcher talks about taste, he or she is referring to the four taste primaries—sweet, sour, salty, and bitter. Now, those can, in fact, be distinguished, even when you totally disregard things such as temperature and texture and color and things of that nature. So the word taste has different meanings to different people. To a taste researcher—sweet, sour, salty, and bitter. That's what they mean by using the word taste.

Recently it has been found that in certain textbooks and in certain discussions of taste, a fifth taste primary has been alluded to. This is a taste primary that has been proposed by Japanese researchers. It's called *umami*, and I just reviewed a sensation and perception textbook where, in fact, they talked about the five taste primaries—sweet, sour, salty, bitter, and umami. Now, umami has been known about for approximately 20 years, but it is only in the mid-1980s that the Japanese researchers felt that they had demonstrated conclusively through research that umami does represent a separate taste, and that it's not just an aggregate of some combination of sweet, sour, salty, and bitter, or something of that nature.

So they claim they now have convincing experimental evidence that umami is a separate taste. The translation of the word *umami* into English would be "savory." So now some people are claiming that we have five taste primaries—sweet, sour, salty, bitter, and savory, or umami.

Let me give you exemplars of the taste primaries. The exemplar for sweet would be a sugar, and if you want to know what sweet tastes like, taste sugar. For salty, you would taste sodium chloride, although there are plenty of things that taste salty that have neither sodium nor chloride in them. For sour, dilute acetic acid or unsweetened lemonade would give you a typical taste of a sour substance, and for bitter, try quinine. The alkaloids are typically bitter in taste, and quinine is a good example of a bitter taste. For umami, I guess the exemplar would be monosodium glutamate, the flavor enhancer that is found in some Asian cooking. Unfortunately, some people have a reaction to monosodium glutamate, and it gives them headaches. Not everybody can handle it, but most of us can, I guess.

Now, we're going to talk about the organization of the taste system on the human tongue. I would just like to mention in passing that the way humans have their taste system organized is not necessarily the way it works in other members of the animal kingdom. For example, flies—these pesky things that invite themselves into our houses without our permission—flies have their taste receptors on their legs, so that when you see a fly walking across some disgusting item with a big smile on its face, it's actually tasting that item with the taste receptors on its legs.

Fish have their taste receptors on the surface of their bodies so that as they swim through the water they are actually sampling what there is to sample with these taste receptors on the surface of the body.

In humans, it's arranged a little bit differently, and before we actually go into the mechanism of taste, again let me share some vocabulary with you. I want to share with you the distinction between taste papillae, taste buds, and taste receptors, because they are actually referring to quite different things, and some people actually confuse them. In fact, I recall once seeing a full-page ad in a quite prestigious magazine for a particular brand of coffee, and it showed a steaming cup of coffee; it showed a mouth open with the tongue exposed, and it said, "Give your taste buds a treat." What you could see were those pink spots on the model's tongue. The pink spots on the tongue are not taste buds at all. They are actually taste papillae. You cannot see the taste buds on the tongue, and you cannot see the taste receptors on the tongue. All you can see are the taste papillae.

Now, what are taste papillae? Well, taste papillae are bumps on the tongue that tell you that there are taste moats in that region. It's as if the papilla is actually a castle surrounded by a moat, and these moats are there to trap molecules of the substance to be tasted. So the papilla just tells you that there is a moat there, and in that moat are two to four taste buds. Taste buds are goblet-shaped affairs which are on their sides, lining the walls of this taste moat around the taste papilla, and these goblet-shaped affairs contain 20 to 24 cells. These are supporting cells, and in the middle, in the very middle of the taste bud is the actual taste receptor cell, and you can identify the taste receptor cell because it is the only cell in a taste bud that has little hair-like tufts sticking out of it. These little hair-like projections actually help the taste receptor to come into physical contact with the molecules of the substance to be tasted.

You see, the substances that we can taste are only substances that go into solution in saliva. You can't taste just anything. For example, if you have a marble, and you clean all the grease off it, and you clean all the dirt and anything else off it, and you put that marble in your mouth, you will feel its weight, you will feel its temperature, because of course we have temperature receptors in the mouth, but it will be tasteless to you, because we can only taste things that dissolve in saliva, that go into solution in saliva, so that their molecules can find their way into this taste moat where they are likely to come into physical contact with a taste bud and be entrapped by the little hair-like tufts on the end of the taste receptor.

A healthy, young adult human tongue contains about 10,000 taste buds, thus it contains about 10,000 taste receptors, because typically there is one taste receptor per bud. Now, why am I hedging my bets? Why am I saying that a healthy, young adult human has 10,000 taste buds, therefore 10,000 taste receptors—because that number is different in children, and it's different in the elderly. It'll take a bit of explaining, so let's save that for a little bit later.

So we have these papillae on the surface of the tongue. Now the papillae in different locations on the tongue have different names. The papillae on the tip of the tongue, the ones that perhaps you are more likely to look at in the mirror when you brush your teeth or stick your tongue out, these are called fungiform papillae. The papillae along the edge of the tongue are known as foliate papillae, and we also have some papillae at the back of the tongue, called circumvallate papillae.

Okay, so I've said we have papillae on the tip of the tongue, the edges, of the tongue and the back of the tongue. What about the middle of the tongue? It turns out that the middle of the human tongue is taste blind. It contains no papillae, it contains no taste buds, and it contains no taste receptors. Why have we been able to go through so many decades of life and not be aware that the middle of the tongue is taste blind? Well, it's very simple. When you put something in your mouth, you chew it up and the saliva carries it all over the tongue, and so we assume that the whole tongue is involved in the taste process. That's not true.

In taste experiments done in a laboratory restrict the portion of the tongue that the stimulus is delivered to. There are a couple of ways you can do this. You can dip little pieces of filter paper in different tasting solutions, and then you can place that filter paper on a specific population of taste papillae; if you take one of these little pieces of filter paper dipped in taste substances and put it in the middle of the tongue, you can't taste it at all. The other way that taste stimuli are delivered to subjects in the laboratory is they have a thin rubber tube or a glass tube or a glass pipette of some sort, and they run the liquid stimulus onto a specific part of the tongue, but not the entire tongue. In this case you can easily demonstrate that the middle of the tongue is taste-blind—it doesn't taste anything.

Now, let me tell you something about taste receptors. They have a relatively short lifespan. Taste receptors only live for between seven and 10 days, and then they die. Now, when a taste receptor dies, what happens is the most mature of the supporting cells—the 20 to 24 remaining cells that fill out the taste bud—the taste supporting cell with the most seniority, if you will, moves into the middle of the bud, grows hair-like tufts on it, and becomes the new taste receptor cell. Every seven to 10 days taste receptors die and are replaced by new taste receptor cells. One of the implications of this is even if you've been smoking for 20, 30, 40, 50 years and you give up smoking, your taste sensitivity will return to normal within two weeks. Former smokers are amazed to find what things really taste like after they give up smoking.

Something else about taste receptors is they undergo rapid adaptation. Usually when we put something in our mouths, we chew it and we swallow it in a relatively short period of time. If we were to just let that substance linger in the mouth, we would find that from 1½ to 3 minutes taste experience would fade to nothingness. We would just feel a lump in our mouths. Taste receptors show relatively quick adaptation; one and one-half to three minutes is the amount of time it would take for most stimuli that we would ever taste to adapt. If something is incredibly strong, it might last a little longer than that.

Now, let me tell you about a taste-related phenomenon that has been of more than passing interest to psychologists since the 1950s—the "sweet tooth" phenomenon. The reason psychologists first became interested in the "sweet tooth" phenomenon—that is, the preference that most people have for the taste of sweet—was because a learning theorist by the name of Clark Hull, back in the 1940s and 1950s had what he called his "drive reduction theory of learning." He said animals would only learn certain behaviors, or learn any behaviors, for a reward that would reduce some primary drive—hunger or thirst or something of that nature.

Along came another psychologist who said, "Professor Hull, look at this. I have rats that have just been fed, they've just been watered, but watch this," and he showed that those rats would work for the taste of saccharine. Now, saccharine is non-nutritive, it has no caloric value, it doesn't satisfy any basic need, and so the Hullians were amazed. Why would a rat learn to work for saccharine if it wasn't hungry or thirsty—because it had an appetitive feeling for the taste of sweet—the "sweet tooth" phenomenon. So psychologists wondered, "Why do animals have a preference for sweet?"

One theory was well, maybe the first thing animals taste is mother's milk, and mother's milk is sweet, so animals associate the sweet taste with satisfaction of hunger needs and survival and so on. An example of one of the experiments that was done back then is as follows. They took some pregnant rats, and they adulterated their diet with quinine, and they put quinine in the mother-to-be rat's water, and they would periodically give her subcutaneous injections of a quinine liquid, so all of her body fluids tasted bitter, and when she gave birth her milk tasted bitter. So here were these baby rats drinking bitter-tasting mother's milk, and they wondered, when these rats grew up, if they would prefer bitter over sweet. So here was the test. They gave the rats a choice of a bowl of sweet-tasting liquid and a bowl of bitter-tasting liquid, and the rats overwhelmingly went for the sweet, so it appears that the "sweet tooth" is something we are born with.

Now, is it something that just occurs in rats—certainly not. You all know perfectly well that the "sweet tooth" is prevalent in humans. In fact, the "sweet tooth" seems to be an almost universal phenomenon. Horses have a sweet tooth, dogs have a sweet tooth, monkeys have a sweet tooth, rats, mice, humans—we all have a "sweet tooth." One notable exception is the cat. Cats do not have a "sweet tooth," and this, in fact, has been a source of curiosity to scientists for some decades, and there were different theories. Maybe the cat's tongue has receptors for sweet, but there's some kind of a disconnect between the receptors in the tongue and the parts of the brain that analyze this. Or maybe the cat doesn't have receptors for sweet. Or maybe the cat is just too snooty to admit that it has a craving, like the rest of us, for something as common as sweets.

Well, in 2005, last year, researchers finally discovered why cats don't show this "sweet tooth" phenomenon that most of the rest of us do. As a result of a genetic mutation, the receptor sites on the cat's sweet receptors cannot respond to sweet. Sweet does not bind to the receptors the way it should. This is the result of a genetic mutation, and it's not only house cats. It turns out that it's also tigers and ocelots and cheetahs and other cats. They just have a genetic insensitivity. It's not that they don't like sweet; it's that they can't taste it. If you give a cat a choice between sweetened water and regular water, it's 50–50 what the cat will drink from and how much it will drink.

So does this influence in a negative way the cat's ability to satisfy it's nutritional needs? Not really, because cats—house cats and the other cats that we mentioned—are for the most part carnivores, and so they manage okay without being aware of the sense of taste, or having their eating habits guided by the sense of taste.

So we appear to be born with this "sweet tooth," and as a survival characteristic, it's pretty good, because in nature, animals don't have any guide to tell them what's good or bad to eat. In nature, if an animal is programmed to approach sweet, it's likely to eat things that are good sources of energy, because sweet things generally have sugar in them. You could also program an animal to avoid bitter-tasting things, because in nature bitter tasting things can be poisonous. Not all bitter tasting things are poisonous, but poisonous things tend to be bitter tasting.

So if you were to design a rat, or any animal, and you wanted it to survive on its own, you would program it to approach sweet and to avoid bitter, and that animal would have a better chance of survival. You might also want to program that animal to have an appetitive feeling toward salt, because sodium chloride is necessary. Incidentally, it turns out that wild animals have a strong "sweet tooth;" they also have a positive reaction to salt. We have a less well developed preference for salt. We prefer sweet a great deal, and we prefer salt a little bit. Baby rats have an aversion to sour and bitter, and so do baby humans, so it appears that these preferences are not random. They seem to be built into us.

Another taste-related phenomenon that I want to mention is sometimes referred to as the "wisdom of the body" phenomenon. This refers to an animal's ability to know when it is suffering from some kind of nutritional lack, when something is missing in its diet, and to actively seek out that particular substance. Let me use the example of salt. Farmers know, and game wardens and forest rangers know, that if you put salt blocks out in the woods, that the deer will travel large distances to come and lick those blocks of salt. Farmers know that if they put salt blocks out in the pastures, that their cows will travel large distances to come and lick those blocks of salt.

Now, do the animals make a conscious decision? "Boy, I may be low on sodium chloride. I'd better go lick this block of salt." I doubt that very much. As a matter of fact, this craving for salt—and that's what it must be because it causes deer, who are usually very, very wary animals, to expose themselves, and come out of the woods to go over a lick a block of salt—this appetitive feature of deer for salt is so great that there are laws against private hunters putting out salt blocks just before hunting season—to have the deer used to coming to this particular part of the forest— then the hunters, when hunting season starts, sit there with their guns, and it's easy for them to hunt the deer. You just can't put out blocks of salt.

How do the animals know they need this? What would possibly possess a cow that would make it leave its nice, warm barn and go out through the snow, perhaps, to lick a block of salt out in the pasture.

If you were to ask the cow, "Why did you do that? Why did you leave the warm barn and go out to the cold pasture to lick a block of salt?" Do you know what that cow would say? "Moo." Sorry, I couldn't resist that. But the cow doesn't know. It doesn't know why it's doing that. It's some kind of innate feeling that this would be a good thing to do.

Rats do it too. If you treat a rat with a drug known as metyrapone, which produces an adrenal insufficiency, that rat will increase its sodium chloride intake. See now, the adrenal gland, in addition to secreting adrenaline, also secretes hormones that aid in normal sodium chloride metabolism, so if you have adrenal insufficiency, your health, and even your survival is at risk if you don't take in larger quantities of salt, so a rat with adrenal insufficiency somehow knows to eat more salt.

This wisdom of the body phenomenon has also been demonstrated in humans. There is a tragic case of a young boy whose parents were very concerned because he took in large quantities of salt. He started, for instance, taking the top off the salt shaker and dumping a quantity of salt in his hands and eating it. He took to licking the salt off saltine crackers. They were aware that something was amiss here, so they took this young boy for an examination, and when the doctor heard the symptoms, he had the boy hospitalized. While in the hospital, this young boy died. The autopsy determined that he had a tumor of the adrenal gland and that, in fact, was why he was taking in these large quantities of salt, and if he had not been taking in these large quantities of salt, he would have died at home. See, what happened was in the hospital he was put on the hospital diet, and the hospital diet, while it's adequate for people without any special nutritional issues, was insufficient to maintain this young boy's life, and he died of a deficit of sodium chloride.

There is a disease called "Addison's Disease," that has a number of different symptoms, but one of the characteristics of Addison's Disease is adrenal insufficiency. So people who have Addison's Disease find that they have a craving for salt also.

Now, so far we've been talking about this wisdom of the body phenomenon as if it only involves salt. That's not really true. In laboratory studies, rats have been deprived of necessary vitamins. Then the rats are given access to a cafeteria-style feeding situation to different foods, one of which is very high in the vitamin that the rats have been deprived of. What the rats do is to seek out the food that is high in the nutrient they are lacking. How do they know this? What is the mechanism? Is it because you can demonstrate this for a variety of nutrients?

First of all, somebody said, "Well, maybe when the rat or the human or whatever eats the substance that they're deficient in, they quickly feel better. Maybe it has absolutely nothing to do with taste." So this was tested experimentally. Different groups of rats were deprived of different nutrients, and then their taste nerves were cut.

Now, the tongue is different from the other senses, in that to desensitize the tongue totally you have to cut three nerves. The tongue has three nerves. The main taste nerve is the one that goes to the front of the tongue. It's called the "chorda tympani nerve." Now, you may remember tympani from tympanic membrane and what have you, and the reason it's called the "chorda tympani nerve" is because in the course of going from the tongue to the brain, it passes right behind the eardrum. In fact, some humans, who are undergoing medical treatment for a ruptured eardrum or something like that, have actually agreed—because they have this opening in their eardrum—to have researchers record from their chorda tympani nerve while they pour different taste substances on their tongue. So the human taste nerve has, in fact, been recorded from—and if I remember, I'll share with you some of those results—but let me get back on track now.

To desensitize the tongue you cut the chorda tympani nerve; you cut the glossopharyngeal nerve, and you cut a branch of the vegas nerve. Now the animal can taste nothing. Then you deprive the animal of a nutrient, and you again give it access in a cafeteria-style feeding situation. If the animal eats something and feels better, even without tasting it, it should come to prefer that substance. In the absence of taste sensitivity, it never catches on to which substance it should eat, and the animal will die of its nutritional deficit. So the wisdom of the body phenomenon is not simply an example of eating something, feeling better, and continuing to eat that substance. You must be able to taste it.

Okay, now what could the possible mechanism be? Well, let me again go back to the example of sodium chloride because that's the substance that has had the most research done on it in connection with this wisdom of the body phenomenon. Our tongues are constantly bathed in saliva, and saliva contains, as one of its components, sodium chloride. If you hang your tongue out of your mouth for three minutes or so, and let the receptors that are sensitive to salt regenerate back to their full sensitivity, you might be surprised to discover that your tongue is actually 1,000 times more sensitive to salt than you thought. In this state of heightened sensitivity to salt, you can now seek out and find foods with much lower concentrations of salt than you could be aware of when your tongue is covered in sodium chloride.

Some people suggest that when we are deficient in some nutrient, it actually changes the state of adaptation to the tongue, and it makes us more sensitive to that substance; it actually creates a craving for that substance. That is probably the best explanation that exists at the present time for why an animal would actively seek out a substance that it seems to need. It probably changes the reaction of the tongue by altering some of the adaptation process that is usually going on in the tongue.

Okay, let me go back to this business of recording from a chorda tympani nerve of a human subject. What we're in a position to do is pour things on the subject's tongue, and the subject can tell you what he or she tastes and to what extent. For instance, we know that the tip of the tongue is maximally sensitive to sweet. The whole sides and the back of the tongue can also discriminate sweet, but the front of the tongue is the part of the tongue that is best at discriminating sweet. It turns out that the sides of the tongue can tell sweet too, but they are better at sour and bitter. It turns out that the back of the tongue plays more of a role in foods for which hot/spicy/mild/pain components are an important aspect, because, as I mentioned when we were doing our definitional issues of taste in the colloquial sense, pain components do play a role in the characteristic taste of some substances like the mild pain sensations from carbonated beverages, for example.

So, spicy cuisine, like General Tso's chicken, for example, is best appreciated if the pain components from the hot peppers or whatever are permitted to come into contact with the back of the tongue, the circumvallate papillae if you will, because the circumvallate papillae are actually innervated by the vegas nerve, whereas the front is the chorda tympani, and the sides are the glossopharyngeal, which is the nerve that is more likely to be sensitive to pain components. So it's an interesting intermix of sensitivities and different nerve fibers that give us our characteristic ability to enjoy different tastes.

Okay, so we've talked a bit about the structures on the tongue and the nature of the stimuli for taste and some interesting phenomena, such as wisdom of the body, and in our next lecture we will continue our discussion of the taste system, extending our discussion to some of the factors that influence individual differences in taste preferences. Thank you.

Lecture Sixteen
Taste—Factors Influencing Preferences

Scope:

All normal people are born with the same innate taste preferences. Yet by adulthood, people around the world have such different taste preferences that it is hard to believe that at one time they were similar. The following are some factors that contribute to individual differences in taste preference:

- **Age**: An 80-year-old may have fewer than half as many taste receptors as an 8-year-old. This is one reason why the young and the old have different taste preferences.

- **Learned taste aversion**: There is a special relationship between taste and illness programmed into the brain's circuits. Thus, if we experience a taste and become ill even hours later, we will develop an aversion to that taste, even though the taste may have had nothing to do with the illness. This is not only true for humans but also for many other animal species.

- **Cultural factors**: Different cultures teach their members to like certain tastes and to be repulsed by others. Learning and cultural programming can easily override the preferences we are born with.

- **Familial genetics**: Taste blindness for certain tastes runs in some families, as do extreme taste sensitivities. This has been well documented for the taste of bitter, and it may also be the case for other tastes.

- **Special foods**: Many people, mostly women, have strong cravings for chocolate. There is more at work here than just the sweet-tooth phenomenon. These cravings have been reported to be especially strong when a woman is sad, has been jilted, or is experiencing premenstrual syndrome (PMS). The chocolate craving appears to have an emotional component. Some researchers think the cravings are due to the phenylthylanine in chocolate. This substance is apparently produced in the brain when we are in love, resulting in a "heady" feeling.

Outline

I. A healthy, young adult human has approximately 10,000 taste receptors on the tongue. Children may have more than 10,000 taste receptors, and the elderly may have fewer than 10,000 taste receptors.

    A. In addition to taste buds on the tip, sides, and back of the tongue, children have taste buds (and receptors) on the inside of the cheeks, the back of the throat, and the soft palate. These additional receptors are lost as young adulthood approaches.

    B. People have fewer taste receptors on the tongue as they pass middle age and approach old age.

        1. Taste receptors die off every 7–10 days and are replaced by new receptor cells.

        2. As we age, the replacement process falls behind the dying-off process.

        3. The resulting decrease in taste sensitivity alters taste preferences in the elderly.

        4. Illness, excessive exposure to x-rays, smoking, and alcohol abuse can also adversely affect the sense of taste, no matter what one's age.

II. Another factor influencing taste preferences is *learned taste aversion*, the ease with which we develop a dislike for a taste that has been associated with illness.

    A. The research literature on learned taste aversion indicates that in animals ranging from rats to human beings, there is a special relationship between taste and illness such that this category of learning occurs far more easily than most of our learned behaviors.

    B. Even if illness occurs 90 minutes after a taste experience, rats still learn to avoid that taste in the future, although the taste experience had no part in causing the illness. This special category of learning has obvious survival value.

    C. Peoples' unique experiences with tastes and illnesses contribute to the range of individual differences in taste preferences and aversions.

        1. The taste does not have to cause the illness for the learned aversion to occur.

> 2. Foods ingested before feelings of nausea caused by morning sickness or chemotherapy become aversive to the affected individual.

III. Cultural factors play a large part in peoples' taste preferences. Different societies condition and program the behavior of their members in many ways, including taste preferences.

    A. The Masai have a fondness for the taste of cow's blood.

    B. Some cultures readily consume horsemeat, snakes, grasshoppers, rodents, bats, and other creatures. Other cultures find these tastes unacceptable and/or repulsive.

    C. In India, many people have a need for protein, yet several hundred million cattle roam the city streets because of the sacredness of such animals in Hinduism.

    D. In the United States, there is a cultural taboo against eating dog meat and horse meat.

IV. Familial genetics can also influence taste preferences.

    A. Phenylthiocarbamide (PTC), a synthetic substance, can be tasted by two-thirds of the population (called *tasters*) but not by the other third (called *nontasters*). Being a taster or nontaster runs in families, and tasters are highly sensitive to bitter.

    B. Some tasters find caffeine and saccharine unpleasantly bitter.

    C. Some taste researchers think that other taste sensitivities and preferences may also have a genetic component.

V. Some substances with unique tastes achieve popularity in some segments of the population because of their special properties. Three such tastes are chocolate, ginger, and puffer fish, or *fugu*.

    A. Many people (mostly women) experience cravings for chocolate.

        1. Chocolate has been described as an "emotional" food, in that cravings increase during periods of sadness, relationship problems, or PMS.

        2. Chocolate contains phenylthylamine (PEA), which is apparently produced when we are in love.

        3. Some researchers believe that PEA mimics the good feelings of being in love.

B. Some people develop an affinity for the taste of ginger through using it to clear the palate or for its presumed medicinal value.

    1. Ginger in various forms has been used to manage seasickness, motion sickness, and stomach distress in general.

    2. Ginger is used as a cough suppressant, a fever reducer, and as an enhancer of immune system functioning.

    3. Ginger appears to have antioxidant properties.

C. A third example of a food that is a culturally acquired taste is the Japanese puffer fish, or *fugu*.

    1. Fugu is extraordinarily poisonous, containing a toxin hundreds of times more powerful than strychnine unless prepared by a licensed fugu chef.

    2. In preparing the fish, a skilled fugu chef leaves just a trace of the poison to tingle the lips of the consumer. More than a trace, however, will kill the consumer.

    3. Despite the fact that fugu is very expensive and can be poisonous, it continues to be popular in Japan.

Suggested Reading:

Ackerman, *A Natural History of the Senses*, pp. 125–172.

Colavita, *Sensory Changes in the Elderly*, chapter 6.

Questions to Consider:

1. Can you think of practical applications of the learned taste aversion phenomenon?

2. Why might the issue of seasoning the food at a family reunion be problematic?

Lecture Sixteen—Transcript
Taste—Factors Influencing Preferences

Hello, and welcome to Lecture Sixteen. As you recall, in Lecture Fifteen we went over some of basics of our gustatory sense, the sense of taste. We talked about the taste primaries—sweet, sour, salty, and bitter—and about the recommendations of Japanese researchers that we include a fifth taste primary, umami. We also dealt with some vocabulary issues, looking at the difference between a taste papilla, a taste bud, and a taste receptor. We also talked about the fact that the middle of the tongue is taste-blind, and that most taste substances will adapt to nothingness in between 1½ and 3 minutes.

In the present lecture, we're going to extend our discussion of taste and talk about some of the factors that contribute to individual differences in taste preferences. When you think about it, we all start life as infants with a preference for sweet; we have a "sweet tooth" that we are born with. We have less of a preference for salt, but it's still a mild, innate preference, and we need salt, too. Most of us, in fact all of us, are born with an aversion to bitter and sour.

Starting with that in common, look at how we end up as adults, with the wide range of taste preferences that people experience all over the planet. It's absolutely amazing. We're going to look at some of the factors that contribute to differences in taste preferences. One thing that contributes to differences in taste preferences is the aging process, starting from the young age and going to an old age.

In the previous lecture, I mentioned to you that a normal, healthy, young adult human has about 10,000 taste buds, which means effectively 10,000 taste receptors, because each taste bud contains one taste receptor. Now, the reason I specified young adults is because the number of taste buds and receptors is different as we age. In children, for example, children have taste buds not only on the tip of the tongue and the edges of the tongue and the back of the tongue, but children have taste buds on the sides of the cheeks, the back of the throat, and the soft palate. A baby's oral cavity is just crammed with taste buds and taste receptors, which means that they have much more stimulation from taste substances than we do. Now, this may be a strategy on the part of Mother Nature to make sure that children don't neglect to eat and become malnourished so they have lot of sensory stimulation from their food.

As we age, the number of taste receptors that are located in places other than the tongue begin to die off, and by the time we are adults, taste receptors remain simply on the tongue. Okay, so now we understand why children have more taste buds and receptors than young adults.

How about the opposite end of the continuum? Why do the elderly have fewer functioning taste receptors than young adults or than children? Well, you may recall that taste receptors have a very short life span—7–10 days—and then they die. The way that the replacement process works is that in the taste bud, of the 20–24 supporting cells, the most mature—the oldest of the supporting cells—moves to the center of the bud, grows the little hair-like projections that trap molecules of the substance to be tasted, and forms a synaptic connection with a taste nerve fiber going to the brain.

When you are a healthy young adult, the replacement process can keep up with the dying off process, so a taste receptor will die every seven days, and a supporting cell will move in and replace it in relatively short time. As we age, however, the replacement process begins to fall behind the dying-off process, and this should come as no surprise. As you age, cuts heal more slowly, broken bones heal more slowly, and taste-supporting structures become taste receptors at a slower rate. So as we age, we end up having a net loss in the number of functioning taste receptors at any time. Now, there are no exact figures I can give you on this because there's a great deal of variability.

There are certain environmental experiences that are going to reduce the turnover of taste receptors in anybody. For instances, certain illnesses slow down the replacement process, exposure to X-rays can slow down the replacement process, smoking can slow down the replacement process, and I knew of one individual who claims to have totally lost his sense of taste from years of drinking very strong moonshine whiskey. So if these things can slow down the replacement process in a young person, they can do it in spades for an older person. All we can say for certain is that in our 80s, we have significantly fewer taste buds and taste receptors functioning than we did when we were young adults, and certainly fewer than we had when we were children.

Now, one stratagem that some older folks use to try and keep from finding mealtime bland and boring is to experiment with new seasonings and new spices and try different ethnic cuisines to have that different taste. I think this is a highly valuable and positive thing to do, and I'm moving in that direction myself. So, age is one factor that determines taste preferences. Young people, for example, except for this craving for sweets that sometimes will explode in an orgy of candy eating, prefer bland food because spicy food would overwhelm them with all those taste receptors that young people have. So, yes, taste differences certainly show up in different age groups.

Another factor that can contribute to individual differences in taste sensitivity is a phenomenon called the "learned-taste aversion" phenomenon. This is somewhat complicated, so what I'll do is first share with you the reference experiment—the first laboratory demonstration of the learned-taste aversion phenomenon—and then I will attempt to make it more clear what point I'm trying to make.

The demonstration I'm talking about was done by a professor named John Garcia back in 1966. Garcia gave rats exposure to what he called "bright, noisy, saccharine-tasting water." Now, that sounds like a bizarre combination but it's actually quite simple. He put these rats in an enclosure with a dish of saccharine-flavored water. Now, rats have a "sweet tooth," just as people do, and just as most animals do—with the exception of cats—and so the rats, of course, began to drink this water. While they're drinking the water they're also exposed to a flashing light right in front of the water container, and a pulsating tone over the rat's head. Thus, Garcia used the explanatory label, "bright—the flashing light, noisy—the pulsating tone, saccharine-tasting water." While the rats are drinking the bright, noisy, saccharine-tasting water, Dr. Garcia is exposing them to C-rays. He's giving them a sufficient dosage to produce radiation sickness. Now, he doesn't want to kill them, but he wants to make them good and sick. Now, radiation sickness does not come upon you immediately, and you can't feel the radiation while you are being exposed to it. So what happens is the rats drink the bright, noisy, saccharine-tasting water; they are bombarded with X-rays; they're put back in their home cages; and 90 minutes later they begin to show symptoms of radiation sickness. They become dizzy, show nausea and they just don't feel well.

What Garcia then does is, when the rats are recovered enough to be retested, he puts them back in the environment. They go over, take one taste of the saccharine solution and turn their noses up at it. They're not going to drink that stuff. He tests them with the flashing light. They show no fear or aversion. He tests with them with the pulsating tone—again, no fear or aversion.

Dr. Garcia proposed that this was a special case of classical conditioning, that the taste of the saccharine somehow bridged a 90-minute time lag, and was paired with these feelings of illness. So he wrote this article and submitted it for publication to what was then the most prestigious journal in the biological end of psychology. The editor rejected that manuscript of Dr. Garcia's and actually wrote Dr. Garcia a rather snotty rejection letter. A partial quote from that letter was, "Dr. Garcia, your results are no more likely than finding bird droppings in a cuckoo clock," except the editor did not use the word droppings. He used a four-letter word that maybe means the same thing as droppings.

So the thing is, Garcia's conclusions were revolutionary at the time—to say that this is an example of classical conditioning, where a taste occurs, and then an hour and a half later the sickness occurs, and somehow the brain bridges that gap. People were thinking in terms of Pavlovian conditioning. When Pavlov rang a bell or a tone, he would give the dogs meat powder 500 milliseconds later (.5 sec). People say, "Well, what do you think would happen if Pavlov presented the tone and gave the dogs meat powder an hour and a half later? Would they ever learn to salivate to that tone? So how can Garcia call this classical conditioning?" Well, the point that Garcia was making was that not all stimuli are equally associable with all responses, and there's some special relationship between taste and illness—the learned-taste aversion phenomenon.

It turns out that follow-up research demonstrated that Garcia was absolutely correct. You can demonstrate the same phenomenon in any number of ways, and I guess he finally received the recognition and appreciation he deserved when, years later, the editor of that journal—the journal will remain nameless, and the editor will remain nameless—upon his stepping down as editor, he wrote a farewell editorial on the first page of the journal, and he said, "You know, in all my years of being editor of this journal, the one thing I regret is the way I handled Dr. Garcia's finding of learned-taste aversion. It is for real." So this is the learned-taste aversion effect that was demonstrated in the laboratory, and my point is that it can be operating in people every day.

Let me give you some practical examples of this. Take a woman who is pregnant and is experiencing bouts of morning sickness. She's eating her breakfast—she's eating oatmeal or something like this—and she has a wave of nausea. That woman may very well develop an aversion to the taste of oatmeal. That actually happened to somebody I know, as did this: she's eating scrambled eggs for breakfast, and she has a wave of nausea, and she ends up developing an aversion to the taste of scrambled eggs. So these are examples of the learned-taste aversion phenomenon.

You see, this is another one of Mother Nature's survival mechanisms, like Mother Nature programming animals to approach sugar and avoid bitter—that's to increase the likelihood that we will eat things that have sugar in them, which has energy, and we will avoid things that are poisonous—because most poisons in the woods are bitter. Here we see the learned-taste aversion phenomenon as another pre-wired mechanism that has survival value. An animal eats something that is poisonous. There are two outcomes that can occur. One, the animal will die, in which case its troubles are over, but if the animal survives, it better not go back and eat that substance again. So occasionally, a substance is inappropriately blamed because it was the thing that the animal tasted before it became sick, as in the case of Garcia's rats. The taste didn't make the rats sick; the radiation did. In the case of morning sickness, it was not the eggs or the oatmeal that made the woman sick.

We see other examples of the learned-taste aversion phenomenon in the real world, if you will. For example, some time ago sheep farmers in the West were having a problem with coyotes preying on their sheep and killing them and eating them. So farmers used to take a rather direct approach. They would just go out and shoot the coyotes. Well, animal rights people and wildlife people said, "Let's try something else. Let's try—when a sheep dies of natural causes—let's lace the carcass of the sheep with lithium chloride, which in sufficient quantities can cause considerable nausea. Then we'll leave it out there for a coyote to eat. The coyote will eat the sheep carcass, it will be sick from the lithium chloride, but the taste of the sheep will be associated with the illness, and then this coyote won't bother your sheep any more." It turns out that's very labor intensive. You have to wait for a sheep to die of old age, and then put lithium in it, and then wait for a coyote to….They went back to shooting them. But in fact the learned-taste aversion phenomenon did work in coyotes.

We also see another example from the real world in the case of cancer patients who are undergoing chemotherapy. Now, chemo can produce considerable nausea and discomfort, and it's not unusual to find a patient undergoing chemo developing an aversion to the last taste he or she experienced before they had the therapy and experienced the nausea.

In the interest of conveying information, I'm going to share two learned-taste aversions that I have. I'm using myself as an example for every person. We can all probably count on having had a taste associated with illness in some time in our lives. The first story involves the fact that I have an aversion to pickles. This goes back to when I was nine or 10 years old. I was coming down with the mumps. I had swollen glands, I was feeling terrible, and my mother had the next-door neighbor, Mrs. Voss over, who always scared me. She was a big, gruff woman who—she just frightened me. So I'm trying to have a drink of water because I'm feeling very bad. My mother said, "Are you feeling any better?" "No, I need a drink of water." Mrs. Voss asked, "What's wrong with him?" and my mother said, "We think he's coming down with mumps." Mrs. Voss said, "I know how to tell. Find me a pickle." Mother told her, "We don't have any pickles," and Mrs. Voss said, "Hold the boy; I'll go next door and bring back a pickle." She ran over to her house and came back with a pickle and said, "Come here, boy. Take a bite of this pickle."

I was scared. She was coming at me with this pickle. I started running. I ran around the dining room table. She chased me. I headed for the back door; it was locked. Mrs. Voss caught me, grabbed me and crammed that pickle into my mouth. She triggered a gag reflex, and I was violently ill. I can still recall the taste of pickle juice. Well, I have a learned-taste aversion to pickles. I haven't had a pickle in over half a century.

The other learned-taste aversion—I'll go ahead and tell you the story because we know each other so well—I had to be three years old because we were still living in the space over my grandparents' house. My mother had to take my little brother to the doctor, and my grandmother said, "Leave the boy. I'll come up and check on him every now and then. He can't get into any trouble."

Well, I could get into a little trouble. My mother used to be a secret chocolate addict, and she would never let us have any—she would tell us it's bad for us, but I knew the drawer where she kept her chocolate. So she was out; my grandmother was downstairs. I went over to my mother's chocolate drawer and opened it, and there were two boxes—a big red one and a little blue one. For some reason I thought maybe she wouldn't notice if I ate some from the little blue box, so I took the little blue box out and took a bite of chocolate. It was my first bite of chocolate. It was wonderful. I ate the whole box. Now, because I was three, I couldn't read that what it really was, was chocolate-flavored Ex-lax. Okay. So I ate a strong laxative, a whole box of it, and I had the appropriate result, which ruined the rest of my day, I have to tell you. Now I have a strong aversion to chocolate. It's not that I can take it or leave it—I leave it—and many people find that unusual. I don't typically tell them the story, but I thought that because chocolate is such a favorite of so many people, that you need to know that individual differences in taste preference can even go so far as to include a perennial favorite such as chocolate.

The robustness of the learned-taste aversion phenomenon is just amazing. I had to be three—that's 64 years ago that I had a learned-taste aversion experience with chocolate. Now, see, it wasn't the taste of the chocolate. It was whatever ingredient they put in it, but what do I know? I know that people think they're doing me a favor when they offer me a bite of chocolate, but I politely refuse. So my point here is that everybody can have a learned-taste aversion story. Okay?

Another factor that can bring about incredible differences in taste preferences is cultural training—the conditioning that you undergo as a function of being a member of this culture as opposed to that culture. Now, cultural conditioning starts so young, and as I said, it's so pervasive that you don't even know you've been conditioned. You think everybody should eat what you eat and not eat what you don't eat, but that isn't the way it works.

Our likes, our dislikes, our preferences, attitudes, opinions, prejudices—all of those are based on cultural conditioning, yet it seems so natural, we feel that we were born that way. That's also the case with our taste preferences. Those early taste preferences for the sweet and salt can be easily overcome by cultural conditioning, and in fact, frequently are. Now, I've been very fortunate in my academic career to have been able to travel to 26 different countries where I've seen firsthand the cultural differences in taste preferences. I've been to a Masai village in Kenya where they were drinking cow's blood out of a bowl, and my biggest fear was that they would offer me some cow's blood, because I saw two choices: either drink it and be ill, probably, or not drink it and hurt their feelings. Luckily, they didn't offer it to me.

I've been to parts of the world where they regularly dine on a variety of species of rodents, on fungus, songbirds, grasshoppers and other insects, snakes, snails, and dogs and cats. I remember being in an upscale restaurant in Beijing that sort of reminded me of an upscale seafood restaurant in this country: You go over to a tank in the seafood restaurant, and you point to your lobster. "I'll take that one," and they fish it out, and prepare it for you. In this restaurant in Beijing, you go over to the tank, and you pick out your snake. That took a little getting used to.

So, what we have is a situation where the food items, the taste items that are acceptable in one country—not only acceptable, but considered a delicacy—might be viewed with repulsion, and be viewed as unacceptable in another culture.

In India, for example, they have 1,200,000,000 people. Now, this doesn't hold, of course, for every individual Indian—but in general, there is a need for protein in that country. There is a shortage of protein, and yet they have millions and millions of cows roaming the streets while some people go to bed hungry. Such a thing would be unthinkable, for instance, in Argentina or in some other countries.

In many other countries they have their own "sacred cows," if you will; whereas in India because of cultural conditioning and the role that the cow plays in Hinduism, they wouldn't consider thinking of the cow as an item to dine on. In the United States our sacred cows take the form of horses and dogs. There are people in the United States who would much rather go hungry than eat a dog or a horse. This probably has to do with our tradition in this country of the cowboy, and the cowboy's reliance on his horse, and the old cowboy movies where we knew the horses' names and what have you. The dog, of course, is considered man's best friend in this country. So, in fact, there is a cultural taboo against dog meat and horse meat in this country.

You can imagine some kids coming home from school and saying, "What's for dinner, mommy?" And she says, "Well, tonight we're having Lassie and Trigger." That wouldn't go over too well. As a matter of fact, I can remember an experience when I was teaching an undergraduate class. One of my students was a deer hunter, and it was winter so the stuff didn't though, but he brought me a couple of deer steaks. I didn't want to say, "Let's construe it as a bribe," you know. So I took the deer steaks. I took them home and asked the kids, "Do you guys want to try deer meat?" "Ugh, eat Bambi? No way." So there are emotional factors that influence what people will and will not eat, and horse and dog are examples.

In addition to cultural factors, there are also genetic factors that contribute to individual differences in taste preferences. I will give you an example. A laboratory worker, some years ago, synthesized a liquid, a synthetic liquid called phenylthiocarbamide. Actually it wasn't a liquid; it can be put into a liquid—phenylthiocarbamide. So he has this stuff, which is abbreviated PTC, and he takes a little taste of PTC; it is so incredibly bitter that he can hardly stand it.

It's such a curiosity that he asks the worker at the adjoining bench, "Hey, taste this stuff. What do you think about it?" So the coworker tastes it, and he says, "What about it?" Then he says, "Didn't you find that incredibly bitter?" And the coworker said, "I couldn't taste anything."

Now, this shocked the first person so bad because it was such an intensely bitter taste, it was highly aversive, that he went ahead and tested PTC on a large number of people. What he discovered was that two-thirds of the people who taste phenylthiocarbamide identify it as bitter, and one-third of the people who taste phenylthiocarbamide can't taste it at all. So the general population is divided into tasters, which is two-thirds of us, and non-tasters, which is one-third of us. It turns out that people who are tasters have near relatives who are also tasters. It turns out that the sensitivity to PTC has a genetic basis, and that people who are sensitive to PTC are highly sensitive to the taste of bitter, and people who don't taste PTC are less sensitive to the taste of bitter, but they can still experience bitter. It turns out that among PTC tasters, some of them are so sensitive to the taste of bitter, that they cannot use saccharine, the artificial sweetener, which to them tastes very bitter. They cannot drink coffee, which to them is uncomfortably and aversively bitter.

Research is currently under way in various laboratories interested in genetic factors in human behavior to investigate the possibility that genetic factors are also involved in other taste preferences and taste sensitivities.

Okay, in addition to genetic factors influencing individual differences in taste sensitivity, there are also some factors that are based on a specific taste having some kind of special property that initially attracts somebody to try it for its special property, and then they end up liking the taste, and continue to eat that. One such example of a taste with special properties is chocolate. Okay. If you question a large number of people, and ask them to write down a food that they occasionally have great cravings for, many of these people will indicate that chocolate is a food that they occasionally have cravings for. Now the fact is that this is not meant to be sexist, but the majority of these people who have cravings for chocolate are women. There are some men—not me, as you may well be able to guess—but some men have these cravings too. I've heard women say to each other, "Do you want to do some chocolate after work?" sounding like druggies talking about doing drugs. "Do you want to do some chocolate?"

It's clear that chocolate is an emotional food. Women seem to have greater cravings for it when they are sad, when they are lonely, when they've been jilted, when they are experiencing PMS—the cravings seem to go up. As a matter of fact—I never thought of it before—but my mother, we were kind of poor actually, and yet that was the only luxury she allowed herself, and she was all of the above. She was lonely and jilted and sad. She was raising two little boys alone, and our life was not a bowl of cherries, and she ate chocolate. I never understood that until late in my own life.

All right. So anyway, here's the theory of why people develop these cravings for chocolate. There is a chemical known as phenylthylamine—PEA—and apparently phenylthylamine is produced in the brain when we are in love. In fact, it is PEA that is supposed to be responsible for that heady feeling of walking on clouds and so on when you're in love. Now, when the love stops, the PEA production in the brain stops, and the theory is that there are special times in a woman's life—or I guess it could be anybody's life, but it seems to happen more frequently in women—when you miss those good feelings produced by the PEA when you were in love. Since chocolate contains PEA, by eating chocolate you can kill two birds with one stone, You can taste something sweet and delicious, and you can also increase your PEA levels and have a good emotional feeling. The truth of the matter is that there are other tastes that also contain PEA, but apparently none of them taste as good as chocolate. So that's one theory for the chocolate cravings.

Another taste with a special property that is supposed to contribute to why people end up liking it is ginger. Ginger is a functional vegetable. Ginger is used between courses to clean your palate in restaurants. Some people swear by ginger as a precaution against motion sickness. Ginger is supposed to have the properties of being a cough suppressant and a fever reducer and a booster of the immune system and an antioxidant. I have taken, with my wife, two around-the-world sea voyages. When people heard we were going to be at sea for months and months, many people said, "Take caramelized ginger with you. It's a guaranteed way to minimize sea sickness." So we did, in fact, take caramelized ginger with us, and a number of our fellow passengers apparently had received the same advice, because they brought caramelized ginger with them. It turns out that the people who used caramelized ginger experienced far less motion sickness. Just recently I read a scientific study where one gram of powdered ginger root was compared with Dramamine™ as to its effectiveness in minimizing or eliminating motion sickness. It's real. I know of people who started out eating ginger for one of its other medicinal properties, and ended up liking it, and now they eat caramelized ginger regularly.

Here's one more example of a food with a special property. We're going to be focusing on something that is more or less peculiar to Japan. That taste is the taste of puffer fish—puffer fish or fugu. Now it turns out that fugu has the special property, if it's not prepared exquisitely carefully, of killing you; that's the special property. Fugu, it turns out, or puffer fish, contains a deadly toxin so that if the fugu chef, who must be licensed in Japan, doesn't prepare it properly, you run the risk of dying. Apparently, this is the enticement for young Japanese males who are the primary purchasers of fugu. It turns out that fugu contains a toxin hundreds of times more powerful than strychnine or arsenic or any of the poisons that we're familiar with. An expert fugu chef can actually leave just a taste of the toxin in it, so that when you eat it you can feel a tingling in your lips, and you know that you've just looked the Grim Reaper in the eye, but you're still there to chew your next piece of fugu. So people start out with this stuff—which tastes just like pompano, but it's many times more expensive—they start out with it because of the, I guess the rush of almost dying, of having a near-death experience, and they end up liking the taste. Some cities in Japan have a law that if you die of fugu poisoning, they can't bury you for three days, because in three days the toxin wears off, and some people come back to life.

Okay. So we have spent our lecture talking about some of the factors that contribute to individual differences in taste preference. In our next lecture we will talk about the sense of smell, which I call the unappreciated sense, because people don't realize just how important smell is. Thank you.

Lecture Seventeen
Smell—The Unappreciated Sense

Scope:

If people are asked which of their senses they would miss the least, many choose smell. As we will see, smell is actually more important for humans than most of us realize. If we became blind and deaf, most of us could learn to identify friends and family members by smell. We could also learn to identify people from different cultures by smell because our scent is, in part, determined by what we eat, and as we saw in Lecture Sixteen, different cultures have different dietary habits.

The stimuli for smell are airborne and gaseous. The receptors for smell are located in the olfactory crypt on the olfactory epithelium, a patch of tissue measuring 2.5 square centimeters. Because the olfactory epithelium is located out of the mainstream of inspired air, we must create eddy currents to carry molecules of odorous substances to the receptors by producing a sharp "sniff" to maximize smell sensitivity.

Smell can enhance our experience in a variety of situations. Incense is used in many formal religious ceremonies. Used-car dealers spray artificial "new-car scent" in their vehicles to make them more attractive to buyers. Realtors know that the odor of fresh oven-baked bread in the kitchen will make a prospective purchaser more likely to buy.

Neuroanatomically, the sense of smell is organized in a manner suggesting its participation in a variety of important areas in both humans and lower animals. Smell information goes directly from the receptors to the cerebral cortex, without first passing through subcortical relay stations, as does information from all the other sensory systems. Smell data are then sent to 20 different parts of the brain, including areas involved in memory, emotional reactivity, and motivation.

Outline

I. Smell (or *olfaction*), along with taste, represent the chemical senses in humans.

A. Unlike the other senses, smell stimuli do not have unique names, as colors or tastes do, but are likened to other things (e.g., flowery, fruity) or other experiences (e.g., putrid, burnt). We can identify 10,000 different odors.

B. We have 10 million smell receptors. They are located on a 2.5-square-centimeter patch of tissue called the *olfactory epithelium*, which is located out of the mainstream of inspired air. Smell sensitivity is enhanced by a sharp "sniff," thus creating eddy currents that bring odorous molecules into contact with the receptors.

C. Smell stimuli are airborne and gaseous.

D. Until fairly recently, research on the sense of smell has lagged behind research on the other senses. There are several reasons for this.

    1. Smell stimuli are hard to control—how do you turn a smell on or off?

    2. The receptors are relatively inaccessible.

    3. There is an inadequate technical vocabulary to describe smells.

    4. Historically, smell has been considered less important than the other senses.

II. Olfaction in humans is considerably more sensitive than we realize.

A. We all have heard descriptions of the incredible smell sensitivity of dogs. There are also documented instances of incredible smell sensitivity in humans.

B. An individual human smell receptor is as sensitive as an individual dog smell receptor. Dogs, however, have 1,000 times as many receptors as we do.

C. If it becomes necessary, we can make far greater use of our sense of smell.

    1. Blind people become able to recognize family and friends by smell, not because they have a better sense of smell, but because they must depend more on this sense.

    2. With practice, one can identify people from different cultures by smell because our diets influence our body odors and different cultures have different diets.

    3. Human subjects can recognize their own worn T-shirts by smell.

4. Experiments suggest that women have a better sense of smell than men.

D. Smell may influence people without our conscious awareness.
   1. A phenomenon known as the *McClintock effect,* named for Martha McClintock, the psychologist who discovered it, suggests that odor cues result in menstrual synchrony among female students living on the same dormitory floor.
   2. Thus, McClintock is credited with being the first person to demonstrate the existence of a human *pheromone.*
   3. Pheromones are odorous stimuli that can produce a physiological response in some other species member.

III. Cultural factors are a major determinant of the degree to which people make use of olfactory information.

A. Generally speaking, babies show a preference for pleasant and familiar odors at a very early age.

B. Our sense of smell peaks at age 8.

C. Many Western cultures mask olfactory stimuli with deodorants and room fresheners.

D. We teach our children not to use olfactory cues.
   1. Children naturally use smell to investigate novel objects or foods.
   2. Children are frequently told, "It's not polite to smell your food. Just eat it."

E. *Ayurvedic medicine* (the holistic health care system developed in India thousands of years ago and still in use) uses smell as an important part of examining patients and diagnosing diseases.
   1. Around 250 years ago, Western physicians began to feel that using smell to help diagnose illness was unscientific and undignified.
   2. Some medical conditions (such as phenylketonuria [PKU], diabetes, and kidney disorders) are associated with a particular odor that can help in diagnosis of the condition.

IV. Although Western cultures may downplay the primary importance of olfaction, smell stimuli are utilized nevertheless to enhance various significant experiences.

    A. The aroma is an important component of a good meal.

    B. Scented candles enhance romantic interludes.

    C. Incense is used in many formal religious ceremonies.

    D. Used-car dealers use aerosol "new-car scent" sprays to make their cars more attractive to customers.

    E. Realtors claim that the odor of fresh baked bread in the kitchen is effective in turning lookers into buyers.

V. Neuroanatomical studies of the brain suggest that olfaction is far more critical for normal human functioning than previously realized.

    A. Smell receptors have direct connections with the cerebral cortex without initially passing through various subcortical relay stations, as is found in all the other senses.

    B. By means of the olfactory bulbs, which are the structures that receive input from smell receptors, odorous stimuli generate neural activity in 20 different parts of the brain.

        1. The olfactory system projects to parts of the brain involved in memory.

        2. Olfactory signals reach parts of the brain involved in emotional response.

        3. Brain structures involved in motivated behavior also have connections to the olfactory system.

    C. Examples exist wherein the sense of smell in animals overrides the strength of their other senses.

Suggested Reading:

Goldstein, *Sensation and Perception* (6th ed.), pp. 473–481.

Sekuler and Blake, *Perception* (4th ed.), pp. 542–572.

Questions to Consider:

1. It has been shown in the laboratory that people can tell the difference between around 10,000 different odors. Why do you suppose most people are surprised to learn this fact?

2. Data suggest that, in general, women are more sensitive to odors and are better at identifying odors than men. No physiological explanation for this sex difference has been identified as yet. Do you have any ideas or opinions about this difference?

Lecture Seventeen—Transcript
Smell—The Unappreciated Sense

Hello, and welcome to Lecture Seventeen. In Lecture Sixteen we talked about some of the factors that contribute to individual taste preferences. I marvel at the fact that we all start life with little more than a preference for sweet and an aversion to bitter, and decades later we end up with the wide array of different taste preferences that we see in humans.

In Lecture Seventeen we're going to begin talking about the second of our two chemical senses; namely, the olfactory sense, or smell. I call smell "the unappreciated sense" because many people are really unaware of the importance of smell. I hope that some of the information that I'll share with you in this lecture will convince you that maybe smell is a little more important than we think.

One interesting difference between smell and many of the other senses is there are no smell primaries. I mean in taste we have sweet, sour, salty and bitter, and maybe umami, and in vision we have red, green, and blue, and the skin senses—touch and pressure, vibration, etc., but we don't have any analogue in smell. There are no smell primaries. We can identify, the human nose can actually identify— and this has been demonstrated in laboratories—10,000 different odors. So we have a broad range of sensitivities, but sense of smell is sometimes referred to as "the mute sense" because we don't have a vocabulary to express these smells.

When we refer to a smell we usually refer to it by referring to something else. We say, "That smelled fruity"; "that smelled disgusting"; "that smelled medicinal"; "that smelled flowery." We don't have a vocabulary to describe smells. We have 10,000,000 smell receptors, and these 10,000,000 receptors are able to permit us to identify 10,000 different odors by having broad ranges of sensitivity and by firing in patterns. So, as a matter of fact, this turns out to be about the only way the sense of smell could work, because most smells that we think of as being clear and distinct are actually made up of a large number of separate volatile components. Take the odor of coffee, for example, so recognizable you would think that that's kind of a unitary component, but coffee, the odor of coffee is actually made up of 60 different volatile components.

Now these 10,000,000 smell receptors that I just alluded to are located on a 2.5 square centimeter patch of tissue high up in the olfactory crypt, way up in your nose on an area of skin called the olfactory epithelium. The olfactory epithelium is out of the direct pathway of inspired air. So when we breathe normally, our smell sensitivity is really not so good.

If we want to maximize the opportunity to smell something, we must voluntarily produce a sharp, distinct sniff, because a sniff, a distinct sniff sets up eddy currents, and the molecules of the odorous substance are then caused to drift upward and come into contact with the receptors on the olfactory epithelium. The stimuli for smell are airborne and gaseous, so they're traveling in the air, and in order to put them in contact with the appropriate receptors, we have to take the initiative and sniff. Similarly, if you are in the presence of something that doesn't smell too good, you can breathe through your mouth, and you won't be setting up those eddy currents, and you're less likely to experience that unpleasant odor.

Research into the sense of smell has lagged. In fact, there is less research on smell than there is on the cutaneous sense. Now this is changing. Recently, more interest has been shown by researchers in the sense of smell for a couple of reasons. For example, new data suggesting a connection between smell and memory has caught the attention of researchers, and some researchers are now beginning to investigate in the laboratory some of the claims of a phenomenon called aromatherapy, and we'll come to that a little bit later. But historically, smell research has been quite scarce, and there are a number of reasons—I mean, this is understandable.

First of all, researchers like stimulus control, for instance, a vision researcher. If you want to turn a light on, you push a button and the light goes on. You want to turn the light off, you push a button and the light goes off; it's the same with hearing, the same with the touch and the skin senses. But in the case of smell, how do you turn a smell on, especially when the subject has to give a sharp, distinct sniff, and then when you're ready to try another stimulus, how do you get the old odor to dissipate and get it out of there? So there are, in fact, legitimate problems with stimulus control that would give a researcher pause before specializing in smell.

It's also the case that the smell receptors are rather inaccessible. I mean they are high up. You can't reach them with your index finger, as I've seen some people trying to do. Smell receptors are actually way up in the olfactory crypt. This means that it's difficult to put electrodes up there, even in the nose of a rat or a rabbit or some animal that you might want to record directly from the receptors. The receptors are rather inaccessible.

The lack of an adequate vocabulary is another reason. Scientists like to use precise terms to describe things that everybody knows the exact meaning of. When you have a sensory system where you have no primaries and no names for the smells other than fruity and putrid and resinous and spicy and medicinal—that's not very appealing to somebody who is more comfortable with precise vocabulary terms. Another reason that research on smell, up until recently, has lagged is the general belief that in terms of the hierarchy of the senses, smell is relatively unimportant.

Okay. Now, the epitome of a good smeller, the epitome of a creature that is known for its olfactory sensitivity is the dog. The feats of bloodhounds are legendary. They can track somebody by smelling the odor of an article of clothing this person wore. They can track somebody through the woods hours or even days after that person has made his escape or whatever has caused him to run off into the woods.

In the laboratory you can demonstrate the following. You can take a good strong soap, wash your hands and remove all the greases and oils or anything that might provide an olfactory cue. You wash your hands and dry your hands thoroughly. Then you pick up a stick, you hold it for about two seconds, you put the stick down, and then you go in a lineup with other people, and the dog comes into the room, smells the stick, and walks over and points to you. They are really quite good.

I remember another story about the exquisitely sensitive olfactory abilities of the dog. This took place back when Berlin was partitioned into East Berlin and West Berlin. One of the problems was smuggling and the black market, and one item that brought a high price was real coffee. Apparently, in those days it was very difficult to find real coffee. One of the border dogs that was used to sniff for illegal contraband was named Geisha, and some people still remember what Geisha did one day that was so impressive as a feat of olfactory sensitivity. Geisha was able to discover a bundle of contraband coffee wrapped in plastic, covered with gasoline-soaked rags, under a wagonload of coal. Geisha went over—"Woof-woof. There. Coffee,"—and she was right. I guess Geisha was a girl.

At this point I shall keep a promise I made to you earlier, and tell you about my Halloween costume story. It involved a dog. I'll try and do this quickly. It was, in fact, Halloween time, and I decided to wear a Frankenstein costume. So I went to a friend's house, and I put on a full-head Frankenstein mask. I borrowed this guy's work boots. His feet were much bigger than mine, so I could fit two balled up pairs of socks in the heels, so I was standing several inches taller than I really am, plus the work boots had heels to begin with, so it made me maybe four inches taller than I usually am. I put on an oversized jacket with shoulder pads, and I decided to go fool my wife. I left the friend's house, and I came back to my own house. I thought, "I'll ring the bell rather than just walk in." So I rang the bell. The dog heard the bell and came running to the front door, barking. I heard my wife's footsteps. She opened the door. The dog immediately smelled that it was I and wagged its tail, and sat down beside me. My wife wasn't quite sure, because I was four inches taller than usual, and I didn't say anything. I saw these expressions change on her face: "Is it he? Who is it? Is this some kind of a threatening situation?" She didn't know what to do.

Finally, I broke the ice by saying—and I tried to change my voice— "Lady, I haven't eaten in three days." She recognized my voice and quickly came back with, "Force yourself." This made me start laughing; that made her start laughing, and the dog just sat there looking back and forth. See dogs have a great sense of smell, but their sense of humor still needs a little work. Anyway, that's my dog story.

The fact of the matter is that if you compare the sensitivity of an individual human smell receptor with the sensitivity of an individual dog smell receptor, they're of equal sensitivity. Why, then, does the dog have such greater olfactory ability than we do? Well, the reason is because the dog, on its olfactory epithelium has 1,000,000,000— that's billion with a b—1,000,000,000 receptors, whereas we have 10,000,000. The dog has 1,000 times more smell receptors than we do, and the dog's sense of smell is close to 1,000 times better than ours. It's incredible.

By the way, even though dogs have better olfactory sensitivity than we do, there are still some really impressive demonstrations of smell sensitivity that humans have done. It turns out that most of these humans who have accomplished incredible feats using their sense of smell are blind. but I'm going to tell you right up front that there is absolutely no basis for believing that when you go blind your sense of smell becomes better. It's just that when you are blind, you are forced, of necessity, to make more use of smell information, which is difficult. It requires concentration, and practice. It's not as easy as looking or listening, but when you are forced to use your sense of smell, it turns out to be able to provide you with incredible information.

Well, let me give you some examples. We've mentioned Helen Keller before, and I may have mentioned that Helen Keller was able to identify friends and family when they entered the room on the basis of smell. I may have told you that Helen Keller, as she was driven through the country side in an open carriage, could identify trees and plants and crops and farm animals on the basis of smell. Helen Keller also reported that she was able to identify the occupation of a stranger who was brought in to see her. She could tell what kind of work people did by their smell because she said that we carry with us little bits and pieces of odorous material from wherever we work. So she claimed she could even tell what you did for a living by smelling you.

The other two instances of extraordinary human olfactory ability that I want to share with you have to do with two laundry workers. These were both blind women. They didn't work in the same laundry. They didn't know each other. One worked in what was called an "insane asylum" at the time. The other worked in a long-term care facility, so they were both dealing with the same clients day after day. Both of these women were able to sort the laundry of individual residents in their facilities by smell after the laundry had been washed. They could actually smell and tell whose laundry was whose after it had been washed. That's quite remarkable.

If you and I had to, and were willing to do the work and we were motivated to do so, we could actually learn to identify different people from different countries on the basis of smell. We could tell, for example, an Eskimo from a Japanese from an Arab from a Northern European on the basis of smell. That might take us a couple of weeks of practice, practice, practice, learning to pay attention to subtle cues that ordinarily we don't pay any attention to.

In a much shorter period of time we could learn to tell a vegetarian from somebody who was a meat eater, and the reason that we could do all these things is because our diets, the food that we eat, actually contributes to our particular body odor. It's subtle enough that you have to look for it, and you have to really be tuned in before you can smell this, but people from what we call primitive societies, which is a pejorative term—they're actually from what we might call non-industrialized societies use their sense of smell more, and they, in fact, can discriminate where you're from by how you smell. I spoke to some Japanese people who were candid enough to tell me that in general the Japanese find Americans to have an unpleasant, buttery odor that comes from the fact that we eat so much more beef with animal fat in it than they do. So we, in fact, have a characteristic smell to them. We're not tuned in enough to olfactory cues, but we could become more tuned in to olfactory cues.

It's also the case that research has suggested we have smell capabilities right now that we don't even know we have, and probably wouldn't believe we had if somebody told us. Let me give you a couple of examples. There have been experiments done at universities where professors either hire, or in some way ·coax students into participating in experiments where the students will wear the same T-shirt for a week—something like that—under their regular clothing, so that nobody knows you're wearing the same thing every day. At the end of the week, all of these students throw their T-shirts into a big pile, and they're mixed up. Then the instructions are, "Find your T-shirt." And they say, "How can I do that?" "Well, just try." It turns out that students, on the basis of smell, can in fact find their own T-shirt.

And then another request to students who have worn these shirts and thrown them in a pile is, "Find T-shirts that were worn by males, and find T-shirts that were worn by females." Again, they think, "Gee, I can't do that."

But when they do, it turns out that they are, in fact, able to on the basis of smell distinguish T-shirts worn by a male from T-shirts worn by a female. This type of experiment has been done a number of times, so it is a real phenomenon; it isn't just one fluky, fluky thing.

One thing I will tell you, these experiments tend to suggest that women have a better sense of smell than men. This is a recurring finding that we're going to see through the ages of human beings, that women are a little bit more olfactory than men. For example, mothers of young children have been tested. The clothing of the children is mixed up, and mothers are told—even if the clothing is identical, so you can't tell it on the basis of brand name or color or what have you—"Find your kid's clothing." So they can smell it, and mothers can find their own children's clothing in a big pile of other clothing. Men can't do that. Fathers can't do that. So here again we see an example of the female sense of smell being more acute than the male.

There is also experimental evidence suggesting that odors can influence us, and influence our behavior, without any conscious awareness on our part of exactly what is influencing behavior. One example of that is a phenomenon called the "McClintock effect." A psychologist by the name of Martha McClintock made the following observation. She demonstrated that women in college who lived on the same dorm floor, over the course of a semester, exhibited synchronicity of their menstrual periods. At the beginning of the semester their periods were all at some different level of the cycle. By the end of the semester all of their menstrual periods were congruent. They had achieved synchrony, so to speak.

Her suspicion was that this was based on some chemical signal. Chemical signals that animals give off are called pheromones. Most people, when they hear the word pheromone, they think, "Oh, sex pheromones." The sex pheromones are an example of one type of pheromones, but territorial animals mark their territories with pheromones also. Martha McClintock followed up on her initial finding of this synchronicity, and is credited, in 1998 I believe, with being the first person to demonstrate the existence of a human pheromone. So we have them, too. It isn't a sex pheromone, but it is a pheromone. Pheromones are "odorous stimuli that can produce a physiological response in some other species member." It doesn't always have to be a sexual response. It can be obeying a territorial boundary, or it can be in this case somehow contributing to the synchronicity of some biological process.

Okay, if we have all these smell abilities, why don't we make more use of them? Well, it turns out that we are a non-smelling culture. Cultural factors are responsible for the fact that we don't make more use of smell information. As a matter of fact, we are predisposed from birth on to use smell and to be more tuned into odors around us, but our culture breeds that out of us in ways that I'll get to in a minute.

There is data suggesting that newborn babies use smell to make decisions. Newborns can do this. How is such an experiment possible? What happened was in one experiment, mothers of newborn babies had agreed ahead of time that, yes, they were going to breast feed, and yes, they would agree to have one of their nipples washed, so that it didn't have the odor of the mother on it. And the experimenters—on one mother would wash the right nipple, on the other the left nipple. So they were ruling out the possibility that babies had a position preference of always turning right or left or what have you.

Then they would bring the newborn to the mother, and they would put the baby equidistant to either breast, so that the baby was not closer to one than the other. What this experiment demonstrated was 75% of the babies went for the unwashed breast—the one that had the mother's smell still on it.

By the way, there is an analogous finding with baby rats. Baby rats, of course, by instinct crawl over and begin to nurse, but if you wash the mother rat's nipples, the babies don't attach. So apparently it is smell that leads the baby rat to the nipple and to nurse, because if you washed the smell of the mother rat off, the baby will starve. So it isn't intelligent behavior; it is apparently what they call a species-specific behavior.

Anyway, my point is that at one hour, or whatever, of age, a newborn baby is capable of making a decision at some level based on smell. One-day-old infants will show a facial expression suggesting disgust at the odor of a rotten egg. You give the baby the smell of the mother, and it will smile. You give it the smell of a rotten egg, and it makes a face suggesting disgust.

Infants also show disgust and distress at the smell of smoke and at the smell of acids. Acids are caustic substances that can cause trouble, and of course, smoke means fire. Babies who have neither smelled acid nor smoke before, show alarm and distress, and are disturbed by the smell of smoke and acid, suggesting another one of Mother Nature's built-in defense mechanisms. Just as we are programmed to approach sweet and avoid bitter—because sweet is energy, and bitter may be poison—so we are programmed to approach the smell of the mother, and we are programmed to avoid the smells of things such as smoke and acid.

Another interesting thing about infants and smell is even though the myelin sheath is not fully developed until they are 12 years old, a child's smell sensitivity reaches its peak four years earlier than that. Children are excellent at smelling by the time they're eight years old. They're as good as they're ever going to be. Why, then, are we not a more olfactory-oriented culture—because we apparently come equipped to make decisions from birth on, based on smell. Well, for one thing, we have made the decision some time ago to mask odors that other cultures would find full of information. So we use room fresheners, and we use under arm deodorants, and so on, plus we verbally chastise our children for using their sense of smell.

What do I mean by that? Well, I've seen in restaurants—they take this child out for dinner, and the child is served a strange food that it's never seen before. I've seen the child pick up a piece of food and smell it. Then one of the parents will say, "Don't smell your food. That's bad behavior. Just eat it. It's not good manners to smell your food."

I was in a doctor's office once, and a woman had her young son on her lap. The young boy leaned over to the woman next to him, and he said, "You smell funny." The mother apologized profusely, and scolded the kid, and told him how terrible that was, and "Don't you ever say anything like that again." So, we spray away odors, and we punish our kids for continuing to make use of smell information.

Other cultures make use of information that we ignore or spray away. For example, we talked about traditional Chinese medicine as being a holistic health care system that's over 5,000 years old. There's another one that's twice as old as traditional Chinese medicine, and that is the holistic health delivery system known as Ayurvedic medicine from India. Now, an Ayurvedic practitioner will, in the course of examining a patient, smell the patient—smell the patient's skin, smell the patient's breath, smell the patient's urine, smell the patient's sweat—and it turns out that they use smell as an important adjunct to making a diagnosis.

Actually, up until about 250 years ago, Western physicians used to use smell to help in making diagnoses, because there are certain medical conditions that are associated with a characteristic odor. Let me give you a couple of examples. Phenylketonuria—PKU—this is an inherited metabolic disorder in children that, if not caught in time and corrected by a special diet a phenylalinine-free diet—results in mild to serious mental retardation. Well kids with PKU give off a characteristic odor that's been characterized as a "horsy, stale gymnasium odor." It's easy to distinguish.

Diabetics have a special odor. Kidney problems, digestive problems—all of these medical conditions are associated with a characteristic odor, and could be diagnosed, or the diagnosis could be based, in part at least, on smells. Somewhere along the line, Western medicine made the decision that using smell to diagnose medical conditions was unscientific or perhaps not dignified enough, or something like that. So, typically, we don't do it.

In spite of the fact that our culture does not seem to grasp the importance of smell, per se, we do use smells to enhance other activities. For example, the aroma of your meal is greatly enhanced by the smell. We use scented candles to enhance the mood of romantic interludes. We use incense in religious ceremonies. Used car dealers buy aerosol cans of "new car" spray to spray inside their used cars, and they can ask a higher price for them. Realtors know that if a kitchen in a house that's for sale has the odor of fresh-baked bread in it, people who look at that house are more likely to buy it. There are also neuroanatomical studies suggesting that smell is more important than we typically give it credit for.

Smell has the most direct connections between the receptors and the cerebral cortex. It doesn't have to go first through the thalamus as every other sensory system does. A smell stimulus will produce electrical activity in 20 different parts of the brain, and some of these parts of the brain are the parts of the brain that are known to be involved in memory, in emotional reactivity, and in motivation.

I have a few more facts that I want to share with you in the context of demonstrating the importance of smell even in animals that see and hear as well as we do. It is the case that some animals with eyes and ears in a conflict situation will go with the information provided by their sense of smell.

One example is seen on cattle ranches. Picture this somewhat tragic event. A mother cow gives birth. The calf lives, the mother cow dies. Another mother cow gives birth. She lives, the calf dies. So now we have a live mother and a live calf, but they are not related to each other. Can we take that calf over to the mother and she will raise it as an orphan? No. She rejects it. But what we the cattle ranchers do is they will skin the dead calf, and tie the skin of the dead calf around the live one, and now the mother cow will accept it, and she will nurse it. The evidence of her eyes is saying, "Somebody tied my dead baby's skin around this strange baby calf. I should really be incensed," but no, she smells the skin and permits the baby calf to nurse. There's an example of the evidence of smell overriding the evidence of one's eyes.

Another example occurs to me from a sailing trip that I took that passed some islands off the coast of Alaska. One of these islands was covered, wall-to-wall, with seals, and seals were diving off the island into the water, and crawling back onto the land. Some of these seals were baby seals, and I thought to myself, "How is that baby seal ever going to find it's mother?" because all the seals looked alike to me. I wondered, "Do they call out, and the mother answers? Or do they stand on a rock and look around, or what?" I had a biology professor with me, so I asked the biology professor, "Is this a problem, the babies being reunited with their mothers?" He said, "No, not at all. They'll do it quite readily." I said, "How on earth do they do that?" and he said, "The baby seals follow a scent trail, and they go right back to their mothers."

So we find that smell is the preferred mode for reuniting with a parent or recognizing an offspring over and above vision and hearing, or instead of vision and hearing, again suggesting that we need to take a second look at our preconceived notions about the importance of smell.

In our next lecture we will see more evidence and examples of the importance of smell to humans. This lecture deals with the consequences of anosmia. For those of you for whom that is a new term, anosmia is the technical term for "a loss or diminution of the sense of smell." You can become totally anosmic or partially anosmic. One way to appreciate the importance of something is to see how your life changes when you lose it. So the lecture on the consequences of anosmia should make a believer of you if you're not already convinced that smell is a very important sense. Thank you.

Lecture Eighteen
Smell—Consequences of Anosmia

Scope:

The sense of smell has neural connections with brain regions involved in motivation, emotion, and memory. Research with animals has revealed some of the significance of these connections. A relationship between sexual behavior and smell has been identified in animals ranging from insects to nonhuman primates. Chemical odorous sex attractants called *pheromones* are produced and released by females of many species to attract males during the breeding season. Evidence for the importance of pheromones in humans is scanty at best, but perfume manufacturers take advantage of the possibility in their advertising. Sexual behavior is abolished in rats and hamsters following removal of the olfactory bulbs. The control of sexual behavior of humans is far more complex than that of lower animals, but it appears that 25 percent of people who become anosmic lose their sex drive.

A relationship between smell and human memory has also been documented. Some individuals have powerful *olfactory imagery*, whereby a particular odor can recall in vivid detail some event from the past. In addition, recent evidence suggests that a decline in smell sensitivity correlates with the onset of memory impairment in people with Alzheimer's disease and other forms of senile dementia.

The aging process has been shown to diminish smell sensitivity. This diminishment has negative implications for the elderly in a number of areas, such as carelessness with personal hygiene due to a reduced ability to smell body odor; risk of inadequate nutrition due to loss of pleasure in eating; less joy in daily life because of decreased ability to smell flowers, fresh bread, and other pleasant odors; and greater risk of sickness or injury as a result of reduced sensitivity to the smell of smoke, gas, hazardous chemicals, or spoiled food.

Outline

I. In laboratory experiments, *anosmia* (loss of the ability to smell) has been shown to alter significantly the behavior of animals.

A. Following removal of the olfactory bulbs, territorial animals neither mark their own territory nor respect the markings of other animals.

B. Rats and hamsters made anosmic no longer engage in sexual behavior.

C. The sexual behavior of many animal species, ranging from insects to nonhuman primates, is strongly influenced by pheromones, odorous chemical attractants.

    1. There is no strong evidence that pheromones are a significant factor in human sexual behavior.

    2. Perfume manufacturers would have you believe otherwise.

D. Although the mechanism is not understood at this time, statistical evidence indicates that approximately 25 percent of humans who become anosmic as a result of injury or infection lose their sex drive.

II. Recent evidence points to a connection between smell and memory to the point of suggesting that declines in smell sensitivity sometimes correlate with declines in memory.

    A. Some individuals possess powerful olfactory imagery, such that encountering a particular smell will reinstate the clear memory of some event or experience that may have happened decades ago. This phenomenon is called the *Proust effect*, named for a similar incident described in *Swann's Way*, a work by French author Marcel Proust.

    B. There are now a number of reports indicating that declines in smell sensitivity occur at the same time that memory impairments begin to show up in people with some form of senile dementia, such as Alzheimer's disease.

        1. Scientists acknowledge the possibility that tests of smell sensitivity may be able to predict the onset of memory impairment at an early stage of memory loss so that remediation techniques can be applied sooner.

        2. To date, such smell tests have shown about an 80 percent accuracy rate, as good as any test currently available to predict memory loss.

    C. Discoveries in the realm of neuroscience also suggest a relationship between smell and memory.

1. For centuries, it has been believed that the adult human brain is incapable of producing new brain cells.
2. Recently, it has been demonstrated that two regions of the adult human brain are, in fact, capable of producing new cells. These two parts of the brain are the olfactory bulbs and the hippocampus.
3. The olfactory bulbs receive input from smell receptors.
4. The hippocampus is a forebrain structure known to be critical for the consolidation of short-term memory into long-term memory.

III. There is a form of holistic therapy called *aromatherapy*, defined as the therapeutic use of the essential oils of plants to affect mood or health. Proponents of aromatherapy claim that certain odors can alleviate conditions ranging from personality disorders to digestive problems. Although most of the claims of aromatherapy remain untested, there is some laboratory evidence that motivation and emotion may be responsive to different odors.

A. Aromatherapy dates from the 1930s, when French chemist Rene-Maurice Gattefosse, who worked in a family perfume manufacturing company, discovered what he considered the curative properties of plant oils.

B. Not all scientists agree with the claims of the benefits of aromatherapy.

C. However, the odor of green apples has been shown to lower blood pressure and to promote relaxation.

D. The odor of lavender has been demonstrated to raise the basal metabolic rate, to facilitate concentration, and to increase alertness.

IV. Smell sensitivity has been shown to decline as a consequence of the aging process.

A. Olfactory sensitivity is quite variable among the elderly.
1. After the age of 55, the sense of smell declines precipitously in men, whereas women retain their smell sensitivity for about 20 years longer.
2. The decline in smell sensitivity varies considerably, however, and some individuals in their 70s and older perform as well as middle-aged subjects on tests of smell sensitivity.

B. In general, in the elderly, the olfactory epithelium gets thinner and individual receptors are lost.

C. At any age, some environmental experiences, including blows to the head, infections of the olfactory epithelium, exposure to x-rays, use of such drugs as steroids, and use of tobacco products can reduce smell sensitivity, although such harmful agents have a worse effect on older people.

D. Age-related olfactory deficiencies have potentially serious consequences.
 1. We lose the ability to smell our own body odor and risk causing people to avoid us.
 2. We lose much of the pleasure of eating and risk nutritional deficiencies.
 3. We lose the joy of smelling positive smells (such as babies, flowers, fresh bread, and so on).
 4. The reduced ability to smell smoke, gas leaks, spoiled food, and hazardous chemicals poses a safety risk.

Suggested Reading:

Ackerman, *A Natural History of the Senses*, pp. 3–64.

Colavita, *Sensory Changes in the Elderly*, chapter 5.

Questions to Consider:

1. Some people believe that pheromones have an effect in humans and some people doubt such an effect. Why do we know more about smell-related animal sexual behavior than we do about smell-related human sexual behavior?

2. Do you think that when aromatherapy appears to have positive consequences it is the result of the placebo effect or the therapeutic consequences of smell stimuli?

Lecture Eighteen—Transcript
Smell—Consequences of Anosmia

Hi. In Lecture Seventeen, I referred to smell as the unappreciated sense. In Lecture Eighteen, I'm going to continue that theme by sharing with you some of the data suggesting the consequences of either losing your sense of smell entirely or having your sense of smell diminished significantly.

One way to learn to appreciate something is to see how it changes your life when you lose it. There are documented instances of humans who have been unfortunate enough to be rendered anosmic by some kind of accident that shears off the olfactory bulbs or some kind of a metabolic problem or a bad infection that wipes out the olfactory epithelium. Some of these people turn out to have been gifted writers, and they write very poignant accounts of how their lives have been changed by becoming anosmic. You can only imagine what it must be like not to be able to smell your baby or your spouse or the different foliage as the seasons change or the odor of roast turkey at Thanksgiving. I mean, we just can't imagine it; but some of these writings make it more real for us.

Another way to appreciate the consequences of anosmia is to see what it does to experimental animals that have been rendered anosmic through surgical means. The typical subject in such an experiment is some kind of a rodent—a rat, a hamster, a guinea pig or something of that nature. What we see is, if we produce anosmia in an animal that is territorial by nature, some important changes take place. This animal no longer marks its own territory and no longer respects the territorial markings of another animal. Now, this puts the poor anosmic creature at risk because he or she is going to blunder into some other animal's territory and be attacked, because animals become especially aggressive if their territory is infringed upon. Also, this animal is not going to mark his or her own territory, so other animals will be unaware and wander into this territory, and this creature is going to have more fights than it needs to.

Another finding from the animal literature is that when you render an experimental animal anosmic through surgical means, it totally abolishes their sexual behavior. This is the case in rodents. Now, in non-human primates, rendering a monkey anosmic will significantly reduce, but not abolish a monkey's sexual behavior. It turns out that in the animal kingdom there are odorous stimuli called "pheromones," and one pheromone is to stimulate sexual behavior in conspecifics—other animals of that species that might smell that pheromone.

Pheromones were first discovered in bugs, and of course this was put to a commercial use. Once people discovered pheromones in bugs, they would synthesize that particular chemical pheromone and put it in a bug bag along with some bug killer, and then they would sell these bug bags to people to put in their gardens. A male bug smells the pheromone, and he flies into this bag thinking he's going to have a good time; instead, he is poisoned.

So pheromones were first discovered in insects, but they have also been shown to contribute to the sexual behavior of rodents—well, in everything up to and including non-human primates. However, the more intelligent the creature is, the less totally dependent on pheromones it is, and the more important social factors become. So even with female monkeys in heat, the male will smell the female monkey, and he'll be interested, but if he's in the zoo, for example, and there are people watching, he will not engage in sexual behavior. By the time we come to humans, social factors become so important that even if there were such as thing as human pheromones, they would play a minimal role in human sexual behavior. As a matter of fact, at the present time there is no, absolutely no evidence for a human sex pheromone in spite of what the perfume manufacturers would have us believe.

The pheromone discovered by Martha McClintock was not a sex pheromone. None has been discovered, as I said. In spite of the fact that there is no evidence for a human sex pheromone, there does appear to be some kind of a connection between smell and sexual behavior. There are statistical records suggesting that of humans who are made anosmic by one sort of accident or infection or illness or another, 25% of them lose their sex drive. Twenty-five percent of humans who become anosmic are at risk for total loss of their libido. As I said, the mechanism is not understood, it's still under investigation.

This reminds me that when I was in college, there was a story in a local newspaper about a construction worker who—in an on-the-job accident—was hit on the head by a 2x10, or something like that. His lawyer was suing the company for safety violations, and they were claiming damages, of course, for the time he was off from work, and they were claiming damages because he no longer was interested in having sex with his wife. Now at the time, I remember that those of us who were discussing this article felt that this was another sleazy example of a lawyer trying to up the size of the settlement by claiming that being hit in the head can abolish sexual behavior. It turns out that it was probably a legitimate claim, and if I could remember that lawyer's name I might write him a letter of apology—probably not—anyway, there does seem to be a relationship between olfactory trouble, anosmia, and loss of sexual behavior in some humans.

Another very important smell-related issue these days is the connection between smell and memory. This seems to be a growing area of interest for smell researchers. Let me share with you some of the literature and some of the findings. First of all, it's been known for some time that some people possess incredibly powerful olfactory imagery. By this I mean sometimes you can be minding your own business, and all of a sudden you will smell something, and that smell will elicit in you a vivid memory from some previous episode in your life that you weren't thinking about at all. This phenomenon actually has a name. It's called the Proust Effect. The French writer, Marcel Proust, has had his name attached to this effect—this vivid olfactory memory—because of a very accurate and well written description of such an effect in one of his novels, a novel entitled Swann's Way. In that novel, Proust described the feeling that came over a person when he smelled an odor, how it re-established a memory from long ago that this person had not thought of for quite a while.

Not everybody has experienced the Proust Effect because olfactory imagery is what we psychologists call normally distributed in the population; that is, some people have incredibly vivid olfactory imagery, some people have little or none, and most of us are somewhere in between. I have had one Proust Effect experience myself, and I'll share it with you to see if it resonates with any smell-related memory experiences you have had. In 1964 I had just obtained my doctoral degree, and a good friend of mine had just obtained his law degree, and we decided to take a road trip together. We borrowed the new lawyer's father's Cadillac, which had air conditioning—I'd never been in an air-conditioned car before—and we took off to go across the country. It was a wonderful time, a freeing time. We saw some beautiful sights, and the smell of auto air conditioning occasionally re-elicits that feeling and that memory of driving across the country in this air-conditioned car.

Now, the thing is, in those days the coolant in auto air-conditioning was Freon. That has now been determined to be harmful to the ozone layer, and auto air-conditioning is now based on some coolant other than Freon. Whatever this new stuff is, the smell of it doesn't do anything for me, so I may never have that Proust Effect memory again, unless I go find some black market Freon and sniff it or something like that. That might not even work either, because the Proust Effect is unconscious and involuntary. You cannot actively seek out the smell and then take a whiff of it with the intention of creating that memory. It comes by itself when it wants to. It's really quite interesting.

By the way, it's not just olfactory imagery that is normally distributed. Visual imagery shows the same phenomenon. Some of us have wonderfully vivid visual imagery where we can see things in living color. Some of us see things, can imagine visual experiences, but they're kind of washed out. Some of us see visual experiences in black and white, and some people have absolutely no visual imagery. So humans differ on these dimensions. I don't mean to let you think that everybody is the same.

I never even knew that some people had no visual imagery until a young couple in one of my classes had a minor spat. He was going away to summer camp—he was in some military program, and the young lady said, "Before you go to sleep every night, I want you to imagine my face." He started laughing, and she became angry because she thought he was making fun of her. It turns out he was laughing because he had never been able to imagine anything visually, and when they explained this to each other, the spat was patched up. But I discovered by listening in on this conversation that this young man had no visual imagery. I guess that means there are some people with no olfactory imagery. I don't know.

Okay. Another interesting connection between smell and memory is seen in some of the recent literature linking various senile dementias, including Alzheimer's, to smell deficits. The interesting point here is that if, in fact, there is some kind of a correlation between decreases in smell sensitivity and the onset of senile dementia, then by measuring smell sensitivity it might be possible to identify people who are at risk for senile dementia, or who are just starting to show signs of senile dementia. Here, I will allude briefly to the work of a gentleman by the name of D. P. Devanand, who is co-director of the Memory Disorders Center in the New York State Psychiatric Institution. Professor Devanand has been following 223 subjects for the past five years. What he does is at intervals he tests these people with a scratch-and-sniff test, and every time they're tested, it's the same 10 odors. It isn't that they can't smell them; what he's concerned about is when they can smell them but don't remember what they are. So when we talk about failure of odor memory, we don't mean an inability to smell it, but an inability to remember it.

The odors that Professor Devanand gives these people when they are due for a regular testing include lemon, strawberry, smoke, soap, menthol, clove, pineapple, natural gas, lilac, and leather. So they're fairly common odors. What he finds is, when it's time to test these people, some of them begin to show confusions and inabilities to identify certain odors, and it is his finding that these are the people who are in the very near future likely to start showing the symptoms of Alzheimer's Disease.

Now, why is this an important thing to do? Why should Professor Devanand and others in the field be working on scratch-and-sniff tests to predict who's going to have Alzheimer's when there's no cure for it anyway? As a matter of fact, Professor Devanand's test is about 80% accurate at detecting who is at risk for symptoms of senile dementia. Now, is that good enough? Well, not necessarily, but it's as good as any tests are at the present time.

At the present time, the tests that are used to try and identify people at risk for Alzheimer's disease are what are called neuropsychological test batteries. These sometimes take five or more hours to administer, and they are only 80% accurate themselves. So here is a scratch-and-sniff test, which can be administered in minutes, and its predictive validity is as good as tests that are currently in use that may take five or more hours to administer.

So the thing about early recognition of such people is, with Alzheimer's, since there is no cure, they can work on reducing and minimizing the symptoms, and the sooner you start working on these symptoms, the more you can slow the progress of the disorder. Also, early identification of people who are likely to become symptomatic for Alzheimer's gives the family a chance to do some long-term planning about care and things of that nature. The other thing is at the current time research is going on. There are promising drugs in the pipeline that may actually prevent or slow down the course of Alzheimer's Disease, so it's good to find out who is at risk in case these drugs suddenly become available. They can immediately start the course of treatment.

There are other areas of research suggesting the relationship between smell and memory. One of these is of a neurophysiological nature. First, let me share with you that for hundreds of years the belief has been that at birth we have every brain cell we're ever going to have, which is one of the reasons why a baby's head is so big that it makes the birth process as uncomfortable as it is, because the baby's head contains a hundred billion brain cells, and that's the same number that we carry—well, it's not really the same number we carry through the rest of our lives, because over the course of our lives we lose brain cells—but we start out with a 100,000,000,000 brain cells.

The wisdom has been for a couple of hundred years that we never have any more brain cells, that when we start losing cells from our starting pot of a 100,000,000,000 of these things, that's it, it's all downhill. More recent evidence that has been acquired over the past decade suggests that there are two parts of the human brain where it is possible to produce new brain cells. This was a revolutionary finding, and I'm sure some people still don't believe it. It's not the cerebral cortex, unfortunately—the smart part of the brain, the part that controls the higher mental processes and so on—but the two parts of the brain where evidence suggests—now, first this evidence was discovered in rat brains, but it has now been identified in human brains, too—evidence suggests that we can in fact produce new brain cells in the olfactory bulbs—smell, and the hippocampus, which is the part of the brain that is critically important for memory consolidation and memory retrieval. So in terms of the two parts of the brain that can elaborate new brain cells—smell and memory— very interesting to me.

The next part of this discussion that I'm going to share with you is actually based on a student question that I had some time ago. The student came up after class and said, "Is it true that as we lose our sense of smell we're at greater risk for illness and failure of health?" I guess I misinterpreted this student's question, because I said, "Well, yes, as we lose our sense of smell, we're less able to smell smoke and we're less able to smell electrical fires, and we're less able to—" And the student said, "No, no, no, no, that's not what I mean." Then she showed me a little pamphlet that she had on aromatherapy—a little 20-page pamphlet. She says, "This booklet suggests that if you smell this, it will cure this; and if you smell this, it'll fix this; and if you smell this, it will make you healthier here and here." Then I realized that she wasn't asking a question about anosmia, and smelling acids or smoke or spoiled food, she was asking a question about aromatherapy, and it occurs to me that perhaps many people have questions about aromatherapy, and perhaps some people have never even heard of it.

The young woman who showed me the booklet—the booklet contained a total of 90 ailments that the publishers of the booklet claimed could be cured by either rubbing on a certain plant extract oil or smelling it or putting it in your bathwater or something like that. Just on the first page, I remember the ailments included things such as depression, constipation, diminished libido—meaning no sex drive, bronchitis, memory impairments, and pain. I remember thinking, "This is going way beyond the data as I understand it."

So let me talk a little bit about the current status of our understanding of aromatherapy. First of all, let me define aromatherapy for you. It is defined as "the therapeutic use of the essential oils of plants to affect mood or health." Now, when they say essential oils—I may have mentioned this previously—but they don't mean essential in the sense of "you need it to stay healthy or to have a nutritional diet." They're talking about the "essence of the plant"—essential. They're talking about the essential oil as the volatile aromatic component of this plant's oil.

Here's a brief history of aromatherapy. Aromatherapy is thought to have started in France in the 1930s, and the gentleman credited with coining the term aromatherapy, although he said it in French, of course, was a gentleman by the name of René-Maurice Gattefosse. This gentleman was actually a chemist working in the perfume business run by his family. The story goes—and I have no reason to doubt it—that he was working in the laboratory one day and accidentally burned his forearm very, very badly. He was in pain, as people who burn themselves are. He was looking for some source of relief for this pain burn when he saw a vat of lavender oil that was used in the elaboration of some perfumes or something. So he ran and stuck his burned arm in this vat of lavender oil. The story is that the pain was immediately diminished, and that the arm healed faster than he had expected, with no scar. He was so impressed with this turn of events—how the lavender oil had helped him—that he discontinued his interest in the perfume business and spent the rest of his professional career studying plant oils and their healing and curative properties.

Now, what can we say about the merits of aromatherapy? Well, that depends on whom you ask. If you asked a staunch proponent of aromatherapy, they would say that what you're actually doing when you extract this essential oil from the plant is you're taking a distillate of the plant's vital force; and that when you use this yourself, the essential oils from the plant are purging negative vibrations from your body's energy field. Now, that whole thing leaves me cold, because I'm not sure what the definition of any of those words are—the "plant's vital force" and our "negative vibes from our energy field."

At the other extreme from people who have this highly positive view of aromatherapy, there are scientists who have signed a statement that in a sense said, "We are incensed that legitimately sick…" Now what do they mean by "legitimately sick"; they mean as opposed to hypochondriacs who are not hurting anybody if they buy this stuff— "We are incensed that legitimately sick people may be putting off seeking scientific treatment, thereby endangering their health and life by participating in this quackery."

There are intermediate views on aromatherapy. Some people say, "Well, I can trigger pleasant memories, and I can promote a state of general relaxation." The truth of the matter is that for the most part the scientific community believes that the claims of aromatherapists and aromatherapy are exaggerated, that there may be some minor benefits, but that they blow them all out of proportion for their own aims.

Let me share with you the only two well constructed, well run, well interpreted experiments on aromatherapy that I know of. These were done in legitimate laboratories that know about science, and know how to design an experiment. One reported the finding that of all the things tested, the odor of green apples seemed to produce a lowering of blood pressure in the people who smelled the odor of green apples. The other experiment—well constructed experiment—there are many that are either anecdotal or equivocal and interpreted in ways that perhaps a scientist would have a problem with—the other experiment suggested that the odor of lavender increases alertness when you are doing a sorting task that requires concentration. So, if you're going by the rules of science, there's not a whole lot of evidence for major, major health benefits from aromatherapy. But you know what? If it smells good, and you like it, it's certainly not going to do you any harm.

Let's now change our focus a bit, and talk about what happens to smell, not when you have senile dementia or Alzheimer's or what have you, but smell in the individual undergoing normal aging. In the case of men—and it turns out that men and women are affected differently with this—our smell sensitivity remains relatively constant. There may be a modest decline in smell sensitivity until the age of 55. Then the decline becomes more precipitous, but till age 55 there's not a whole lot going on in terms of smell sensitivity in men. The thing is, men have poorer olfactory sensitivity than women probably over their entire lives.

In the case of women, smell sensitivity stays relatively good—again there are modest declines—until the age of 75. Women retain much of their smell capability, much of their olfactory sensitivity for a good 20 years longer than men do. As a matter of fact, at the age when men are beginning to show serious declines in smell sensitivity, women are still able to do something that men never could do, and that is detect the scent of fear on another woman. Let me tell you how this experiment was done.

Women were asked to wear underarm pads, and then they were divided into two groups. One group watched a normal movie and the other group watched a scary movie—Freddy Krueger or something like that. At the conclusion of the movie, another group of women was asked, on the basis of smell, to try and figure out which women saw the scary movie and which women saw the nondescript movie, and they were able to do it with a high degree of accuracy. Men couldn't begin to do that.

I indicated that smell sensitivity begins to decline in men after 55, precipitously, and in women after 75. I also need you to know that that's a general statement, and that there are great individual differences in smell sensitivity and in the rate with which smell sensitivity diminishes as a consequence of age. Some people in their 70s still have the smell sensitivity of a person in middle age.

All right, now what happens to our sense of smell to cause this decrease in smell sensitivity with age? Well, one thing that happens is the olfactory epithelium begins to become thinner. Now, there's a way to tell just by visual examination when smell sensitivity is beginning to decline. In a healthy young person whose smell sensitivity is within normal limits, the olfactory epithelium has a yellowish appearance. As we begin to lose our sense of smell, the color of the olfactory epithelium begins to fade. So this nice yellowish color begins to fade, and that's a visual clue that physiological changes are taking place, and that smell sensitivity is being affected.

The other change in addition to the olfactory epithelium changing color and becoming thinner is that we begin to lose individual receptors. Now, we start with 10,000,000, so we can afford to lose a few, but this does in fact precipitate a decline in smell sensitivity.

Okay, now there are certain environmental events that are known to be harmful to smell and smell sensitivity. Repeated blows to the head, for example, so boxers you would expect, would be having trouble with smell sensitivity. Infections of the olfactory epithelium, exposure or overexposure to X-rays or steroids—sometimes people are forced by one medical condition or another to use steroids—these can hurt smell sensitivity, and smoking is also harmful to our smell sensitivity. Now, I've just listed for you some situations that are harmful, not only to smell sensitivity in the elderly, but in anybody. The problem is our sensory systems become more vulnerable with age, so those things such blows to the head and X-rays and smoking and infections and steroids—they're going to have a worse effect on an older person's smell sensitivity than on a younger, and we should all avoid that stuff as much as possible.

Now, what are the consequences that befall an older person who, through living long enough, has, in fact, experienced a decline in their smell sensitivity? By the way, you don't become anosmic simply as a consequence of growing older. It just means you will need a stronger concentration of the odorant to experience it. Some older people who used to be able to smell a substance at a very weak concentration now may need a concentration nine times that strong, but they can still smell it, so it's not as if you totally lose your sense of smell.

One of the consequences of having partial anosmia is that you are now much less likely to be aware of your own body odor. I am sad to report that my mother-in-law lived to be 92, and she was in a personal care home for the last few years of her life. I guess she or whoever her caretakers were, were not careful with her personal hygiene. Sometimes we would go to visit her, and she would smell really bad. We would say, "Nana, you know, you don't smell so good," and she would say, "But I took a bath." The thing is she was much too incapacitated to step into a tub to take a bath. She didn't smell herself, so I guess she thought that was good enough.

The other problem with the elderly having a diminished sense of smell is they take less pleasure in eating because they don't experience the full flavor, and I make the same suggestion here that I did in talking about smell, that people experiment with different seasonings and spices and ethnic cuisines and so on, rather than just write eating off as a source of pleasure.

In general, a loss of smell can also diminish your overall joy in life because, let's face it, there is great pleasure in smelling a freshly washed baby or in smelling flowers or smelling pizza—maybe not everybody loves that, but I love the smell of pizza—or freshly baked bread. So the absence of those smells does take away something from your overall joy of life.

Last but not least, when your smell sensitivity declines, it does put you at risk. The answer that I gave to that young woman in class who was asking about aromatherapy, and I misinterpreted and thought she was asking about anosmia, the answer to the question I thought she was asking was, "We are at greater risk for not detecting the smoke of a fire, for not detecting a natural gas leak, for not detecting that this food is bad or spoiled, and for not detecting that we are in the presence of toxic, hazardous chemicals." So there are legitimate safety concerns about our diminishing sense of smell in our later years.

In our next lecture we will begin talking about a new sensory system, the vestibular system. Thank you.

Lecture Nineteen
The Vestibular System—Body Orientation

Scope:

The vestibular system responds to changes of the body's position in space. This system is made up of two components with two different functions. Both components are housed in the inner ear, which is why most medical problems involving the inner ear affect both auditory and vestibular functioning.

One component of the vestibular system is the *semicircular canals*. This system provides us with sensory information about the acceleration and deceleration of the body and about the direction in which the body is moving. The semicircular canals do not respond to constant rates of movement, only changes in the rate of movement.

The second component of the vestibular system is made up of two inner-ear structures known as the *utricle* and *saccule*. These structures tell us when we are not in an upright position with respect to the pull of gravity. The utricle and saccule cannot function in a gravity-free environment, nor do they provide information about body orientation when we are underwater. Seasickness, other forms of motion sickness, and the "bed spins" experienced by people who drink too much alcohol and lie down with their eyes open all involve the vestibular system.

The elderly generally dislike the vestibular stimulation from swings, roller coasters, and so on that young people are fond of. This preference change is due more to the loss of stomach muscle tone, fat accumulation, and changes in the ability of connective tissue to prevent greater motion of the internal organs than to vestibular sensitivity changes per se.

Outline

I. Several human sensory systems are concerned with the detection of movement.

   A. The auditory system responds to movement at a distance from the body.

   B. The cutaneous system responds to movement on the surface of the body.

C. The vestibular system responds to movement of the whole body.

II. The two portions of the vestibular system are responsive to two different categories of movement. Both portions are housed in the inner ear, near the auditory receptors. (Figures 19a and 19b)

    A. The vestibular structures that respond to velocity changes are the *semicircular canals*.

       1. There are three semicircular canals in each inner ear: the superior, the posterior, and the lateral.

       2. Each canal is in a different orientation, making it more responsive to movement in a particular direction.

          a. The superior canal goes from front to back.

          b. The posterior canal goes from left to right.

          c. The lateral canal goes from side to side.

       3. At the base of each semicircular canal is a distinctive swollen region called the *ampulla*.

       4. Each of these canals is attached to a reservoir and is filled with an incompressible fluid, *endolymph*.

       5. Inside the ampulla is a gelatinous structure called the *cupula*, which can block the canal so that fluid cannot move through it.

       6. The vestibular hair cells embedded in the cupula are bent by movement of the endolymph in the canal caused by body motion.

       7. Because the hair cells and cupula are "spring loaded," the semicircular canals are sensitive to changes in velocity, not steady-state motion.

       8. Research has shown that animals of all kinds, with the exception of frogs, have semicircular canals that signal movement in two opposite directions.

    B. The *utricle* and *saccule* are the portions of the vestibular system that respond to changes in bodily orientation with respect to the pull of gravity or the upright. They are sometimes labeled the *gravitational receptors*.

       1. Hair cells in the base of the utricle and saccule have their tips imbedded in a flexible membrane.

       2. The surface of the membrane is covered with tiny calcium carbonate particles called *otoliths*.

       3. When we lean, gravity shifts the otoliths and bends the hair cells.

4. With our eyes closed, deviation from the upright cannot be detected in a zero-gravity environment.

III. Gravity is not the "curse of the elderly," as it is occasionally called.

   A. The force of gravity is necessary for maintenance of normal muscle tone.

   B. Astronauts are severely weakened by an extended stay in a gravity-free environment. On occasion, they are too weak to exit the space capsule without help.

IV. As we saw in Lecture Seven, there are several commonalities between the auditory system and the vestibular system.

   A. The auditory and vestibular systems share the same cranial nerve.

   B. Both sensory systems are located in the inner ear.

   C. Both require physical stimulation of hair cells for transduction to occur.

   D. Both the auditory and the vestibular system require the presence of endolymph.

   E. Anything harmful to one of these two systems, such as ototoxic drugs, is usually harmful to the other.

V. Certain categories of vestibular stimulation are responsible for motion sickness, with its resultant feelings of headache, chills, nausea, and muscular weakness.

   A. Motion sickness (including seasickness) is far more likely to occur from passive movements, rather than active movements.

   1. Vertical movements produce a greater effect than lateral movements. Movement in several planes simultaneously produces the worst effect.

   2. Slow, oscillating movements are more potent for sickness than short, rapid movements.

   3. Animals show motion sickness as well.

   B. "Bed spins," which can be experienced by lying on one's back with open eyes after a bout of heavy drinking, is also a vestibular phenomenon.

   1. Alcohol is infused into the endolymph of the semicircular canals, changing its specific gravity.

2. The equilibrium of the system is disrupted, resulting in the hair cells bending over.
3. The discontinuity between the messages sent to the brain from the bent hair cells that movement is occurring and the messages from the eyes that no movement is occurring results in the experience of the room spinning.
4. The sensation of spinning in the opposite direction occurs as the alcohol leaves the endolymph, although the affected individual is usually asleep for this part of the experience.

VI. It is widely known that our preferences for sources of vestibular stimulation, such as riding on roller coasters or swinging on playground swings, changes as we age. There are several reasons for this.

A. There are degenerative changes in the vestibular portion of the eighth cranial nerve, just as there are in the auditory portion.

B. Vestibular receptors are lost as a function of age

C. Calcium deficiencies, which are more frequent in the elderly, change the properties of the otoliths in the utricle and saccule.

D. Loss of tone in stomach muscles, the accumulation of abdominal fat, and the reduced ability of connective tissue to hold the internal organs firmly in place add to the aversiveness of certain types of vestibular stimulation among older people.

Suggested Reading:

Carlson, *Physiology of Behavior* (8th ed.), pp. 219–222.

Colavita, *Sensory Changes in the Elderly*.

Questions to Consider:

1. There are documented instances of scuba divers in murky water becoming disoriented and swimming down when they mean to swim up. How is such a "malfunction" of the vestibular system possible?

2. Would it be possible to perform the tasks of daily life if an individual were to lose all functioning of the vestibular system? What adjustments would have to be made?

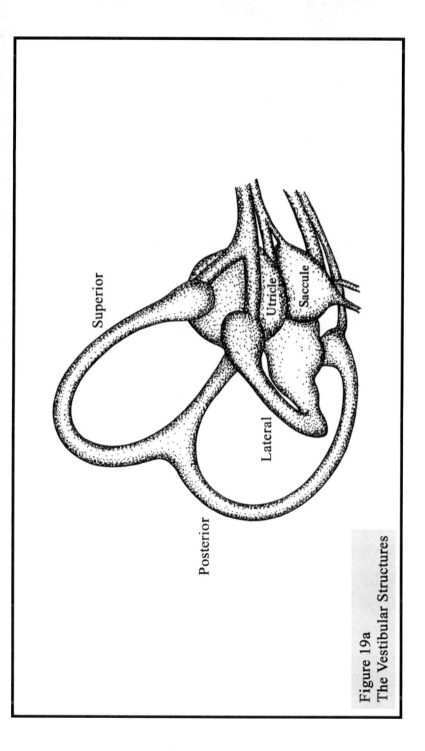

Superior

Utricle

Saccule

Lateral

Posterior

Figure 19a
The Vestibular Structures

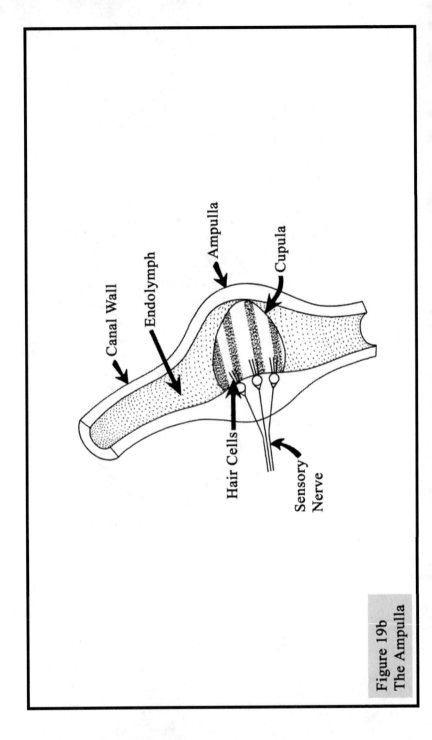

Figure 19b
The Ampulla

Lecture Nineteen—Transcript
The Vestibular System—Body Orientation

Welcome back. Lecture Eighteen marked the conclusion of our coverage of the chemical senses, smell and taste. In Lecture Eighteen we talked about some of the consequences of anosmia, the consequences not only for experimental animals but also for humans.

In Lectures Nineteen and Twenty we're going to discuss two senses that many people have never even heard of. These are the vestibular sense and the kinesthetic sense. Actually, the vestibular and the kinesthetic senses represent the last two of four human senses that are concerned with some aspect of movement.

Remember, the auditory system is actually concerned with movement—movements of objects at a distance from us that create pressure variations that signal the ear in the form of sound waves. The cutaneous system is also concerned with movement—movement of objects on the skin.

The vestibular system is concerned with movement of the whole body in space, and when we come to the kinesthetic sense you'll see that it's concerned not with the whole body but with the individual body parts, the limbs.

So let's begin our discussion of the vestibular system. Actually there are two divisions to the vestibular system. One is concerned with detecting changes in velocity—acceleration and deceleration—and the parts of the vestibular system concerned with detecting changes in velocity are called the semicircular canals. Now, these are rather difficult to describe. People have the picture best when they look at a three-dimensional model, but I will try as hard as I can to explain them, and I need you to try as hard as you can to understand what I'm talking about.

There are three semicircular canals in each ear. These semicircular canals are only about one centimeter in height. They are semicircles. One of them is called the superior canal, and it is a semicircle that goes from front to back; it's a little canal going from front to back. Another canal is called the posterior canal, and instead of going from front to back, it goes from left to right. So we have the superior, the posterior, and then a third canal is called the lateral canal, and it is, of course, located going sideways. So we have a superior, posterior, and lateral in the right ear, and a superior, posterior, and lateral in the left ear.

Just to give you the dimensions of these canals: most of the semicircular canal is about .28 millimeter in width, a little bigger than a quarter of a millimeter. However, at the base of each canal there is a swelling, known as the ampulla. At the ampulla, the canal swells from .28 mm in diameter to .9 mm in diameter, a significant increase in size. Now, these canals are attached at both ends to fluid-filled reservoirs, and the canals themselves are fluid filled, and the fluid that they are filled with is known as endolymph, an incompressible fluid.

So the picture now is that we have a canal that is attached at both ends to a reservoir and filled with endolymph. Let me call your attention to the ampulla, that swelling—the .9 millimeter-in-diameter swelling. Inside the swelling is a gelatinous structure known as the cupula. The cupula actually blocks the canal so that fluid cannot move through it. The cupula is fixed at one end, and able to move at another end. I can't think of a better analogy, so think of the cupula as—when I was a kid I remember we used to have these Bozo punching dolls. They had sand in the base, and you could punch the doll in the nose, and it would fall over, and then spring right back up again. This is what we mean by the cupula being "spring loaded." It can move, but it will then regain its original position. Okay. So think of the cupula as an obstruction in the canal that under certain circumstances will move out of the way and permit the endolymph to move.

Now, here's another picture to imagine. Hold a glass of water that's filled right to the brim, and everything's at equilibrium and the water is flat and nothing spills. But then you decide to move forward, and you move forward. Because of inertia, you and the glass move forward, but the water doesn't, so it splashes backwards, perhaps splashing on your hand or your sleeve. This is what happens in the case of the semicircular canals. They are filled with incompressible endolymph. The system is at equilibrium. The gelatinous cupula is closed. Now, you move the body forward. Again, inertia causes the endolymph to be a little slow, so the endolymph is actually going to slosh backwards like the water in the glass, and it's going to bend open the gelatinous cupula, and permit the flow of endolymph in this closed system. In the base of the cupula where it is attached to the wall of the ampulla, the vestibular hair cells are embedded, so when the cupula bends, the hair cells bend, and the hair cells send signals to the vestibular part of the eighth nerve—the vestibulocochlear nerve—and the brain is made aware of the fact that you just moved forward. Now as I said, the semicircular canals are concerned with changes in velocity, not steady state, and that's because of the spring-loaded nature of the cupula.

Perhaps a better example might be to think of a freshly planted sapling, a little, skinny, baby tree there in an open field, and a gust of wind comes and blows the sapling over. Now, if the wind does not increase in velocity, the sapling will show this spring-loaded feature, and it will spring back up to its erect position. The only way to keep the sapling bent over is to continually increase the velocity of the wind. That's the way the semicircular canal and the spring-loaded cupula operate. The only way to keep it open and to keep the fluid moving and to keep the hair cells bent is to continue to accelerate.

For example, let's say you won the lottery and you buy a Bentley and you have a chauffeur. You are blindfolded in the back of your Bentley on a perfectly smooth road, and you tell the chauffeur, "Accelerate up to 60 miles per hour." The car is at a stationery position, so the vestibular system is at equilibrium. You begin moving. The endolymph bends the cupula, the cupula bends the hair cells, and you are aware, even being blindfolded, of movement. The car accelerates up to 50 miles per hour. You continue to experience the sensation of movement—you're moving. You reach the agreed-up speed of 60 miles per hour, and when the car reaches 60 miles per hour, the spring-loaded cupula closes, you are no longer aware of the sensation of movement. Now you tell the driver, "Slow down," and the driver slows down, and the process happens in reverse. Now, inertia causes the fluid to lag behind, and again the cupula will be bent the other way, and you experience the sensation of a reduction in velocity.

The physical operation of the semicircular canals was first explained by two researchers named Steinhausen and Dolman in 1875, if you can believe it. What Steinhausen and Dolman did was to take a fish, a pike as a matter of fact, and they dissected the head of the pike until they had exposed the semicircular canals—the three canals, the superior, posterior, and lateral canals. Now, the bony walls of the semicircular canals in the pike were so thin that they were translucent. They could essentially see what was going on in the canals.

So Steinhausen and Dolman injected India ink droplets into the semicircular canals of these fish, and then they put the fish on—well, think of a lazy Susan—one of those devices that you spin around to move food from one person to another without having to stand up and walk around. They could see the India Ink droplets, and they watched, and they saw that when they spun the fish in a forward direction, the India ink droplets moved backwards, and opened up the cupula, just as we know today happens, and when the lazy Susan reached a constant velocity, the spring-loaded cupula closed, and had that fish been alive and well, it would not have experienced any movement at that steady-state velocity. When they slowed the lazy Susan, the endolymph pushed the cupula in another direction, and the fish would have been aware of a reduction in velocity.

Interestingly enough, Steinhausen and Dolman were doing these observations before it became possible to actually record from the vestibulocochlear nerves, but their observations suggested that each canal can signal direction of movement either forward or backward or left or right or up or down or what have you. See, by virtue of having six canals, three in each ear, a pattern of firing can tell the brain about movement in virtually any direction. So Steinhausen and Dolman were suspicious of the fact that a single canal could tell you about two directions of movement, which turns out to be true. So we know when we're moving forward, and we know when we're moving backward, left or right, up or down.

Later on, when experimental technology permitted actually doing electrical recordings from the vestibular system, we could verify this. It has now been verified in a number of animals—well, in a whole series of animals—that in fact, each canal signals by virtue of changing its pattern of electrical firing to the brain, signals movement in two directions, two opposite directions.

This has been discovered in all mammals and in rodents, and it's been discovered in birds and in fish, that the semicircular canals can signal forward or backward. Now you may think, "Why would a bird or a fish need its brain to be aware when it's moving backwards?" I have given this some thought, and I've seen shore birds, for example, flying along and suddenly a gust of wind of unusual strength comes up, and can actually blow the bird backwards. Birds need to know when they're going backwards so they can increase their efforts and continue going in a forward direction. The same thing is true of fish. A fish can be swimming forward and suddenly hit an unusual current that's stronger than anticipated and the fish can actually be moved backward. They need to be aware of this to increase their efforts.

The only animal that I'm aware of whose semicircular canals only signal information in one direction—of all the animals that have been tested—is the frog. If a frog were to hop backwards, it would apparently be unaware of the fact that it was hopping backwards. To my knowledge, no frog has ever hopped backwards, so it's just as well. Okay, so that's the first division of the vestibular system—the semicircular canals that give us information about acceleration and deceleration.

The second division of the vestibular system is concerned with telling us about our orientation in space with regard to the pull of gravity. The gravitational field is taken as the zero point, and if we lean left, the system tells us, or right or forward or backward. The structures for the detection of deviations from the upright with the pull of gravity being the zero point, is made up of two bony sacs that are located right under the semicircular canals. These two bony sacs are called the utricle and the saccule. The utricle is the bigger of the two. It can be envisioned as sort of a small, elongated bird egg. The saccule looks more like a small, bony kidney bean. It doesn't have the symmetrical shape of the utricle. The utricle is bigger. The utricle contains 26,000 hair cells. The saccule is smaller, containing only 11,000 hair cells, but they both seem to function in helping us to detect deviations from the upright. Now, sometimes the utricle and saccule are referred as the gravitational receptors, because they tell us about deviations from the pull of gravity, and they also require a gravitational field to work. Let me explain how this comes to pass.

Picture the utricle, which is bigger and maybe easier to visualize. In the base of the utricle are hair cells. The hair cells are very similar to the ones found in the semicircular canals and also similar to the ones found in the auditory system. So we have a layer of hair cells in the base of the utricle. Over that layer of hair cells is a thin, flexible membrane. This membrane is malleable enough that it can be pushed on, and when you push on the membrane you displace the hair cells that have their tips in physical contact with the membrane.

So we have the hair cells and a flexible membrane. On top of the flexible membrane are calcium carbonate particles, like little grains of sand made out of calcium carbonate. These are known as otoliths, which is a Latin word for ear rocks, little ear rocks. The system is incredibly simple. When you lean to the right, the otoliths shift to the right, and they depress the membrane to the right, and the hair cells are bent to the right, and the brain is made aware of the fact that you have bent to the right. If you straighten up again, the otoliths resume their even distribution on the surface of the flexible membrane. If you lean left, the hair cells bend left because the membrane has bent left under the weight of the otoliths, which have now shifted to the left. An incredibly simple mechanical system, but it does require the presence of gravity.

What does this mean? It means in a zero gravitational field, this portion of the vestibular system doesn't work. It means astronauts, for example, who are floating weightless in space with their eyes closed don't know whether they're right side up or upside down, because their utricle and saccule require gravity to operate.

There's an interesting story. I saw an interview with one of the astronauts who was being questioned about what it's like to be in weightlessness, and to just float around, not knowing up from down unless you open your eyes. He answered these questions candidly, and he said something very interesting about how they slept at night. Astronauts sleep in the space capsule at night, just floating around wherever they happen to be. This gentleman had a great deal of trouble falling asleep because he was used to the feel of a pillow on his head. The way he creatively handled this situation was to take a little pillow and a velcro strap and strap a pillow to the side of his head, and this permitted him to sleep at night. Now, he was in the habit of waking up halfway through the night and turning over on his side and having the pillow on the other side of his head when he was back on Mother Earth with a gravitational field. So what he had to do is was in the middle of the night in space, wake up, un-velcro the pillow from the right side, switch it over the left and re-velcro it, then he could complete sleeping in this Zero G environment.

In addition to the gravitational sense not working in space, I will say that smell doesn't work in space either, because, remember, smell needs volatile molecules to somehow find their way to the olfactory epithelium. So smell is not operative in a Zero G environment either.

I'd like at this point just to take a few minutes and put in a plug for gravity, because I've heard gravity maligned. I remember reading somewhere that somebody referred to gravity as "the curse of the elderly." Now what did they mean by this? Well, they were talking about the fact that as we age we seem to sag and our shoulders slump and our posture becomes stooped and we take little shuffling steps as if the Earth is trying to pull us down. That's not the fault of gravity. That's because we have not been careful about maintaining bone density and muscle tone. As a matter of fact, in the absence of gravity, we would all be as weak as kittens, because our muscles need to exercise against something, and gravity gives some of us the only exercise we're going to have.

I'm reminded of this because of the fact that when astronauts complete a mission in outer space one of their biggest fears is that they're going to be too weak to walk out of the capsule under their own power. So what Zero G does is to make us weak. So I submit that gravity is not an enemy, but that gravity keeps us able to function and able to "locomote" because in the absence of it, the muscles would certainly atrophy. Okay. That's the end of the pitch for gravity.

Let's go back to talking about the vestibular system. The operation of the utricle and saccule is pretty well known. Part of our understanding of the utricle and saccule came about because of the discovery that certain crustaceans—such as lobsters and prawns and crayfish and so on—instead of having a utricle and saccule, have a single organ that takes the place of both of these structures called the statocyst organ—but it works just like the utricle. The crustacean's statocyst organ has a layer of hair cells in the base. It has the flexible membrane, but instead of having calcium carbonate particles it has what are called statoliths. Now, some of these crustaceans secrete their own statoliths, which serve the function of otoliths. Some creatures do not secrete their own, but rather, if they are ocean-dwelling creatures, utilize sand from the bottom of the ocean, and some of these crustaceans have a species-specific behavior—a reflex or instinct, if you will—where in order to make sure that their statocyst organ has enough sand in it to do the job, they will actually pick sand up and load up their own statocyst organ with grains of sand.

This permits us the opportunity to do a laboratory experiment. We take one of these crustaceans, and we shake all the sand out of its statocyst organ, and we put it in a container, and on the bottom of the container we have steel filings, little bits of metal filings. The creature follows its instinct, and it will dutifully load up its statocyst organ with these metal filings. When it is finished it will sit there pleased with itself, and now we can do our mischief, because we can look at this animal, and you can guess what we're going to do. We're going to take a big magnet and we're going to hold this magnet beside this creature's head. Of course, that pulls all the metal filings to the right—it bends the hair cells under the flexible membrane in its statocyst organ—and the creature's brain receives the message, "Hey, you're falling over to the right," and the creature will make scrambling movements and attempt to right itself. If you want to be mean or mischievous, depending on your definition, you switch the magnet over to the other side. Now this creature's brain is receiving a message from the statocyst organ that it's falling to the left, and the creature will scramble back the other way, and you can—if you want, you can play a little dance music, and—no, you don't want to do that. Anyway, this demonstrates exactly how the statocyst organ works, and you can generalize exactly to the utricle and saccule.

Okay, now we've alluded previously to the fact that the vestibular system has a lot in common with the auditory system. Let me just review some of this. First of all, they share a common cranial nerve. Half of the eighth cranial nerve is for hearing, and half is for the vestibular sense. They also share the same type of receptor. They both use hair cells as the receptor—the auditory system and the vestibular system—and both the semicircular canals and the utricle and saccule, which means that everything we said about ototoxic drugs in the context of hearing and hearing loss also holds for the vestibular system. The other thing is that they both share a similar incompressible fluid to do their job. The bottom line is because of these close correspondences between these two systems, anything that's harmful to one is most likely to be harmful to the other also.

Okay. Let me deal with another phenomenon that is related to the vestibular system, the phenomenon of motion sickness. The most common variety of motion sickness that many people have experienced is seasickness, so many of you will know what the symptoms of motion sickness or seasickness are, and they include such things as headache, chills, nausea, and muscular weakness, and

©2006 The Teaching Company.

in general it's a bad time. Well, there have been enough studies of motion sickness and the vestibular system that I can make some general statements.

First of all, if you're passive in a situation, you're going to be sicker than if you're active in a situation. For example, if you're in a car with bad springs, and it's bumping up and down and so on, you're much more likely to experience motion sickness if you're sitting as a passenger than if you're actually driving. I'll talk about why that seems to be the case in a bit. Another thing we can say about motion sickness is that movement in the vertical plane, up and down movement is worse than, in terms of making you sick, movement in the lateral plane from side to side. Movement in several planes simultaneously is the worst. Slow oscillating movements are more likely to promote motion sickness than short, rapid movements, and the reason for this is because the way the eyes operate when they're scanning the environment is short, rapid movements, and so if short, rapid movements tended to make us motion sick, every time we scanned and flicked our eyes around we would be at risk for this.

So the other thing I want to say about motion sickness is animals show it, too. This is just not some human invention or the result of our suggestibility or our worry about having it. Animals show motion sickness too. Motion sickness appears to be Mother Nature's way of keeping us from harmful parts of the environment, such as earthquake zones or ice floes or rough seas.

How does Mother Nature accomplish this? Well, the brain is wired as such that when discontinuities occur between the information that the vestibular system is sending to the brain, and the information that the motor system—through receptors that we will talk about in our next lecture, through the information that the motor system is sending to the brain—this discontinuity is a sufficient condition for motion sickness to occur.

This is why the business between active and passive is so important. You know, if you're standing on a boat or sitting on a boat, and the boat is rocking up and down and left to right, you're likely to be motion sick. But you can replicate those same movements by walking and bending up and down. You're, in fact, duplicating the same movements, but now the motor system is saying, "It's okay. I'm doing it." When you're passive, the motor system says, "Hey, I'm not doing that. This must be either an earthquake zone or rough seas or something. I'd better make you sick so you won't do this any more." So it's the discontinuity of information between the vestibular and the motor system that is responsible for the condition known as motion sickness, or seasickness.

There's a special kind of motion sickness that is best known to college students, and periodically they ask me about this. "Professor, what's the deal with bed spins?" Now, the first time I heard that I had to say, "What are bed spins?" This is when a student drinks too much, goes in, lies down on his or her bed, and the room seems to be spinning around. Well, I didn't know, so I looked it up. Here's the explanation for bed spins. When you've had too much to drink, that alcohol begins to infuse into the semicircular canals, into the endolymph, and it changes the specific gravity of the endolymph. That system is at equilibrium with the specific gravity as it's supposed to be. When you go messing with it, and then you lie down, instead of remaining in a rigid position, the cupula falls over because the specific gravity of the endolymph has been changed. So now you're receiving discontinuity of information between the visual system and the vestibular system, because you're lying in bed looking up, and the eyes are saying, "Hey, I'm not moving," but the vestibular system is saying, "Something is moving," and again we experience motion sickness. If those students were still awake when the alcohol began to evaporate and be metabolized and leave the endolymph, they would experience a spinning in the opposite direction as the specific gravity of the endolymph was restored, and the cupula swung to its closed position. So that's the story on bed spins. Then, as I indicated earlier, apparently ginger is able to minimize motion sickness in some way that I'm afraid I don't understand.

Let me quickly talk about some age-related changes that take place in the vestibular system, and by the way, anybody who has aged knows that such changes do occur. For example, when you were young, remember how you used to love to ride on swings and roller coasters and things of that nature? Now, the thought of that is not very appealing. Why is that the case? Well, there are a number of changes that have taken place since you were last on a roller coaster or a set of swings. First of all, nerve and nerve fiber degeneration takes place. Individual nerve fibers in the vestibular part of the eighth nerve are either thinning out so they carry information more slowly, or dying entirely, so you're not having the precise vestibular feedback that you used to have, and this causes some uncertainty in the brain as to how to interpret the sensations that it's receiving. In addition to the nerves beginning to show degenerative changes, you lose vestibular receptors as a function of age.

Another problem that sometimes accompanies changes in our comfort with vestibular stimulation with age has to do with the fact that as we grow older we tend to experience calcium deficiencies, and remember the otoliths are calcium carbonate particles, so sometimes we can improve our vestibular situation by making sure that we don't have a calcium deficiency. Now, some of the changes in our comfort with vestibular stimulation are actually due to factors other than changes in the nerves or the receptors or the calcium carbonate particles. They have to do with changes in the tone of the connective tissue that hold the internal organs in place. With age, connective tissue loses its tone, if you will, and it permits greater movement of the internal organs, and this is a source of discomfort.

Another change that accompanies the aging process is we lose tone in our stomach muscles, which again permits more movement of the internal organs. Finally, many of us acquire abdominal fat, and so what swings and roller coasters are doing that make us uncomfortable, in addition to the less precise information from the vestibular system, is letting our internal organs slosh around in our stomachs, which doesn't feel very good.

Experiments have been done on subjects of different ages where you are blindfolded and put in a dental chair, if you will, and the chair is slowly tilted. Now, for instance, when you were a healthy young person, you could perceive a tilt of maybe two degrees or three degrees, but with some older people who have experienced some of the changes that I'm talking about—you may actually tilt that dental chair 14 degrees before they experience a tilt. So there is definitely a decrease in the precision of vestibular information that the brain is receiving as a function of age.

In our next lecture I will begin talking about the kinesthetic sense. Some people call that the muscle feedback sense, but it is actually far more than that. It is the last of the sensory systems we're going to talk about that is concerned with sending information to the brain about the location of the limbs in space based on movement. Thank you.

Lecture Twenty
The Kinesthetic Sense—Motor Memory

Scope:

The kinesthetic sense is sometimes called the "muscle memory" sense, but it is far more than this. The kinesthetic sense sends to the brain continuous sensory feedback from receptors located not only in the muscles but also in the tendons, ligaments, and joints. This sense is crucial for the ability to perform daily activities, such as sitting, standing, walking, and climbing stairs, where coordination of antagonistic muscle groups is necessary and cooperation between body parts is required to maintain fluidity of motion. The kinesthetic sense also provides the information needed for Olympic-caliber gymnasts and divers to perform their amazing physical feats.

It is not possible to master a complex motor activity simply by reading a book. We must practice the requisite motor movements over and over until the brain learns from kinesthetic feedback what it feels like when we finally do it right. Even then, hundreds or even thousands of additional repetitions are required until the phenomenon of *automaticity* is established in the frontal lobes. When automaticity is established, we can use the cognitive and volitional capabilities of the brain for strategic planning, rather than for moment-to-moment monitoring and orchestration of individual limb movements. The establishment of automaticity represents a neurological distinction between a novice and an expert in such activities as tennis or golf, where both motor skill and strategy are essential.

Laboratory studies indicate that precision of input from the kinesthetic system reaches its peak in the middle to late teens and begins to show almost imperceptible declines by the late 20s. There are no top Olympic gymnasts and divers in their 30s. By the time we are in our 50s and beyond, we must substitute experience and strategy for youth in such activities as tennis and golf. We can no longer have complete confidence in the accuracy of kinesthetic feedback. This change translates into, among other things, shortening one's backswing in golf.

Outline

I. The kinesthetic system provides the brain with information about the position and movement of the limbs in space.

   A. The kinesthetic sense is sometimes called the "muscle feedback" sense, although it has other important functions.

   B. In addition to monitoring activity in the muscles, the kinesthetic system measures tension and force in the ligaments and tendons and the direction, speed, and angularity of movements involving the joints.

II. The kinesthetic sense depends upon receptors located in muscles, tendons, ligaments, and in the joint capsules.

   A. Receptors in the muscles, called *muscle spindles*, respond to the degree of contraction in a given muscle. Data from the muscle spindles permit cooperation between antagonistic muscle groups to permit fluidity of movement.

   B. Receptors known as *Golgi tendon organs* are located in the tendons.

      1. Golgi organs monitor the moment-to-moment force exerted by muscles on tendons (tendons attach muscles to bones).

      2. If a tendon experiences an unfamiliar or unusually heavy load, the Golgi tendon organs trigger a "clasp-knife" protective reflex that causes the muscle to collapse to prevent injury.

      3. Part of athletic training is to teach the Golgi organs to accept higher and higher muscle loadings without firing the protective reflex.

      4. Another goal of athletic training is to teach the Golgi tendon organs to accept the higher muscle loadings that accompany the "follow-through" motion.

   C. Ligaments attach bone to bone at the joints.

      1. There are stretch receptors in the ligaments and joints that respond to changes in the angles at which a joint is bent.

      2. These same receptors are sensitive to the velocity of movement and the degree of limb rotation.

III. Kinesthetic feedback to the brain permits us to improve the efficiency and effectiveness of motor activities through practice.

A. It is not sufficient to read a book on how to perform skilled motor activities, such as playing golf or tennis.

B. We must perform a skilled motor activity over and over again so that the brain develops an awareness of what the kinesthetic feedback feels like when we "do it right."

C. The precision and sophistication of kinesthetic feedback required to perform different physical activities shows enormous variation.

    1. Most of us have sufficient kinesthetic sensitivity to learn to operate a standard-shift transmission.

    2. Very few of us have sufficient kinesthetic sensitivity to be an Olympic-caliber gymnast or diver.

IV. The human brain is also capable of a function called *automaticity*.

A. Initially, a coordinated sequence of motor responses requires that each component of the sequence be planned and thought about separately.

B. After sufficient repetitions, the kinesthetic feedback associated with the whole motor sequence has become familiar enough that the motor cortex can produce the motor sequence without the need for continuous monitoring by the cognitive portions of the brain.

C. This function, automaticity, leaves our cognitive capacities free for strategic planning and represents a major difference between novices and experts in various sports, including gymnastics, diving, tennis, and golf.

    1. Novice athletes work at the nuts and bolts of the sport.

    2. Expert athletes work on the strategy of the sport because they have established automaticity.

    3. Automaticity is a robust cognitive phenomenon. Once you have thoroughly memorized a poem or learned an activity, such as riding a bicycle or driving a standard-shift car, you do not forget or lose the ability to perform the activity.

V. The aging process plays a major role in kinesthetic sensitivity.

A. Evidence suggests that maximum sensitivity of kinesthetic feedback is achieved in humans at around the age of 12, the age at which the myelin sheath is fully developed.

B. Laboratory studies show that people in their mid to late 20s display very small decrements in the accuracy of kinesthetic feedback.

C. By the 40s, amateur golfers and tennis players notice a difference in their games.

D. Older athletes can still achieve success in their sports, but adjustments must be made.

    1. Older athletes in such sports as golf and tennis must substitute accuracy and control for speed and power (e.g., shorten the backswing).

    2. Older athletes must use more experience and strategy in place of pure athleticism.

    3. Older athletes find satisfaction in competing in sporting events that have age categories.

    4. In normal aging, the kinesthetic changes that we undergo pose little or no major impediment to everyday life in people up to and through their 80s.

Suggested Reading:

Colavita, *Sensory Changes in the Elderly*, chapter 9.

Jerome, *The Elements of Effort*, pp. 38–41.

Questions to Consider:

1. Kinesthetic feedback is responsible for the success of virtually every move we make, yet most people have never heard of the kinesthetic system. What does this say about human curiosity?

2. Can you think of examples of automaticity at work in your everyday life?

Lecture Twenty—Transcript
The Kinesthetic Sense—Motor Memory

Hello, and welcome to Lecture Twenty. As you may recall, in Lecture Nineteen we talked about the vestibular system, the sensory system that has two components; one that tells us about velocity and direction of movement and has receptors are housed in the semicircular canals, and the other component telling us about our position with respect to the upright, sometimes called the gravitational system, with the receptors housed in the utricle and saccule.

Today we're going to talk about another sensory system that tells us something about position in space. But the kinesthetic system, the subject of today's lecture, tells us about movement of individual body parts. Every single body part that contains either a muscle or a joint or both is sending moment-to-moment feedback to the brain about where that body part is in space or whether the muscles are tensed or relaxed or what the tension on the tendons is or what have you. The kinesthetic system, which most people have never heard of, is critically important for our ability to engage in the activities of everyday life.

For instance, I'm now going to send commands from my motor cortex down to the toes. I'm going to say, "Wiggle those toes." How am I going to know that that command was actually carried out? It turns out that the kinesthetic system is sending information to my brain from the toes that are wiggling, and is saying, "Mission accomplished." In the absence of kinesthetic feedback, though, how would we know whether those toes actually wiggled?

Okay. Now, some people call the kinesthetic sense the muscle feedback sense, and I suppose it is that, but it's actually a good deal more than that, too. The kinesthetic system does provide us with sensory information about what the muscles are doing, but it also sends information back from receptors in the tendons, from the ligaments, and also from receptors in the joints, so that we are constantly receiving moment-to-moment feedback about a variety of things.

Let's go back to my wiggling of the toes example. Every body part has two categories of nerves. Every body part that's capable of moving or flexing or contracting receives motor input from the primary motor cortex in the frontal lobe, and it also has a sensory nerve that carries information back from that moving body part to the brain saying, "Mission accomplished." So, for instance, I want to wiggle my toes, and suppose the sensory nerve in my leg was cut, so I could send motor messages to the toes and say, "Wiggle," but with that severed sensory nerve, I wouldn't know that the toes were actually wiggling unless I looked.

The receptors in the muscles that tell us about the state of contraction of the muscle are called muscle spindles. The muscle spindles are very sensitive to the state of contraction in that muscle, and they can give us information across the full spectrum of muscle contraction from "The muscle is totally relaxed," to "The muscle is contracted to its maximum." That's the job of the muscle spindles, to tell us about moment-to-moment changes in muscle contraction.

This turns out to be a critically important piece of sensory information to the brain because every limb has antagonistic muscle groups, and you don't want both of those muscle groups contracting at the same time or, for instance, your locomotion would not be smooth and fluid. Suppose that the antagonistic muscle groups in my legs were both contracted at the same time, I would have to walk like this, and we don't want that. The way that the brain is able to keep antagonistic muscle groups from contracting simultaneously and cooperating, if you will, is by attending to this moment-to-moment feedback from the muscle spindles.

You've probably heard the expression, "So-and-so froze with fear," or if you're unlucky enough to have had that experience, maybe you've told someone else, "I froze with fear." When somebody does freeze with fear what's happening is the emotional situation that they're encountering is so great that they lose control or sensitivity to what the muscle spindles are saying, and all the muscles tighten up. Antagonistic muscles tighten up, and the person is immobilized. So the muscle spindle makes it possible to do such things as walk and eat. All the activities that we take for granted, which involve antagonistic muscle groups, are due to the coordination possible because of feedback from the muscle spindles.

Let's talk about the receptors in the tendons. Tendons, by the way, are those tough, sinewy tissues that attach muscle to bone, so each muscle is attached, both at its origin and at the insertion, by tendons to the bones. Well, there are receptors in the tendons also, and these receptors tell us about the state of tension that a contracting muscle is putting on the tendon. This is also important information. The Golgi tendon organ is the receptor in the tendon that monitors contraction and pressure and force on the tendon. The Golgi tendon organ has a protective function. If the Golgi tendon organ in the tendons in the body detects an unusually heavy load, and fears that the muscle may actually be ripped loose from its attachment, the Golgi tendon organ triggers what is called a clasp-knife reflex; that is, the muscle just quits. The muscle stops. Well, rather than attempting to explain it, maybe I can describe some situations where you may have experienced this.

Perhaps there was a time when you decided to get back in shape, and you were going to start doing pushups and lifting weight, and so on. So here you are, you're doing pushups, and you want to squeeze out one more, and you're pushing and pushing, and all of a sudden— boom—the muscle just collapses. That was the Golgi tendon organ firing this protective clasp-knife reflex. Or suppose you're doing bench presses and you're there and you're doing them and you're going to squeeze out one more—because you know, "no pain, no gain"—and the Golgi tendon organ perceives this as an unusually heavy load, a dangerous load, and it fires that clasp-knife reflex and—boom—the weights come right back down—or curls, too, the same thing. So this is an example of what happens when the Golgi tendon organ detects an unfamiliar load. It doesn't even have to be really dangerous. Sometimes if it's an unfamiliar load, that clasp-knife reflex will fire, and the muscle just collapses.

One of the goals of athletic training is to teach the Golgi tendon organs to accept higher and higher loadings without collapsing. This takes place through repetition, repetition, repetition, and the Golgi tendon organ learns that this is not a dangerous loading.

Another issue in athletic training that involves the Golgi tendon organs has to do with the follow-through motion that is so necessary in sports such as golf or tennis or even bowling. You can tell just by looking that somebody is a novice if they take a little short back swing in golf, and then don't take a big follow-through in golf; or somebody that takes a little choppy shot at the ball with a tennis racket; or in bowling, somebody that doesn't give the big full follow-through that is typical of people who are experienced in those activities. So the Golgi tendon organ is, in fact, an important receptor for gaining proficiency in certain skilled activities.

Let's talk a bit about the ligaments and the joints. Ligaments, by the way, are those "structures that hold bone to bone at a joint," and of course the joints are the "places where a bone comes together." There are receptors in both the ligaments and the joints known as stretch receptors. Now these stretch receptors in the ligaments and joints are also providing instant-to-instant feedback to the brain about things such as the angle at which a joint is being held, about the rotation taking place, for instance, in the shoulder joint or the wrist, and about the velocity of movement.

We take these things for granted—the kinesthetic feedback—and yet this kinesthetic feedback about muscle contraction and about joint angles and about velocity of movement and rotation at the joints is critically important in the mastery of complex motor sequences. This is one of the reasons why the kinesthetic sense is so vital to improving through practice. You must make the motor response over and over again, and then you visually assess the outcome.

So you hit a golf ball, and then you look and see. "Did it go where I want? Was it as far as I wanted? Was it too far left or too far right?" And when you come to the point where you are hitting the shot properly, then you have to tune in and see how does that feel? You're tuning in to the kinesthetic feedback. How does it feel when I make the proper response? You see, you cannot just read a book and then be proficient at a complex motor activity. You can read about the theory of it, and the book can make suggestions, but the only way to become proficient at a complex motor skill is repetition, repetition, repetition. You need to find out what it feels like when you do it properly, and the kinesthetic feedback makes itself so aware to you that you can repeat that same move.

My children took tennis lessons once, and the tennis pro told them, "After you hit a shot properly, try and think how it felt so that you can repeat it. When you are so proficient that you can hit the shot properly whenever you want to, then you must do it a thousand more times to own that shot," so that the brain, in fact, has a good template to examine when you've done it properly—what it feels like, and when you don't do it properly what that feels like.

Kinesthetic sensitivity, the precision of kinesthetic feedback, differs considerably from one person to another. Just as smell sensitivity and taste sensitivity and auditory sensitivity differs from one person to another, so does kinesthetic sensitivity. Most of us have sufficient kinesthetic precision to learn to drive a standard shift car, for example, but a few unfortunate souls don't. Their kinesthetic feedback is not sufficient to permit them to acquire the motor skills necessary to drive a standard shift car. But most of us do, and it is a complex activity. You're steering with one hand, you're shifting with the other, and you have the clutch pedal, the brake pedal and the gas pedal to work out between two feet. It depends significantly on your awareness of how much pressure you're putting on the gas, and how much pressure you're putting on the brake, and how fast or slow are you letting out the clutch, and coordinating all that stuff. Without kinesthetic feedback, you couldn't learn to drive a standard shift car.

As a matter of fact, without kinesthetic feedback you couldn't even walk. You would have to learn to walk all over again. How do we know this? Well, because there are some unfortunate individuals who—because of some neurological problem or other—have lost kinesthetic feedback. In one instance, this poor person had to take to his bed. He didn't even trust being up and out of bed because he no longer knew what his limbs were doing. He no longer was able to count on having the feedback telling him that he was feeding himself properly or that he was even walking properly.

Finally, this individual marshaled his courage and his resources and began learning to walk again, but he had to learn to walk a new way. Now, instead of having kinesthetic feedback telling him what his legs were doing, and which muscles were doing what, he had to monitor visually: the left leg here in front, and then the right leg in front, and then the left leg in front, and then the right leg. He never did come to the point where he could drive a car, which would be too dangerous. He wouldn't know how hard he was stepping on the gas or the brake or whatever, even in an automatic transmission car.

But he did become so far that by monitoring visually he could walk downstairs, walk to a bus stop, and step on a bus, but he would have to watch his left leg to make sure it moved up and stepped on the step, and he would have to watch his right hand go out and reach the safety rail that people used to hoist themselves up on a bus. He did advance so that he could ride a bus again, but his quality of life was diminished greatly. He had to learn to feed himself all over again by watching what the right hand was doing and what the left hand was doing. He could no longer count on that kinesthetic feedback that you and I take for granted.

Speaking of driving a standard shift car, which I remember very well as a teenager—at first you have to cognitively, consciously focus on every move you're making, and you have to remember when you put the brake on you have to push the clutch in or the car will stall. When you let the clutch out you have to give it gas or the car will stall. You have to remember to shift gears with your right hand, and you have to remember you don't shift into first while the car is moving. I had to remember all that stuff. It was so demanding that I could not drive with the radio on—it was too distracting—and I certainly couldn't drive and have a conversation with a passenger. That was a recollection that I have of learning to drive a standard shift car.

Imagine the precision and the fine tuning of the kinesthetic feedback needed for an Olympic gymnast or diver to do those incredible feats of motor skill that they perform with such apparent effortlessness—the twisting and turning and flipping and spinning—and meanwhile, their kinesthetic system has to be sending moment-to-moment feedback to the brain. They do all this and still maintain the grace and balance of a ballerina. It's absolutely incredible. The accuracy and precision of that kinesthetic feedback is way beyond what most of us have.

I look forward to the Olympics every four years to watch the gymnasts and the divers because I am so aware of the precision and the marvelous sensitivity of their kinesthetic system. If I don't want to wait to wait for the next Olympics—I say this in all seriousness—I watch all of Jackie Chan, the Chinese actor—I watch all of his movies. The plots are relatively transparent and little bit simplistic, but he does his own stunts and he is a marvelous athlete. He does the most incredible feats of motor skill and makes them look easy. You can turn the sound off, but I really enjoy watching Jackie Chan movies, especially the older ones. He's a little older now, and that has consequences for the sensitivity of kinesthetic feedback, but I find him marvelous.

The ability to perform complex motor skills such as a gymnastics routine or a diving routine or even driving a standard shift car depends upon an ability of the brain that cognitive psychologists are very much interested in called automaticity. It's the way that complex motor sequences that originally have to be consciously monitored every step of the way become self-propagating. They run off by themselves. How does this happen? Well, at first you have to learn segments of the total behavior, and then you practice and practice and practice, and over learn these segments, and then you put the segments together. You do this over and over and over again and eventually this interesting cognitive phenomenon, called "automaticity," is initiated in the brain, and the only voluntary, cognitive, conscious decision you have to make is when to start the sequence.

For example, in driving a standard shift car, after automaticity has kicked in, what happens is that each momentary instance of kinesthetic feedback signals to the brain to produce the next momentary instance of motor outflow, and all you have to do is decide when to start the sequence, if the sequence has been over learned and automaticity has been attained.

You can tell when a gymnast, for example, goes to the line, and they compose themselves; they're about to make the only conscious decision that they have to make during that whole sequence. You see that sometimes they'll raise their hands and lean forward, and you know the routine is going to start, and then they take the first step or move or jump or run, and the rest of the sequence just runs off automatically. Automaticity—it's an amazing thing.

It's the same with divers. You can tell when a diver has made the voluntary decision to initiate the sequence. They rise up on their toes a little bit and lean forward, and then off they go, doing this beautiful, beautiful motor routine. The fact of the matter is that you and I have experienced automaticity over and above driving a standard shift car, which is also an example of automaticity. The light turns green and you decide, "Well, we'd better be going," and the kinesthetic system and the motor system cooperate and coordinate, and off you go, shifting gears, perhaps listening to the radio and carrying on a conversation with a passenger. That's automaticity.

Let me share with you examples that you may remember from your life experiences of automaticity. I've had this experience—maybe you have too. You've had a busy day at work, you have a lot of things on your mind, and it's time to go home. You get into the car, you turn on the ignition, and the next thing you know you're pulling in your driveway, and you don't a memory of a single move you made going home. You did the whole thing under automatic pilot, sort of. That's automaticity. The motor responses are so ingrained and so automatic that you can spend your cognitive energy, not thinking about, "Well, I'd better put the turn signal on; I'd better stop for the stop sign." You can be thinking about that problem that you left at work, or thinking about what you're going to do for the evening. So, yes, automaticity is something that we've all had experiences with. It's not just for Olympic gymnasts.

Another example of automaticity of a motor activity can be seen. Think back to when you were in junior high school, and maybe you were the one who was chosen to recite a poem at an assembly, and initially you had to learn every one of those words in the poem separately. You had to combine small groups of words, but you rehearsed and you rehearsed and you rehearsed, and came the assembly, and you stood up there and you made the conscious decision, "I'm going to start, 'When in the course of human events…' or The Gettysburg Address, 'Four score and seven years ago…' " Whatever it was, once you make the decision to start and you say the first word, the rest of it ran off with virtually no effort on your part. That was automaticity.

One of the major differences in athletic competition between players who do really well and players who do less well is the degree to which they have established automaticity. Novices in a new sport must waste their cognitive activity thinking of concrete things such as in golf, for example, weight on your heels, left arm straight, head down, shift your weight, swing through the ball. What's the expert doing with his or her cognitive capacity while the beginner is talking themselves through each and every step of the motor sequence? The expert is saying, "Better loft the ball so it doesn't roll when it hits the green. Better aim to the right of the pin because the green seems to slope left to right." So the novice is working on the nuts and bolts of the motor activity, and the expert is planning strategy.

It's the same in tennis. The beginner is thinking, "Watch the ball hit the racket, remember to follow through, remember your top spin, twist your wrist and your shoulder so you can put top spin on the ball." The expert is thinking, "Hit to the back hand, rush to the net, put it away with a cross-court drop shot." One is thinking nuts and bolts; one is thinking strategy.

The automaticity circuits, which are presently being studied by cognitive psychologists and cognitive neuroscience, wherever they exist in the brain they must be incredibly robust, because once a motor sequence has achieved automaticity, it seems to linger for a long time. You know you've heard people say, "Once you learn to ride a bicycle, you never forget." There is a grain of truth in that. Once you learn to drive a standard shift car you'll never forget it. There's a grain of truth in that, too. Once you've learned a poem to the point where automaticity is involved, and you say the first word, and the rest of the poem sort of runs itself off, you'll probably remember that the rest of your life. I still remember the Gettysburg Address. I still remember "In Flanders Field the poppies grow...," although I haven't recited those pieces in more than half a century. Automaticity is a very robust cognitive phenomenon.

Now, part of our concern is with automaticity and kinesthetic feedback and the aging process, so let's talk a little bit about that. Evidence suggests that maximum precision and sensitivity of kinesthetic feedback can be seen in a young child around the age of 12, which is just about the age when the myelin sheath, the protective insulating substance that covers nerve fibers and keeps them from short-circuiting, just about the time that that is completed too. So, theoretically it would be possible for a 12-year-old child to represent his or her country in the Olympics. Now, usually it takes them a few more years, because even when your kinesthetic feedback is at its peak, you still need a couple of years of experience under your belt before you can perform at an international level, but it is not all that uncommon to encounter 13-, 14-, 15-year-old gymnasts representing their countries in the Olympics. It's truly, truly, amazing. Well, the kinesthetic system seems to be in place and intact by the time you're 12. Whenever I give you a number like that, remember, that's a ballpark estimate. A little sooner in some people; a little later in others; 12 is a ballpark estimate.

The system is in place at a relatively early age. It also begins to show declines at a relatively early age. Now, experiments in the laboratory—and by the way, that's where you have to conduct these experiments because the declines I'm talking about are initially too small to be seen in the outside world— have indicated small, but measurable declines in kinesthetic sensitivity by the time you are in your mid- to late-20s.

Is that discouraging? Well, the fact of the matter is that for most people those declines are totally unnoticeable, because if you're a skilled athlete, and even though you're maybe experiencing very slight kinesthetic declines in your 20s, the fact of the matter is that your experience and your self-confidence are probably high enough that you're still going to perform in a quite acceptable manner. However, it is rare indeed to encounter world-class athletes, in sports that require the mastery of complex motor sequences, who are in their 30s. By then, the deficits in precise kinesthetic sensory feedback have reached the level where it's hard to maintain a national ranking when you're in your 30s.

At the amateur level it's rare to find athletes in their 40s still maintaining a national ranking. Now, of course, it differs from one sport to another. Some sports require extraordinary kinesthetic feedback. As it would be out of the question to be a gymnast or a diver and still perform and be nationally ranked in your 30s or 40s.

In tennis, some rare individuals can still do it. I am thinking, as I say this, about the women's tennis player, Martina Navratilova. She is now close to 50, and Martina Navratilova is still competing in professional tournaments. She's competing against young women in some cases who are close to one-third of her age, and she is acquitting herself well. Now, even Martina Navratilova, an outstanding athlete, has had to make some concessions to the aging process. For example, she now plays doubles rather than singles. But her muscle tone is superb, and her percentage of body fat is very, very low, so it's clear that she's still working very, very hard. But she's quite unusual.

In general, we can expect—in terms of kinesthetic deficits—mild decreases in sensitivity through the 30s. Through the 40s these deficits, for most of us, are a little more noticeable, and they become even more obvious through the 50s. Now, how do they measure such a thing? Well, they have all kinds of laboratory equipment where the person being tested is blindfolded, and their arms and legs are put in passive sling-like things that can slowly, passively lift the arms or legs, and you tell when you've detected that movement has taken place. Or at the joint, they can change the angle of the joint, and this can test the stretch receptors' sensitivity when how much the joint angle must be changed before you notice it. These are more passive tests.

They can also do things like give you a hand dynamometer, and say, "Squeeze this thing half as hard as you're capable of," and then they'll say, "Do that again." They'll see if you can squeeze it the same amount time after time. Or they can use a radar gun and say, "Throw a ball at three-quarters of your ability, speed wise," and then they'll see if you can do it over and over and over again, because all of these abilities, repeating the same degree of grip strength, or throwing the ball just as fast, all of these abilities require precise kinesthetic feedback.

There's also a test they use that's like a child's game of pick-up sticks to measure sensitivity of kinesthetic feedback in making small-muscle movements. The bottom line, though, is that kinesthetic changes in sensitivity do occur as a function of age, and the older athlete must make adjustments. The older athlete must learn to substitute accuracy for speed and power, so you do shorten your back swing in golf, or you do shorten that swing and the power on that big booming serve, going more for accuracy than for power. Those people who still care to compete in athletics at an older age may have to settle in competing in sports that have age categories, so they're competing against other people whose kinesthetic systems have undergone age-related decline. Or you take up sports that have less of a need for precise kinesthetic feedback. For instance, give up tennis and start taking up running where the kinesthetic feedback needed is much less sophisticated.

Now, I know that I've given this lecture a good athletic focus. There's a reason for this. If I were to talk about normal individuals and normal aging, the lecture would be quite boring, because, truthfully, the kinesthetic changes that we undergo as a function of age represent no major threat. This is in the case of normal aging, not where there's some kind of pathology or senile dementia going on. In the course of normal aging, kinesthetic feedback is really not going to be much of a major impediment to you performing your everyday activities. Up to and through the 80s, this is the case, so that's really kind of good news.

There may have to be some concessions made. For instance, you may have to substitute an electric razor for a blade razor because of the lack of precision about how hard you're pressing against your skin. You may have more trouble with behaviors that require a very light touch, such as putting in contact lenses and things of that nature, but in all honesty, health failure is much more of a problem for the elderly than lack of kinesthetic feedback.

One final point—we are in the age of biotechnology and robotics and things of that nature, and there are robotic instruments that can beat a human at chess. I would be very surprised if robots or robotic instruments are ever devised that can learn a complex motor sequence like a human being. The difference being, we have this wonderful, exquisite kinesthetic sense that provides us with that moment-to-moment feedback, and a robot would not have this.

Now I did read recently about a robotic arm that is capable of doing microsurgery, and this is all well and good. The full story, however, is that some human is at the controls of this robotic arm, and that human is using his or her kinesthetic feedback to operate that robotic arm, so it's really the human that's doing the intelligent part of that task.

We've been talking about the kinesthetic system in this lecture, the sensory system that provides momentary feedback about what all the moving parts of the body are doing.

In our next lecture we will talk about the structure and function of the brain. We will start acknowledging the brain as the organ of perception, and we will start with Lecture Twenty-One. Thank you.

Lecture Twenty-One
Brain Mechanisms and Perception

Scope:

The human brain represents the result of millions of years of evolutionary changes, but the older parts of the brain do not disappear when new parts develop. The newer parts simply grow over the older parts, which still retain their original functions. The newest part of the human brain, the cerebral cortex, regulates the higher mental processes, including perception.

The human brain exhibits bilateral anatomical symmetry up through the forebrain. The cerebral cortex, however, is slightly asymmetrical. Parts of the left hemisphere are larger in most people. The anatomical asymmetry in the cerebral cortex corresponds to a functional asymmetry that extends to the phenomenon of perception. Research suggests that the perception of language is the province of the left cerebral hemisphere.

Perceptual dysfunction is caused by focal loss of brain cells—loss of brain cells in a certain part of the brain. Therefore, the diffuse loss of cortical neurons inevitably brought about with age is not typically an issue in perceptual dysfunction. Similarly, studies have shown that memory storage is spread throughout the brain, thus making memory less vulnerable to diffuse brain damage.

Outline

I. The human brain represents the highest level of organizational complexity yet achieved on Earth. This complex organ has evolved over millions of years, and some parts of the human brain are far older than other parts.

    A. The oldest part of the human brain is the hindbrain, which controls the vital functions, such as blood pressure, respiration, and heart rate.

    B. The midbrain represents an intermediate level of brain development.

        1. The midbrain also determines our levels of sleep, wakefulness, and arousal.

        2. The midbrain is responsible for reflex orientation to sensory stimuli.

C. The forebrain has three broad categories of important functions.

1. The forebrain regulates the physiological drives, such as hunger, thirst, sex, and temperature regulation.
2. The forebrain is involved in emotional reactivity.
3. The forebrain controls the automatic aspects of our motor behavior, such as balance, postural adjustment, and initiation and fluidity of movement.

D. The cerebral cortex is the newest part of the human brain. It controls the higher mental processes and gives us important inhibitory capabilities.

1. The higher mental processes include thinking, willing, problem solving, concept formation, and perception.
2. The inhibitory capabilities of the cerebral cortex give us the option of dealing with life on a level more civilized than "fight or flight."

II. The cerebral cortex is divided into the frontal, parietal, occipital, and temporal lobes, each lobe being represented in both the left- and right-brain hemispheres. (Figure 21a)

A. The frontal lobes are concerned with motor functions, broadly defined.

1. The planning of motor sequences is a frontal lobe function.
2. Interpreting a map or a blueprint involves the frontal lobes, because this is preparation for motor activity.
3. The frontal lobes also enable us to inhibit motor activity if the timing is not advantageous.
4. The problems with impulsivity seen in AD/HD are thought by many researchers to be the result of underfunctioning of frontal lobe inhibitory circuits.

B. The anterior portions of the parietal lobes receive sensory messages from the cutaneous receptors in the skin. The posterior portions of the parietal lobes are actually visual association areas, meaning that these brain regions are important for certain categories of visual perception.

C. The occipital lobes are the primary visual cortical areas, the first areas to receive sensory messages from the visual receptors. From the occipital lobes, sensory data from the visual receptors are transmitted to the visual association areas for further analysis.

D. The upper (dorsal) portion of the temporal lobe is the primary receiving area for hearing (including speech). The lower (ventral) portion of the temporal lobe is another visual association area.

E. The four lobes of the brain have neural connections with each other and with subcortical brain regions. The complex interconnectedness of brain regions has important implications for perception.

1. The same perception can be evoked by different sensory inputs (for example, the concept of your significant other can be evoked by a picture, a smell, a tone of voice, and so on).

2. Memory can be used to imagine a sight, sound, or smell that evokes a perception.

III. In general, neurologists and neuropsychologists anticipate some type of motor dysfunction following significant frontal lobe damage and some type of sensory or perceptual dysfunction following significant damage to the parietal, occipital, or temporal lobes.

IV. The left and right hemispheres of the human brain appear to be bilaterally symmetrical.

A. True anatomical symmetry in the human brain occurs only at the levels of the hindbrain, midbrain, and forebrain.

B. There are measurable left brain-right brain asymmetries in most humans at the level of the cerebral cortex. These asymmetries have behavioral significance.

1. A neurologist named Juhn Wada discovered two areas where the left hemisphere is consistently bigger than the right.

a. The first area is along the sylvian sulcus or fissure, in the area where we perceive speech.

b. The second area consists of the pyramidal tracks, which are the nerve fiber bundles that carry information from the primary motor cortex out to the peripheral muscles.

2. Most people are right-handed (the left brain controls the right side of the body).

3. Most babies are born with asymmetries favoring the left cerebral hemisphere.
4. Because of plasticity, if a person suffers brain damage to the left hemisphere at a young age, he or she will switch to being right-hemisphere dominant and vice versa.

C. Speech appears to be a left-hemisphere phenomenon in all normal (non-brain-damaged) right-handed individuals and in 70 percent of normal left-handed individuals.

V. Significant brain cell loss in the cerebral cortex can have consequences for perceptual abilities.

A. Some diffuse loss of cortical neurons with age is inevitable.
1. However, such diffuse loss is not typically an issue in perceptual dysfunction.
2. Perceptual dysfunction is caused by focal loss of brain cells, that is, loss of brain cells in a certain part of the brain.

B. All categories of senile dementia involve significant cortical brain cell loss, and all categories of senile dementia result in both cognitive and perceptual impairments, including loss of memory.

C. Karl Lashley, an early physiological psychologist, studied the different parts of the brain as related to memory and concluded that memory storage is spread throughout the brain, thus making memory less vulnerable to diffuse brain damage.

Suggested Reading:

Carlson, *Physiology of Behavior* (8th ed.), pp. 84–85.

Gazzaniga, *The Bisected Brain.*

Questions to Consider:

1. Would it surprise you to learn that there is no strong evidence for hemispheric asymmetry in any animal below the level of humans? If so, why? If not, why not?

2. Children born with a tendency to be left-handed can be trained to become right-hand dominant. Some parents believe that such training will help a child experience less inconvenience in our "right-handed" society. Explain why you agree or disagree with this reasoning.

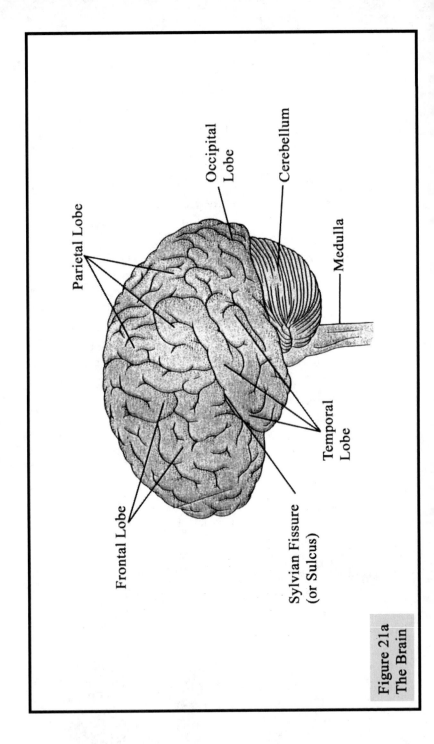

Parietal Lobe

Occipital Lobe

Cerebellum

Medulla

Temporal Lobe

Frontal Lobe

Sylvian Fissure (or Sulcus)

Figure 21a
The Brain

Lecture Twenty-One—Transcript
Brain Mechanisms and Perception

Hi. Welcome to Lecture Twenty-One. In Lecture Twenty you'll recall we talked about the kinesthetic system. That's the sensory system that provides us with moment-to-moment feedback from receptors in the muscles, the tendons, the joints, and the ligaments.

In this lecture, Lecture Twenty-One, we're going to look at the structure and function of the human brain with special attention being paid to the cerebral cortex. We have, on occasion, referred to the brain as the "organ of perception." Today we're going to flesh that statement out a bit, and modify it, because it turns out that the whole brain, of course, is not involved in perception; rather, the highest level of the brain is—the cerebral cortex.

The human brain represents the highest level of organizational complexity that any creature's brain that ever existed on the planet has reached. We're the top of the heap. But the human brain—as it exists today, in its present form—went through many, many stages and changes over millions and millions of years. I'm going to take you on a brief evolutionary trek through the history of the brain.

When we talk about evolution—some people when they hear the word evolution think about animals that used to exist and now they're dead and they've been replaced. Brain evolution is a little bit different. The old parts of the brain didn't just disappear. Rather, they are still in there. We have primitive parts in our brain that have been unchanged for millions of years. In brain evolution, what happens is a newer part of the brain simply grows over the old part and—rather than taking away the functions of the old part—the new parts of the brain establish new functions.

Okay, this will be an over-simplification, but basically accurate, as we go through the different parts of the brain. We've already mentioned a couple of these parts. I've shared with you the information that the oldest part of the brain—evolutionarily speaking and chronologically speaking—is called the hindbrain. When it first appeared on planet Earth, the hindbrain was little more than a cluster of cells that grew on the end of the spinal chord. We still have a hindbrain in there today, in our skulls. The job of the hindbrain is to mediate the vital functions, to keep us breathing, to keep the heart beating, to keep the blood pressure within normal homeostatic limits. This is the job of the hindbrain.

Let's jump ahead a couple of million years from the hindbrain, and another layer of cells evolves, and grows over the hindbrain, and this we call the midbrain, and we've already addressed the midbrain in earlier lectures. The midbrain basically has two broad categories of functions. One, it maintains our level of sleep, wakefulness, and arousal. For example, the spinothalamic tract, which takes impulses from the free nerve endings—the pain messages—goes to the midbrain, and so pain is very effective at increasing our level of arousal and alertness. Pain is a very potent stimulus in that regard.

The other category of functions found in the midbrain involves reflex orientation to sensory stimuli, and we talked about that too, so that the tendency to orient toward a stimulus somewhere in our periphery is reflexive and controlled by midbrain circuits. The tendency to duck and cover when we see something in visual space racing toward our heads is also mediated by midbrain circuits.

Let's move on from the midbrain. Another several million years later, another layer of cells evolved over the midbrain, and what we have now is the forebrain. The forebrain is concerned with a variety of functions. One, the forebrain involves circuits that permit us or cause us to fulfill our survival needs, our basic physiological motives—hunger, thirst, sex, temperature regulation—all of these vital needs that we share in common with lower animals involve circuits in the forebrain. Emotional reactivity—the more primitive aspects of emotion—fight or flight, fear, rage—these are controlled by forebrain circuits, in a region of the forebrain known as the limbic system.

The forebrain is also concerned with the automatic aspects of motor behavior—not the skilled voluntary motor activities that we choose to engage in. For instance, if you're walking, and you trip on a crack in the sidewalk and you stumble, the ability to regain your balance automatically without thinking about it involves forebrain circuits. If I were standing straight up and down as I am, and the room suddenly tipped to the left, rather than fall over, what happens is that the forebrain elicits reflexes to regain that stability. By throwing out your right arm and leg you change your center of gravity and you don't fall over. There are the postural adjustments needed for walking that we don't have to stop and think about. Walking is actually more complex than we give it credit for being, but because automatic circuitry takes care of this, shifting of the center of gravity from side to side as we walk and things of that nature, these are all controlled by neural circuits in the forebrain.

Okay. So now let's grow another layer of cells over the forebrain. Let's jump ahead another couple of million years in evolution, and we're going to grow a two-millimeter-thick layer of cell bodies over the forebrain and we're going to call this the cerebral cortex, evolutionarily speaking, the newest part of the brain. Just as we've done for the other lower parts of the brain, let's state the functions of the cerebral cortex in a sentence or two. Well, one role of the cerebral cortex is to mediate the higher mental processes. This involves such things as thinking, willing, concept formation, perception—now there's a key word for the subject matter of our whole series of lectures—perception—so perception is the province of the cerebral cortex.

In addition to the higher mental processes, though, the cerebral cortex has another important category of functions. It provides necessary inhibitory circuits to the lower parts of the brain. It is the cerebral cortex and its inhibitory circuits that give us options. For example, an angry rat has no choice but to act like an angry rat, but an angry human has a choice. We can either act like an angry rat, because we have those circuits in the forebrain, or we can utilize the inhibitory capabilities of the cerebral cortex and act like an angry human being. A hungry rat has no option but to eat. A hungry human has two options. It can go ahead and eat or the hungry human can utilize the inhibitory circuitry of the cerebral cortex and say, "I'm hungry, and I'd really like to eat, but I'm going to inhibit these primitive tendencies impelling me to eat, because today is a religious fast day," or "…because today I choose not to eat to show solidarity with the homeless," or "…I choose not to eat because of a political protest" or something like this. So we have options that lower animals don't have because of the inhibitory circuitry in our cerebral cortex.

Okay, now let me take this anatomy of the brain a step further, and tell you that the cerebral cortex is divided into four lobes. If you want to know where the frontal lobe is, you hold your hand right over your forehead; you are now covering the frontal lobe. If you want to know where the parietal lobe is, take your hand and put it on the very top of your head; you're now covering the parietal lobe. If you want to know where the occipital lobe is, take your hand and put it on the back of your head; you're now covering the occipital lobe. And if you want to know where the temporal lobes are, take your left and right hands and put them over your ears; you're now covering the location of the temporal lobe in the brain. Okay. We have these four lobes.

Now let's talk briefly about the functions of these four lobes. This may come as a surprise to you, but the major function of the frontal lobe is in motor activity, and some people hear that and they say, "Boy, I thought the frontal lobe was the smart part of the brain where we plan and make decisions and organize and do complex calculations and things of that nature." Well, when we say the frontal lobe is concerned with motor activity, we are using the term "motor activity broadly" defined, because it turns out that most of the things that we plan or organize or arrange are actually preparing us to then do a series of motor activities. For instance, when you wake up on Saturday morning and plan your day, "Well, first I'll have breakfast; then I'll go to the gym; then I'll go to the post office; then I'll have the car washed"—that's all frontal cortex planning because it all involves motor activities. "I'm going to eat breakfast"—a motor activity. "I'm going to go to the gym"—motor activity. "I'm going to have the car washed," etc., etc. Most of the things we plan are motor sequences.

When a student is planning his or her course schedule for the semester, it involves the frontal lobe, because you're planning some motor sequence that you're going to carry out. If you want to plan your major in college, "Well, my freshman year this or this or this, and my junior year…;" that's motor, that's frontal lobe stuff. When you read a map to take you from here to Indianapolis or wherever you want to go, that's preparing you to step into the car and then do a series of motor activities that take you from here to Indianapolis.

If you read a blueprint, and then build a building, it's frontal lobe stuff. So when we say that the frontal lobe is concerned with motor activity, that's motor activity broadly defined.

The frontal lobe also, by the way, has inhibitory circuits that can inhibit motor activity if it's not at an advantageous time for you. For example, suppose you have a job interview for Monday. Monday morning you wake up, and you have laryngitis. If you go to that interview, you're going to make a terrible first impression. So you use the inhibitory circuits of the frontal lobe to decide, "Well, I'd better postpone this and reschedule it for a time that's better for me, that's in my best interest."

The inhibitory circuits in the frontal lobe that have the ability to inhibit motor activity are very, very important to us. Perhaps you can see the importance when I tell you that some respected researchers in the area of Attention Deficit/Hyperactivity Disorder believe that ADHD—the core disorder being impulsivity and lack of impulse control—that ADHD comes about because of under functioning of the inhibitory circuits in the frontal lobe. See, in an individual without ADHD, he or she has an impulse, and says, "Wait a minute. I'd better think that over." Then that person says, "Gee, that's not a good idea. I won't do it." In the case of ADHD, an individual has the impulse, acts on it, and then later, when it's too late, says, "Gee, maybe I shouldn't have done that." Some people think that what makes the difference are these inhibitory circuits from the frontal lobe.

This explains, by the way, the paradoxical effect of Ritalin. Here we have somebody who's hyperactive and has trouble concentrating, and you give them a psychostimulant. How on earth does that work? Well, the theory that seems to have some merit is that you're giving this individual a psychostimulant that's going to increase activity in the frontal lobe, thereby increasing these under functioning inhibitory connections. Anyway, frontal lobe is motor.

Let's go and look at some of the other lobes of the brain. Put your hand on the top of your head. This is the parietal lobe. The front of the parietal lobe is called the anterior parietal lobe and the back of the parietal lobe is called the posterior parietal lobe. The front of the parietal lobe—the anterior parietal lobe—is what we call the primary projection area for the cutaneous senses. In other words, while the free nerve endings are going by way of the spinothalamic tract to the midbrain, the encapsulated end organs, by way of the lemniscal system, are sending precise cutaneous information to the anterior portion of the parietal lobe. So if we electrically excite the anterior parietal lobe, people will feel cutaneous sensations on the skin. Okay, so that's where the skin senses project, in the anterior parietal lobe.

The posterior parietal lobe is actually what we call a visual association area. We haven't used that term before. Visual association areas are concerned not with the basic visual information, but with that basic information combined into complex perceptions. So whenever we talk about a visual association area, you will know that we're not talking about basic visual processes, but rather, we're talking about some complicated perceptual mechanism. We'll have more to say, of course, about visual association areas, because there are more of them in the brain too.

Let's talk about the occipital lobe, which we would locate if we put our hands over the back of our heads. The occipital lobe could pretty much be covered by a little skull cap if you were to wear one back here. The very center of the occipital lobe is what we call the primary projection area for vision. This is where basic visual data go—the middle of the occipital lobe. The periphery of the occipital lobe—the area that surrounds the basic area, which is called the primary projection area—is another visual association area. In other words, the periphery of the occipital lobe is going to be concerned with more complex visual perceptions. By the way, we will definitely not go into any complex visual perceptions in this lecture, but stay tuned for Lecture Twenty-Three, when that's all we're going to talk about.

Okay, let's move on from the occipital lobe, which again has a primary projection area and a visual association area, to the temporal lobe. When you cover your ears with your hands, you're covering the temporal lobe. The temporal lobe is shaped like a wrinkly hot dog bun. It's more elongated, and that analogy with the hotdog bun is not so bad, because you know you can split a hotdog bun down the middle, and you have a top half and a bottom half, the temporal lobe also has a top half and a bottom half. The top of the temporal lobe is called the superior temporal area, and the bottom half of the temporal lobe is called the inferior temporal area. We're not making a value judgment here—we're not saying one is better than the other. Superior is used to refer to the fact that it's the top, and inferior is used to refer to the fact that it is the bottom.

The superior temporal lobe is actually an auditory area. All of the impulses from the auditory hair cells go to the superior portion of the temporal lobe. The ventral bottom—inferior—half of the temporal lobe is another visual association area. Okay? So we have visual association areas in the posterior parietal, in the peripheral occipital, and in the ventral temporal—the inferior temporal—lobe and each of those visual association areas is of critical importance, as we will see in Lecture Twenty-Three.

The interesting thing about all of the lobes of the cerebral cortex is they all have interconnections with each other. So they are not only receiving information from the subcortical regions of the brain, they are giving and receiving information to each other, which has some interesting implications for people. One of the things that the areas of the brain—especially the association areas—one of the interesting advantages it gives us over lower animals is that we are capable of forming multi-modal perceptions, multi-model concepts. For example, I can experience the perception of my significant other either by the sound of her voice or the smell of her perfume or her favorite color or a picture of her. See, because of the fact that we have interconnecting association areas, a number of different stimuli can end up eliciting the same perception. Most lower animals do not have that option in their brains.

Now, based on what I told you, if you were a neurologist or a neuropsychologist—both of these are people who work with head injuries and brain damage—the neurologists are using the high-tech imaging techniques to find out where the damage is. For a neurologist, for example, the report might be, "You have a six gm fissure mass at the base of the third frontal convolution of the left cerebral hemisphere." Neuropsychology is actually a branch of clinical psychology, so the neuropsychologist would say, "As a consequence of that, you are going to have trouble with mathematical operations," or something like that.

So the neurologist is interested in where the damage is, and the neuropsychologist is interested in what is the functional consequence of that disorder. In any event, either of those two people, if they were seeing a patient with frontal lobe damage would be very tuned in and sensitive to the possibility of motor involvement, because we said that the frontal lobe controls motor activities broadly speaking. So somebody with frontal lobe damage—we would be looking for their ability to plan sequences or inhibit motor activity, or if it were in the primary motor area, we might be looking for some paralysis or perhaps deficits in fine-motor speed or motor strength.

Damage to frontal lobe, then, is concerned with primarily with motor deficits. Damage to any of the other lobes, the parietal, the occipital, or the temporal lobes is much more likely to result in some kind of deficit of a sensory or perceptual nature.

Now, let's talk a little bit about the fact that the human brain has a left and a right half. If you were to look at a model of a human brain or a real human brain as a teaching specimen in a medical school course or something like that, to the naked eye, the left and right halves would appear to be mirror images of each other. The human brain appears to have bilateral symmetry. Well, it actually does have bilateral symmetry up to the level of the forebrain. The human brain shows bilateral symmetry at the hindbrain, at the midbrain, and at the forebrain, but it is actually slightly asymmetrical at the level of the cerebral cortex.

The thing is that this asymmetry is not obviously noticeable, and people really didn't notice it until—good Lord!—50 or 60 years ago, when a researcher demonstrated that there are left hemisphere, right hemisphere asymmetries. If you had to guess which hemisphere is slightly larger, you would probably guess the left cerebral hemisphere, because you know that the vast majority of us are right handed, and you probably know that the left half of the brain controls the right half of the body, and the right half of the brain controls the left half of the body. So if you guessed that the asymmetries favor the left hemisphere, you would be absolutely right.

How do we know this? Well, about 50 or 60 years ago, a gentleman by the name of Wada came into possession of human brains from deceased people who had willed their brains to science, and he did careful measurements of the brain rather than just eyeballing it. He found that there were two areas where the left hemisphere seemed to be consistently bigger. One of these was along a region called the sylvian sulcus. You've not heard that term before, but the sylvian sulcus is actually "the border of the superior temporal lobe, between it and the parietal lobe." So in other words, the sylvian sulcus is longer right about where we perceive speech.

The other area in which Wada found asymmetries favoring the left hemisphere was in structures called the pyramidal tracks, and that's probably another term that you haven't heard. The pyramidal tracks are the nerve fiber bundles that carry information from the primary motor cortex out to the peripheral muscles. Okay, now since the left pyramidal tracks are thicker, and because the left side of the brain controls the right side of the body, this makes sense with the fact that most of us are right handed. Can we say that we are right handed because the left pyramidal tracks are thicker? Or do you think it's that the left pyramidal tracks are thicker because we're right handed? It's a chicken or egg thing, and unfortunately Wada's observations, being on adult humans, don't tell us whether we were born with these asymmetries or not.

People originally thought that handedness was probably something that our culture chose for us, or our parents chose for us, and I can see why they would think that because I've had students in my class from India who have said that the schools want you to be right handed in India. I've had a woman in class recently from the Philippines who said that in the Philippines they want you to be right handed. And I know from personal experience. I lived out of the United States when I was younger, and I had to go to a Catholic junior high school, and they were very unhappy if somebody was still using the left hand. So there are cultural forces trying to make more of us right handed. Many parents, by the way, want their children to be right handed because they think it will give them an easier time through life, since most scissors are for right-handed people, and golf clubs are for right-handed people, and desks are for right-handed people.

Then why, who, and when did somebody decide, "Hey, let's make kids be right handed"? Some people say it started with the Romans because the Roman Legions—at one time Rome ruled the known world—and the Roman Legions required that all young men from all the territories that Rome was in charge of serve in the Roman Legions, and the Roman Legions said, "You will carry your shield in your left hand and your sword in your right hand." So if you were the parents of a baby—a boy baby—you would want that baby to be right handed, because he might have to defend himself with his sword in his right hand.

Then why would the Romans want girls to be right handed? Well, I've heard the story that the Romans knew that if a woman holds a baby in her left arm, that the baby is soothed by the heartbeat of the mother, and that frees the right arm to feed the baby or clean the baby or do whatever chores the baby needs done. So some people said the Romans wanted everybody to be right handed. Well, that sounds good in theory, but archaeologists tell us that many of the artifacts from prehistoric times were for right-handed cave dwellers, so the story about the Romans doesn't answer that question.

But the one who did answer it was our friend Wada again. He went back to the drawing board in terms of measuring different parts of the brain. This time he came into possession of the brains of stillborn babies. Now, there's no question that they had learned language or learned to be right or left handed because they were stillborn. He found anatomical asymmetries that we can now call unlearned anatomical asymmetries in the brains of these stillborn babies. Again he found them in the sylvian fissure and the pyramidal tracks.

Let me give you his figures. In Wada's sample of stillborn babies, 65% of them had anatomical asymmetries favoring the left hemisphere; 24% had anatomical asymmetries favoring the right hemisphere; and in 11%, he could find no measurable difference. Can we extrapolate from those findings to humans—to normal adult humans? The answer is no, because these babies were not representative of normal humans, adult or otherwise. Something was wrong with these babies or they wouldn't have been born dead.

If we look in the general population, 10% of us are left handed, and 90% of us are right handed. The implication here is that Wada's percentages are an under representation of the degree to which the left hemisphere is dominant in our culture. Is there any evidence for this? Well, yes. In brain-damaged populations, we find a much higher percentage than 10% being right hemisphere dominant and left handed. Now, I'm not saying that left handed people are brain damaged. Plenty of them are gifted and talented. What I am saying is that in populations of brain damaged as opposed to in the general population we find higher than 10%.

Why could this be the case? Well, let's take a hypothetical sample of 1,000 newborn babies. We can expect that 900 of them would grow up to be right handed, left hemisphere dominant, and 100 would grow up to be right hemisphere dominant and left handed. Let's also assume, tragically, that maybe 1% of them are going to experience birth trauma, forceps delivery or whatever that is going to produce brain damage, and that others of them are going to have early childhood head injuries.

Now, the human brain possesses a characteristic called plasticity. If you suffer brain damage as a child or an infant in the left hemisphere, you're going to switch over, and your right hemisphere is going to be your dominant hemisphere. Similarly, if you experience brain damage in the right hemisphere, you will switch over, and your left hemisphere will be your dominant hemisphere. If we assume 1% in both the 900 left hemisphere dominants and the 100 right hemisphere dominants, we're going to have nine brain-damaged left hemisphere dominant babies switching over and being right hemisphere dominant, and in the right hemisphere dominant people to start with, one of them is going to switch over and be left hemisphere dominant. This is why we have higher percentages of lefties in the brain-damaged populations.

It is known that the left hemisphere is our dominant hemisphere, and the left hemisphere dominance for language is so great that it is the dominant hemisphere for language in all normal right-handed people and 70% of normal left-handed people, ruling out the brain-damaged people. Okay, 70% of lefties are left hemisphere dominant for language. Of the remaining 30% of left-handed people, 15% of them have language in the right hemisphere, and 15% of them actually have language represented in both cerebral hemispheres. This will become significant in Lecture Twenty-Two when we talk about language perception.

Let me say that the aging process is also involved in changes in the brain. As we age, of course, we're going to experience some unavoidable diffuse brain cell loss. However, diffuse brain cell loss is not typically an issue in perceptual dysfunctions, because perceptual dysfunctions frequently require focal brain damage in a specific locus of the brain. So, fortunately the normal aging process is highly unlikely to result in us having serious perceptual dysfunctions. Now that's normal aging. With senile dementias it's a whole different story. In senile dementias, such as Alzheimer's Disease, it's been estimated that elderly people may be losing as many as 100,000 brain cells a day—100,000 brains cells today, and another 100,000 tomorrow, and the day after and the day after—in the senile dementias you are going to have perceptual dysfunction because senile dementias are associated with serious memory problems, and memory, of course, is an important aspect of perception, because perceptions are based on your past experiences with a given stimulus or stimulus situation, and if you can no longer remember those previous experiences, it's going to certainly alter your perceptions.

One of the best known of the early physiological psychologists, a gentleman by the name of Karl Lashley, spent 20 years studying the different parts of the brain as it related to memory and, indirectly, to perception. Lashley devised tests of memory for experimental animals, and he produced experimentally induced brain damage in hundreds and hundreds of animals until he had explored every single conceivable part of the brain.

He published the results of 20 years of brain research on memory in a book called *In Search of the Engram*. *Engram* was the term that physiological psychologists used to use for "the memory trace," so what he was saying was this research is in search of the place in the brain where the memory trace is stored. As a result of his 20 years of research, he came to the tongue-in-cheek conclusion that memory is impossible, because he found no part of the brain that if destroyed would wipe out memory. The reason for this is because what he was really saying was not that memory isn't possible, but that memory is spread out over many different regions of the brain—which is actually good for us because it makes memory that much less vulnerable to diffuse brain damage.

To quickly recap, we've talked about the structure and function of the brain, talked about the evolution of the brain, the lobes of the brain, and left-right differences in brain functioning, and we wound up by talking about diffuse brain damage associated with aging.

In our next lecture we will talk about some very important human perceptual abilities.

Lecture Twenty-Two
Perception of Language

Scope:

Language is made up of verbal auditory stimuli that have become charged with meaning. The perception of speech is clearly an important perceptual capacity for humans. Language is so critical that it has two areas of the brain dedicated to it, one for speech production and one for speech comprehension. The cortical region critical for speech comprehension (*Wernicke's area*) is located in the left temporal lobe in the region known as the *auditory cortex*.

Words are made up of *phonemes*, the smallest distinguishable vocal utterances. Different languages can have different phonemes. The phonemes that a baby hears in the language of his or her caregivers during the first few months of life lead to the establishment of dedicated connections between auditory receptors and neurons in the auditory cortex. A phonemic "perceptual map" is formed, with each phoneme having a specific site in the auditory cortex.

In later life, the ease of acquisition of a second language will depend upon the degree of phonemic overlap between the first and second languages. Most individuals who begin to learn a second language after age 12 are unlikely to speak it like a native.

The aging process has some implications for speech perception. The phenomenon of presbycusis interferes with processing of the high-frequency components of speech sounds, while decreases in auditory nerve conduction speed result in intelligibility problems with rapid speech.

Outline

I. In the 1950s, it was generally believed that human sensory, motor, and cognitive capabilities were controlled by specific centers in the brain. A decade later, we saw that the brain is not divided into centers but that most human activities involve the intercommunication and cooperation of different motivational systems of the brain.

II. There are two exceptions to the finding that the human brain is not divided into task-specific centers.

A. One involves language perception.

B. The other involves human face perception.

III. There are actually two speech centers in the human brain, one center for the production of speech and one for the understanding of speech. (Figure 22a)

A. The center for the expression or production of speech is known as *Broca's area*. It is located (in most people) in the posterior portion of the left frontal lobe.

B. The center for the understanding or reception of speech is known as *Wernicke's area*. Wernicke's area is located along the upper boundary of the left temporal lobe (along the left sylvian fissure).

C. Damage to either speech area produces a neurological condition known as *aphasia.*

    1. Damage to Broca's area produces *expressive aphasia*, in which the individual can understand speech but cannot express it.

    2. Damage to Wernicke's area produces *receptive aphasia*, in which the individual can express speech sounds but cannot understand speech.

    3. If brain damage involves both Broca's area and Wernicke's area, the affected individual can neither generate nor understand speech sounds. Such a condition is referred to as *global aphasia.*

D. The conceptualization system in the brain appears to be separate from the spoken language system, in that people with global aphasia have been taught to communicate using sign language.

IV. Words are made up of *phonemes*, the smallest distinguishable utterances of speech.

A. Different languages are made up of different phonemes and different numbers of phonemes. English contains 43 phonemes, while Hawaiian has only 15.

B. Neonatal infants can produce any phoneme from any language in the course of their random babbling.

    1. Over the first few months or so of life, babies hear only phonemes from the language spoken by their caregivers, and babies are rewarded for uttering noises that sound like the language of the caregiver.

2. During this time period, dedicated connections begin to form between auditory receptors in the inner ear and specific sites in the auditory cortex, creating a phonemic perceptual map. Each phoneme in the baby's native language is represented at a specific site in the auditory cortex.

V. Although it can be modified relatively easily for the next decade, the phonemic perceptual map is well established by six months and completed by the first year of life.

    A. A child's babbling now includes only phonemes found in his or her language.

    B. A child can easily learn two (or even three) languages simultaneously, because multiple perceptual maps can be formed simultaneously and do not interfere with one another.

    C. Learning a second language after the first language has been mastered is more difficult.

        1. The completed perceptual map of the first language makes formation of the second more problematic.

        2. After the age of 12, an individual is unlikely to acquire a second language and speak it like a native.

        3. The degree of difficulty depends upon the overlap of phonemes from the two languages.

    D. After a phonemic perceptual map is formed, we become functionally deaf to sounds not found in our native language.

VI. After the age of 1, children whose caregivers speak to them a lot construct words from phonemes faster than the children of more taciturn caregivers.

VII. Advanced age contributes to some declines in speech comprehension and intelligibility.

    A. Presbycusis results in the high-frequency components of speech sounds being missed by an older listener.

    B. We also develop a general decrease in auditory sensitivity due to the thickening of the eardrum and atrophy in the stria vascularis.

C. Age-related degenerative changes in the auditory nerve result in slower conduction speed, causing problems in the comprehension of rapid speech.

D. The overall decline in hearing sensitivity with age creates problems with speech intelligibility and speech comprehension that are especially troublesome when listening to a soft-spoken person in a noisy environment.

Suggested Reading:

Sekuler and Blake, *Perception* (4th ed.), pp. 484–495.

Questions to Consider:

1. A 16-year-old girl came to the United States 80 years ago, speaking only Polish and a little German. She quickly learned English, became a U.S. citizen, and ran several small businesses. When she died at the age of 93, she still had a heavy Polish accent. Why was she unable to lose her foreign accent after almost 80 years of speaking English?

2. Are you aware of any data suggesting that any animal below the level of a human can acquire and use language (not simply as auditory signals but as symbolic stimuli)?

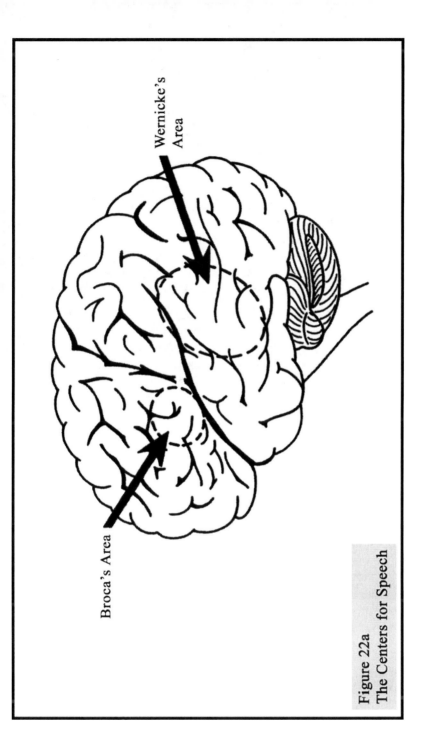

Figure 22a
The Centers for Speech

Lecture Twenty-Two—Transcript
Perception of Language

Hi! Welcome to Lecture Twenty-Two. In Lecture Twenty-One we talked about the structure and function of the brain with special attention being paid to the cerebral cortex. In this lecture, Lecture Twenty-Two, we're going to take some of what we learned about the organization of the brain and apply it to a specific perceptual ability—language perception.

First, here's a little history. Back in the 1950s, physiological psychologists had the belief that the brain was divided up into specific little centers. This belief came about because when they electrically stimulated a region of the brain in the forebrain, called the hypothalamus, they could make animals begin eating even if they weren't hungry. They had what they called stimulation bound eating.

This finding was so important and interesting that it drove research in laboratories around the country. Everybody started sticking electrodes in the hypothalamus and seeing what behaviors they could elicit. Researchers found what they thought was the brain center for eating, and the brain center for drinking, and the brain center for sex, and the brain center for aggression, and the brain center for pup retrieval in female rats. So the belief was that the brain was divided up into specific little centers. It turns out that this was due to a methodological error and a naïve understanding of how the brain worked.

You see, psychologists, when they design an experiment, like to have everything under their control. So if you want to look for the eating center, you put an animal in a cage with nothing but a bowl of food. You stimulate its brain, and if it runs over and eats, you infer that you've found the eating center. Well, it turns out psychologists all over the country had discovered the same center in the brain, even the ones that were studying drinking or sex or aggression or pup retrieval or what have you. How could the same brain center control all of these motivated behaviors? The answer was that what they were doing was short circuiting a general motivational system.

You see, the brain is not divided into specific little centers; it is divided into systems, including a motivational system, which they were short circuiting by sticking a wire in it and passing a current through it. In order for the rat to know whether it was hungry or thirsty or sexy or feeling maternal, it would need information from very many other parts of the brain.

The way that the psychologists discovered this was after some of them had compared notes and found that they'd all found the same part of the brain except having different functions, they put an animal in a cage with food and water and a piece of wood and a member of the same sex and a member of the opposite sex and some baby rats, and they stimulated this particular part of the brain. They couldn't predict what the animal was going to do; sometimes the animal would eat, sometimes it would drink, sometimes it would gnaw the block of wood, and sometimes it would shred the paper. If it was a female rat, sometimes she would take care of the baby rats. If it was a male rat either he'd go fight with another male rat, or he'd run out and buy flowers for the female rat. They couldn't tell what they were going to have; they had an explosion of motives.

That's when they began to realize that the brain isn't divided into specific little centers—that there is a general motivational system that you're short circuiting when you just pass a current through it, and that other parts of the brain are necessarily involved in deciding exactly what the motive is, and how to satisfy it.

Well, it's the same in humans. Generally speaking, the brain is not divided into specific centers. That statement holds true 100% for rats and lower animals. It turns out that there are a couple of exceptions in the human brain. It turns out that there are two perceptual abilities that humans have that lower animals don't have, that are so important to humans that they do have dedicated regions of the cortex devoted to them. In other words, there are two centers in the human brain that humans have and no other animal has.

These two perceptual abilities that have dedicated centers in the human brain are, one, language perception, and two, human face perception. We are the only creatures that are skilled in these two perceptual abilities—the perception and understanding of language and the ability to identify human faces. We are the only animal that can do that, even animals with 20 times the visual acuity of people can't identify human faces the way we can.

To be more accurate, there are actually two speech areas in the human brain, two speech centers, if you will, one for the production of speech, which is a motor function, and one for the reception or understanding of speech, which is more of a perceptual function.

Now, based on what you know from the previous lecture, you can probably guess which cerebral hemisphere has these two speech centers, and if you guess the left hemisphere, you're absolutely correct. You may also be able to guess in what part of the brain the speech center for the production of speech is found, and in what part of the brain the center for the understanding of or reception of speech is to be found. If you were to guess that the center in the left hemisphere for the production of speech is found in the frontal lobe, you would be absolutely correct, because speech production, of course, is a motor function, and the frontal lobe is the motor center in the brain.

The production of sound depends upon the integrity of a region—in the left hemisphere for the vast majority of us—in the frontal lobe known as Broca's Area, after the physician Paul Broca who discovered this connection in 1861. Broca did an autopsy on a deceased individual that he'd been treating for gangrene or something, and the other interesting characteristic about this patient is that he hadn't uttered a word in his entire adult life. In the course of examining the brain, Broca found that this guy had a big tumor at the base of the third frontal convolution in the left cerebral hemisphere, which has now come to be called Broca's Area.

The speech center for understanding speech, comprehension of speech, or reception of speech—those terms are pretty much interchangeable—is found along the left sylvian fissure, which was first pointed out by Wada as being longer in the left hemisphere of most brains. So the receptive speech area is found on the superior temporal surface of the superior temporal lobe in the region that has come to be called Wernicke's Area, for the same reason Broca's Area is called Broca's Area; this is the gentleman who discovered it and identified its function.

Damage to either Broca's Area or Wernicke's Area results in a condition called aphasia. Aphasia is the term used to apply to some "disorder of the associative aspects of language." Now, there are two categories of aphasia, depending upon whether you have damage in Broca's Area or Wernicke's Area. Damage to Broca's Area produces what we call expressive aphasia. If there is total destruction of that center, you're mute, you can't talk at all. With partial destruction of

©2006 The Teaching Company.

Broca's Area you may be able to utter some sounds that in some way, shape or form resemble language, but you're greatly impaired in language ability if you have damage to Broca's Area.

If the damage occurs in Wernicke's Area, along the superior surface of the temporal lobe in the area of the sylvian fissure, you have problems understanding speech. The fact of the matter is, people with damage in Wernicke's Area can still utter words, but the words are what have been referred to as word salad; they don't express anything, they're just essentially sounds. So we have these two categories of aphasia—Broca's Area, which is also called expressive aphasia, and Wernicke's Area, which is called receptive aphasia.

There is another category of aphasia that is diagnosed when the brain damage is extensive enough that it includes both Broca's Area and Wernicke's Area. In this case the term that is used is global aphasia. Study of global aphasia patients has suggested that the conceptual system in the brain is separate from the language system. In other words, you may have aphasia, but that doesn't mean you can't think or express yourself symbolically. The thing is you just can't do it in language. You might be able to do it in writing, or you might be able to do it as was demonstrated in 1975 in a study involving seven global aphasia patients, one of whom was eighty-four years old. Researchers taught these folks sign language, and they were able to communicate. They could understand signing, and they could in turn communicate by signing. So this is why we say that the conceptual system is different from the language system in the brain.

One more point before we stop talking about aphasia. I want to clarify for you that, for instance, if a boxer is punched in the throat and has swollen vocal chords, and can't talk, that's not expressive aphasia. Aphasia refers to an inability to talk due to central factors in the brain. Similarly, if someone is deaf and can't understand language, that is not aphasia. Aphasia is not deafness. You can still hear when you have aphasia. It's just that words no longer have symbolic value. They're just noise. So these are the two categories of aphasia, Broca's and Wernicke's. When sounds acquire symbolic meaning, we call them *words*. Damage to Wernicke's Area takes away that symbolic meaning, and they simply become sounds again.

Now, let's talk about speech and speech perception. Since the focus of our twenty-four lectures together is more on perception rather than motor functions, we will have no more to say about Broca's Area or expressive speech. Let's talk about the reception of speech.

The basic unit of speech is not the word but the phoneme. We're going to do a little vocabulary here. A phoneme is the "smallest utterance that is distinguishable from other utterances." It's not the same as a letter." Phonemes are not the same as letters. Let me give you an example. The /p/ sound in pin is a phoneme. The /ph/ sound in fin is a phoneme. The /b/ sound in ban is a phoneme, and the /m/ sound in man is a phoneme, so they're not the same as letters at all.

Different languages possess different numbers of phonemes—the basic distinguishable utterances of a language—phonemes. Now, the number of phonemes in English has changed over the past few decades. As new words come into the language and into the usage in the language, sometimes the number of phonemes has to be increased. At the present time the number of phonemes in English is 43. As I said, the last time I paid attention it was 28, now it's 43.

The number of phonemes in other languages differs significantly. For example, in the Hawaiian language, the number of phonemes is fifteen. Now, you can see that the number of phonemes in a language can significantly influence the character of that language. Let me give you some examples from Hawaiian, with fifteen phonemes as opposed to forty-three. "Cow-cow" means food in Hawaiian. *Muumuu* /moomoo/ is a long shapeless dress. *Nene* /nā-nā/ is the Hawaiian state bird, sometimes called the *Hawaiian goose—nene*. The most famous of the Hawaiian kings is King Kamehameha. The most famous of the Hawaiian queens is Queen Lili'uokalani. The word for chief is Ali'i. One of Kamehameha son's, who was himself king for a little while, was Liholiho. So what you see in a language with very few phonemes is that the phonemes are used far more frequently than in a language with many phonemes. So you hear that repetition—nā-nā, moo-moo, cow-cow in Hawaiian. That sounds foreign to the English ear as we have so many phonemes that we don't need to repeat them many times in the same word.

Neonatal infants—young babies, a week old or two weeks old, less than a month old—in the course of their random babbling, neonatal infants are capable of uttering any phoneme that has ever been a part of any language on the surface of the planet, new languages or old languages. Babies can replicate the phonemes for that language in their random babbling.

By the first month of life, two processes are going on that constrain the range of phonemes that an infant is capable of using. The first constraint comes about from the phonemes that are spoken by the baby's caregivers. What the baby hears is nothing but the phonemes in the language of the caregivers. The other constraint is that when a baby, in the course of its random babbling, makes a sound that sounds like speech to its parents or primary caregivers, they make a fuss over the baby. The baby is rewarded by this, and even though the baby doesn't know what he or she may have said or almost said, that sound increases in probability of occurrence.

So, for instance, here is a baby making random baby sounds—ge-ge, goo-goo, ga-ga, ma-ma," and the mother runs over. "Oh, you said Mama! That's wonderful! Or in the case of the father where the baby does the random babbling and maybe says, "da-da," again a big fuss is made over the baby. So by the end of the first month, what's happening—through the baby hearing phonemes from the primary caregivers, and repeating some of these phonemes, the ones that have been rewarded—is dedicated connections, dedicated neural connections, begin to be established between the hair cells in the baby's cochlea, and neurons in Wernicke's Area. Dedicated connections begin to be set up.

What is happening is that the beginning of a process called the formation of a phonemic perceptual map is beginning to be established—a phonemic map, a perceptual map in the baby's brain—so that on future occasions when the same phoneme is heard by the baby, the same auditory hair cell receptors are going to send information to the same cluster of neurons in Wernicke's Area. Eventually, each phoneme in the baby's native language is going to be represented at a different spatial location in this perceptual phonemic map. This map is well on its way toward being established by the time the baby is six months old. Now, the baby doesn't know words; this is a passive process that takes place through what the baby is hearing.

How do we know this? How do we know that the phonemic perceptual map is discriminately different in children hearing different native languages by six months of age? We know from EEG studies—from electroencephalographic studies—that have been done, for example, on the brains of children hearing English from their primary caregivers, as opposed to children hearing Swedish from their primary caregivers. At six months of age what the baby is hearing and where it goes in the baby's Wernicke's Area is different depending on if it's hearing Swedish or English.

So the primary of the phonemic perceptual map has been significantly established by six months. Evidence suggests that it is completed by the end of the first year of life, that all of the relevant phonemes are now spread out on this phenomic perceptual map in the baby's brain by the time it's one year old. The fact of the matter is, though, that the brain of a human infant possesses something that we've referred to as plasticity. Remember, we said if you were destined to be left hemisphere dominant, but you had brain damage from birth trauma, you might switch over and be right hemisphere dominant? That's an example of plasticity. Well, that plasticity is also operative in the brain of a newborn baby forming its phenomic perceptual map, so the plasticity remains for the first year of life, meaning that you can learn new phonemes. It's just going to be a little harder.

It turns out that by the end of the first year of life, the character of an infant's random babbling is quite different, in fact, it's no longer random anymore. The child's babbling at one year of life has now acquired the sounds of its native language. Babies still don't know words, and they still don't know that they can communicate using words, but they know that when they say things like "ma-ma, da-da" and "by-by," somebody makes a fuss over them; whereas if they say sounds that have no relationship to the primary native language of the caregivers, nobody makes as big a fuss.

Babies are capable of learning and establishing phonemic perceptual maps for two or even three languages simultaneously. As infants, they can form three—usually it's two—but they can form three perceptual maps and they don't interfere with each other. It turns out that there are enough neurons in Wernicke's Area that these perceptual maps do not intrude and interfere with each other. The implication of this is that it is far easier for a child to learn two languages simultaneously, than it is to learn one, and then later learn the other, because when you've established a phonemic perceptual map for the phonemes in one language, this constrains somewhat the formation of a second perceptual map for another language. It's still doable; it's just more difficult. It's easier to learn them for an infant, for a child, simultaneously rather than successively.

Acquiring a new language after age twelve—and you may remember we said that this plasticity in the brain has dwindled significantly by the time the myelin sheath is in place. The insulation of the neurons from each other around age 12 or 12-ish—after age twelve, a child is unlikely—is not impossible, but it's unlikely—to ever acquire a second language and speak it like a native. You can speak it very well, and you can speak it so that non-natives will think you're doing it perfectly, but it's very difficult for somebody to acquire a language after age twelve, and to fool a native speaker to think that you are, in fact, a native speaker of that language.

Now, of course, there are many factors that contribute to this ability. If the phonemic map of the first language—if the phonemes in that phonemic map—overlap with the phonemes in the second language, it's going to be easier. For example, if you are a Spanish speaker, and then later in life you choose to learn Italian, that's going to be a relatively easy crossover because many of the phonemes are the same in Spanish and Italian. However, if you are a Spanish speaker, and later in life you choose to learn Russian, that's going to be a bit more of a challenge because of the difference in the phonemes between those two languages—between Spanish and Russian.

The fact of the matter is that if you do not hear a phoneme from another language as a child, you will be functionally deaf to that phoneme later in life, and there are examples of this. Let me just share a couple with you. In the English language, for example, the /r/ sound in *rip* is sharp and clear and distinct from the /l/ sound in *lip*. So in English, the /r/ sound and the /l/ sound are going to have spatially separate locations on our phonemic perceptual map.

In Japan, however, the "r" sound and the "l" sound are merged, so it's like "lru" instead of "ru" or "lu." As a consequence, the location of the "r" sound and the "l" sounds in the phonemic perceptual map of a Japanese child, there's going to be a great deal of overlap, and the neurons are going to be all tangled up. A Japanese child and adult will have difficulty actually hearing the distinction between the "r" and the "l" sound. They will be functionally deaf to that phonemic difference. The two phonemes are far apart in the English perceptual map; overlapping in the Japanese perceptual map.

Let me tell you what some of the practical consequences of this are, in fact, from personal experience. My wife and I were in Kyoto, Japan, and we were so proud of ourselves that we had learned to ride the subway, so we were feeling more like trekkers rather than tourists. My wife wanted to go to a large Japanese department store, and she went to the cosmetics section to see what they had that she needed or that weren't available where she was She needed some blush, so she said to the young woman working behind the counter, "I'd like to see some blush," and the young woman said, "Brush?" and my wife said, "No, blush," and the young girl said, "Brush?" And my wife said, "Blush," and she said "Brush." Finally my wife pointed, "Blush," and she brings it. I don't remember if my wife purchased it or not, but I remember the exchange. It was clear that this young woman who was so anxious to be helpful was functionally deaf to the distinction between the "ru" sound, the brush and blush. Now, as we were walking away, I still heard the salesclerk behind the counter working on it herself. "Brush, brush," and she never did understand it.

Now, I happened to encounter a business professor whom I knew, walking around Kyoto. He told me about a trip he took to a Japanese industry with 30 business students, because in many areas of business, we can now learn from the Japanese. So there was an industrial site, and they had a host.

The host said, "First, we will hear an introductory lecture from Professor Tanaka, and in the afternoon we will take you to see the rubber trees." My friend thought, "Why do we want to go see the rubber trees?" Well, of course, what the man said was, "In the afternoon we will go see the laboratories," but it sounded like rubber trees, because of that merging of the "ru" and the "lu" sound.

I'm not picking on or teasing or making fun of the Japanese. We are functionally deaf to their phonemes too. I discovered this also on the same trip to Kyoto. There was one temple—Kyoto, by the way is the city of temples. I highly recommend you visit the city of temples, and see all the beautiful temples. There was one temple that was not near a subway station, so we took the subway as far as we could, and then went and hailed a taxi. I said to the driver, "Ryoanji Temple, please?" He said, "What? And I said, "Ryoanji Temple," then he leaned in, and said, "Where do you want to go?" I said, "Ryoanji Temple," and I realized I wasn't making myself understood, so I leaned forward, and I showed him the tourist map that I had, and it said "Ryoanji Temple." He said, "Oh, Ryoanji Temple." "I thought that's what I said," but then I realized it couldn't have been what I said that I was functionally deaf to the phonemes this gentleman used to say that name. So it works two ways, my friends. They are functionally deaf to some of our phonemes, and we are functionally deaf to some of their phonemes.

This has also been demonstrated in the laboratory. Again, the Japanese speakers and English speakers were wired up with EEG electrodes to measure the electrical potentials in different parts of their brains. It turns out that the EEG record is indistinguishable from a Japanese speaker and an American English speaker if we say "Pan and ban," okay, because those two phonemes exist in both languages and they are at different sites on the phonemic perceptual map. But if you say "rip" and "lip," the EEG records are quite different from the English speaker to the Japanese speaker.

After we have created our phonemic perceptual maps, and we have our phonemes down, it's time for the infant to go to work and start forming words from phonemes. In this regard, some very interesting research by a psychiatrist from the University of Chicago named Janellen Huttenlocher suggests that mothers who talk more to their children actually facilitate those children understanding more words at an earlier age.

She compared two groups of mothers, mothers who were loquacious and talked a lot, and mothers who were more reserved and didn't talk a lot. The babies of the more talkative mothers by age 20 months knew 131 more words than the babies of the mothers who didn't talk to them much. Now, this is not a sexist finding. It could have worked out just as well, I assume, with fathers doing the talking, except she had a group of people for whom the mother was the primary caregiver.

It also turns out that it doesn't matter whether these words are monosyllabic or polysyllabic words. The important thing is that they hear a lot of words. So you can either read to your child from a Dr. Seuss book or from a Tom Clancy book. It doesn't appear to matter—as long as they hear words—how long the words are. The child doesn't understand these words, but what's happening is the neural circuitry is being laid down for the absorption and the storage of more words. It turns out that children are like a sponge. They learn words at an incredible rate. Well, in four months the children whose mothers talked to them a lot went from 131 more words than children who weren't talked to much to 295 words, so they were just sucking up these words.

I have to share a personal experience as a proud grandfather. Some years ago I went to visit my daughter, and my youngest granddaughter was in the kitchen. They had two cats, Sukey and Amy. Sukey was the bigger, older cat, Amy was the littler cat, and the granddaughter was watching the cats. Sukey had cleaned her bowl, and Amy was eating out of her bowl. Sukey went over, and elbowed Amy out of the way and started eating Amy's food. This 3-year-old kid looked at the cat, and said, "Sukey, you're despicable." I was just floored by that, so later on I asked my daughter, "Where did she hear that word *despicable*? When's the last time that you remember using that word?" She thought and she thought, and the only thing she could think of was a couple of days earlier she had read a newspaper article about the recent shenanigans of some local politician, and she used the word *despicable* to describe his actions. And this little child, in one exposure to that word, claimed it as her own. I saw that personally.

Her older sister apparently pulled a similar feat. I didn't see this one, but my daughter told me about it. When this other granddaughter was less than three years old, my daughter was saying something about her stomach didn't feel so good, and this little baby said, "Maybe it's acid reflux." I mean, they're just amazing the rate they learn words.

Okay, on to language and language perception. What happens to language and language perception as we age? Well, it's not a happy story; I mean it could be worse. There are declines in both speech intelligibility and speech comprehension. In other words, we have trouble understanding words, and if we do hear a string of words, sometimes we have a little trouble comprehending exactly what the meaning of that message was.

Where do these deficits in comprehension and intelligibility come from? Some come from presbycusis, the progressive loss of hearing for high frequencies as a function of age, because some components of sounds are in the high frequency range. They also come about because of the general decrease in auditory sensitivity due to that thickening of the eardrum and the atrophy in the stria vascularis kind of tuning down the volume on our sensitivity.

There are also degenerative changes that take place in the eighth nerve—or at least the auditory part of the eighth nerve—making sounds travel more slowly and making it more difficult for us to follow rapid speech. As we age we have the most trouble following soft-spoken people who speak rapidly. My suggestion would be in those situations to say politely but assertively, "Please slow down, speak up, and face me when you speak," because looking at somebody's lips is helpful in interpreting their speech even if your hearing is normal.

In our next lecture we will talk about some other interesting aspects of human perception, visual perception abilities. Thank you.

Lecture Twenty-Three
The Visual Agnosias

Scope:

Our capacities to identify an object by its form, apprehend its color(s), determine its location in space, and estimate its rate of motion all seem to occur automatically as the result of a single act of perception. Actually, this is not the case. Each of these component parts—form, identity, color, location in space, and motion—is analyzed in a different visual association area and integrated with memories of our past experiences with the object in question to create an overall perception.

The contribution of different regions of the visual association cortex to overall visual perception is suggested from instances in the human clinical literature when focal brain damage alters or abolishes one component of a perception, such as color or identity, but leaves the remaining components intact. This literature deals with the *visual agnosias*. *Agnosia* means "failure to know." It does not refer to blindness but to an inability to apprehend a particular aspect of a visual perceptual experience. One category of visual agnosia, *prosopagnosia*, refers to a deficit in the ability to recognize human faces. People with this condition are not only unable to recognize the faces of family and friends but cannot even recognize their own faces in a mirror.

Because visual agnosias result from focal rather than diffuse brain damage, they are not an accompaniment of the diffuse brain cell loss associated with aging.

Outline

I. Our perception of events in the visual field is so automatic and natural that we fail to appreciate the complexity of what we are doing.

   A. A visual perception typically includes an awareness of the color, shape, identity, location in space, and direction and velocity of motion of some object or objects.

   B. Each of the components of the overall perception is analyzed in a different region of the brain; these regions are known as *visual association areas*, all part of the *visual association cortex*.

C. Damage to a particular visual association area can eliminate a single element of a visual perception, leaving the other elements of the perception intact.

II. Focal (as opposed to diffuse) damage to a visual association area does not result in blindness but in a condition known as *visual agnosia*.

III. *Agnosia* means "a failure to know" something. There are six general categories of visual agnosia, each associated with damage to a different visual association area.

IV. Color agnosia (*achromatopsia*) has been seen in patients following damage to the medial (middle portion of the) occipital lobe.

A. Patients with such damage experience no loss of visual acuity, but they see only in black and white. This is not traditional colorblindness, in that, when studied scientifically, the cones are still intact and functioning normally.

B. Achromatopsia results in problems with daily activities, such as coordinating one's wardrobe or obeying traffic lights.

V. There are two categories of visual shape agnosia, both of which involve the inferior (bottom half of the) temporal cortex.

A. In *apperceptive visual agnosia*, the patient can point to an object's location, identify its color, and determine whether or not the object is moving but cannot determine the object's shape. The patient can determine the object's shape if permitted to hold or touch the object. Likewise, the patient can identify people through smell or through voice recognition. Such individuals are functionally blind and cannot perform such everyday activities as driving.

B. In *associative visual agnosia*, the patient can perceive the object's shape, as evidenced by being able to draw the object, but cannot identify the object or tell what it is used for.

   1. In associative visual agnosia, there seems to be a disconnect between the inferior temporal cortex and the language system used for naming objects.

    2. If the object cannot be named, its use is not easily retrieved from memory.

VI. *Spatial location agnosia* has been seen in patients with damage in the posterior parietal lobe. Affected individuals can be shown a visual display with an object in it. The patient can name the object and describe its function but cannot say where it is located in the visual field.

VII. In the condition called *motion agnosia*, the affected individual cannot perceive motion. The experience is somewhat akin to time-lapse photography, in which objects are not seen to be moving but abruptly disappear from one location and instantly reappear at another location. This condition is associated with brain damage at the boundary of the lateral occipital cortex and the posterior temporal cortex.

    A. One patient with such damage had great difficulty crossing streets because cars seemed far away, but as she started across the street, they were suddenly upon her. She learned to use sounds cues to cross safely.

    B. Pouring coffee or tea into a cup was also problematic for this patient because initially, there was little liquid in the cup, and in what seemed like the next instant, the cup was overflowing. Again, she grew to depend on sound cues for help.

    C. Following the speech of others was made more difficult for the patient by the fact that their mouth movements were not in sync with their words. She found it best not to look at peoples' lips as she spoke to them.

    D. Being in a room with a group of people was quite disturbing, in that the people were perceived as disappearing from one spot and reappearing elsewhere whenever they moved. This patient tried to avoid such situations.

VIII. *Prosopagnosia* is a form of visual agnosia characterized by an inability to recognize human faces.

    A. Our ability to recognize human faces is so important to us that a portion of our brain is dedicated to it. The critical brain region appears to be the ventral portion of the right temporal lobe.

B. Patients may see eyes, ears, a nose, and a mouth but may not be able to recognize an individual face.

C. Affected individuals may be unable to recognize their own faces in a mirror.

IX. Normal age-related diffuse brain cell death does not produce the visual agnosias; instead, they are the product of focal damage to a specific cortical location.

Suggested Reading:

Carlson, *Physiology of Behavior* (8th ed.), pp. 190–201.

Sekuler and Blake, *Perception* (4th ed.), pp. 233–243.

Questions to Consider:

1. How can laboratory experiments using animal subjects help us to understand the visual agnosias?

2. What (if anything) can we infer about the way the brain creates our perceptions from clinical cases of visual agnosia?

Lecture Twenty-Three—Transcript
The Visual Agnosias

Hello, and welcome to Lecture Twenty-Three. In Lecture Twenty-Two we talked about language perception, which is, of course, a critically important perceptual ability for humans.

In Lecture Twenty-Three we're going to talk about some aspects of visual perception, which also turn out to be very critical for the normal functioning of the human being. Sometimes we learn about the way that the brain constructs a perception, in this case a visual perception, by being permitted to study through their kindness and altruism people who have experienced brain damage and then allow us to try and learn from their misfortune. That's going to be the case for most of the examples of visual perceptual dysfunction that I'm going to talk about in this lecture.

To give us a hypothetical point of departure, I'm about to create a visual perceptual for myself. I'm going to look out the window and—lucky me—I just saw passing across the parking lot a red convertible. I looked a little closer and I saw that it was a Ford Mustang, and because I have a special affection for Ford Mustang convertibles, I noticed that it was a 1967. So I saw a red 1967 Ford Mustang convertible crossing the parking lot at—I would estimate— a speed of around 10 miles per hour. The perception made me smile, indicating that it also had an emotional component, and I happen to know why it made me smile—because it reminded me of a trip I took from Pittsburgh to Philadelphia in a red Ford Mustang convertible in 1968. The car was a 1967. We took the trip in 1968. I was attending the Eastern Psychological Association Meeting in Philadelphia. I went with my best friend, and we had a wonderful time on the trip there, at the convention, and on the way back.

The perception that I just had included color and size. I knew about the size because of monocular and binocular depth cues. I knew it was a real car 70 yards away rather than a toy car one foot behind the window. So the perception that I just had included color and size and movement and shape and form, which allowed me to identify what this structure was and it had that emotional component. I also could tell in what part of my visual field this car was located—upper left, lower right, whatever. So all of those individual sub-components formed what the Gestaltists would have called a *gestalt*—a unified whole perception.

In fact, it would be unthinkable, unimaginable, to think of that same perception with one or more of its components taken away. It just doesn't seem like that could happen, but yes, in fact, it could happen—unthinkable, but not impossible—because it turns out that each and every component of that complex visual perception that I just had depends upon the functioning of a specific part of what we call visual association cortex.

Different aspects of that visual perception are analyzed by neural circuits in different parts of associative cortex which then compare notes and interact with each other through those lateral connections that we mentioned in an earlier lecture, and create that entire unified gestalt, the unified perception. Remember, the cortical regions also have connections with the emotional circuits in the limbic system of the brain, giving it the ability to make me smile when I saw it because of remembering that trip I took from Pittsburgh to Philadelphia.

Now, it is possible to have that same perception, but in black and white. It is possible to have that same perception, but not be able to discriminate the shape of the object I'm looking at. So I would see a red blob moving across the parking lot. It's possible to see that same perception, but not be able to perceive movement. It's possible to have that same perception, but not be aware of where in my visual field the target object that I was looking at was located. Each of those instances of faulty perception has, in fact, occurred as a result of focal damage to a different part of some individual's visual association cortex.

Now, when we say "focal damage," we're talking about concentrated damage in a specific region of the brain as opposed to diffuse damage, which is spread over a larger area of the brain. What I have just described to you are examples of what are called the visual agnosias. Now, the word agnosia means "a failure to know." I'm sure you've encountered the word. Well, for instance, an agnostic is "somebody who doesn't know whether God exists or not." So the visual agnosias refer to our failure to know something about a perceptual scene that we're looking at.

The agnosias do not have traditional blindness, which usually involves either the receptors or the optic nerve. The visual agnosias represent failures of a specific aspect of visual perception, but it is certainly not the same thing as blindness.

We're going to talk in this lecture about six different categories of visual agnosia, each associated with focal damage to a different part of visual association cortex. The first of the visual agnosias that I want to share with you is called achromatopsia. Now that's the technical term. What it really means is color agnosia. It is possible for someone to look at that same scene that I looked at, and with perfect visual acuity discriminate that they're looking at a Ford Mustang, and that it's moving across the parking lot, and that it is a convertible, and that's it's going about 10 miles per hour, but their perception would have no color. It would be like watching a black and white movie.

You might think, "Oh, that's just color blindness," but no, it is not traditional color blindness, because traditional color blindness involves the cones—the visual receptors that mediate color vision—and it can be demonstrated in people with achromatopsia that the cones are functioning normally. So, how do we do that? How can we demonstrate that the cones are functioning normally? Well, one way is with an ophthalmoscopic examination. You can look in and you can see that the cones are of normal appearance. Well, does that guarantee that they are functioning normally? No, but there's another way to guarantee that.

We talked about the EEG, the electroencephalogram, where you record the brain waves from the brain, and it can tell you things about the formation of a phonemic perceptual map. Well there is also an electrical waveform that we can record from the cornea of the eye; it's called the ERG, electroretinogram, and it tells us about the functioning of the different components in the eye.

How can we record from the cornea of a human without causing them great discomfort? Well, you use what is called a wick electrode. You have a wick, a cloth wick, soaked in saline, and you take a contact lens with a little hole drilled in it, and you stick this wick electrode in it. Then you insert the contact lens so that this cloth wick soaked in saline is gently touching the cornea—no pain involved—and you take the other end of this electrode, you amplify it, and display it on an electronic instrument that displays waveforms. You make the hole in the contact lens off center so you can shine a beam of light into the eye, and you send a flash of light into the eye.

What you have from your wick electrode is the electroretinogram—a very complex waveform. The electroretinogram is used for diagnostic purposes, say in babies who are too young to tell you what they see or what the problem is, or in people in a state such that they will not or cannot cooperate with somebody examining their eyes. What you see in people with achromatopsia is that the electroretinogram is normal. The electroretinogram tells you about the state of functioning of the rods and the cones and the ganglion cells and the pigment epithelium. All of this is normal in these people, but they cannot perceive color, and it's due to damage to a particular part of the visual association area. In this case, it turns out to be in the posterior parietal lobe. We'll see that a number of instances of visual agnosias involve different parts of the posterior parietal lobe—not all of them, but some of them.

Now, what does life hold for people with color agnosia? Well, the first thing to say is, of course, their quality of life is diminished somewhat. They can no longer appreciate the full beauty of a sunset. They can no longer appreciate the beauty of a peacock opening its tail feathers. They can no longer appreciate the beauty of a floral garden in the spring or what have you, but they can still manage.

There are some more practical deficits that people with achromatopsia experience. For instance, they have to learn a new way to obey traffic signals. Instead of obeying the signals by the color—red, green, and amber—they now have to remember the location of the lights on a traffic signal. The other thing is they are going to need help coordinating the color of their wardrobes. Other than that, their visual acuity, as I said, is still as good as it ever was.

Let's move on to another category of visual agnosia, of a failure to know something about the visual stimulus. There are actually two categories of what is called visual shape agnosia. In both cases the inferior temporal cortex, which is another visual association area, the inferior temporal cortex is involved. Remember, the temporal lobe is like a hotdog bun, and the top half is the superior temporal, which is auditory and especially speech perception, and the bottom half, the inferior temporal, is a visual association area. Well, visual shape agnosia seems to involve the inferior temporal cortex.

The first category of visual shape agnosia is called apperceptive agnosia. In this case the individual is unable to discriminate shape or form, so somebody with apperceptive visual agnosia would look out that window, and they would see a red blob moving across the parking lot. They could perceive movement, they could perceive color, they could perceive where in the visual field this thing was located, but they couldn't tell you what its shape or form was, which means they couldn't tell you what its identity was or what it was used for.

Now, I know this seems too bizarre to be true, but there are documented instances, and some of these people have permitted themselves to be studied in laboratories. The thing is, if you sit such a person at a table, and they have apperceptive visual agnosia, and you say, "There are three objects in front of you. Do you see their location?" "Yes." "Can you point to them?" "Yes. There, there, and there." "Can you see the color?" "Yes, I can tell the color." "Do you know what these things are?" "No."

All they see is blurs. So they can't identify people, and they can't identify things. Now, if you let them reach out and touch the objects, then they say, "Oh, yes, this is a lampshade, and this is a telephone, and this is a water pitcher." So they still know what things are, but they have to use touch. The way they identify people is either by the sound of the voice, or if it's somebody they're very familiar with, possibly by the smell. But these individuals are functionally blind.

So apperceptive visual agnosia means these people cannot drive; all they're seeing is shapes. In fact, the way to conceptualize apperceptive visual agnosia is to imagine looking at the world through milk glass, which is what severe cataracts are like, actually. You can see shades, you can see movement, but you cannot discriminate form or identity of the things that you're looking at. The thing is, actually, apperceptive visual agnosia is not as debilitating as severe cataracts, because these people do have normal color discrimination. They just can't tell what they're looking at. So, it's not traditional blindness. You can guarantee this again by doing an examination of the retina using ophthalmoscopic techniques, and also using the electroretinogram. You can see that the retina is functioning, and that this functional blindness is, in fact, due to a disorder of one of the visual association areas.

The second category of visual form agnosia is called associative visual agnosia. This is pretty unusual too. In associative visual agnosia the individual can, in fact, perceive the shape and form of the object, but they can't tell you what it is, and they can't name it.

In this case it still appears to involve the inferior temporal cortex, but there appears to be a disconnect—as if a fiber bundle is either atrophied or cut or something— so that the inferior temporal cortex cannot communicate with the language centers of the brain for naming of objects. The fact of the matter is if you can't name an object you're at a great disadvantage in retrieving that name, which tells you what the object does, what its identity is.

Now, how do we know these people can discriminate the form and the shape? Because in experiments with people showing this category of visual agnosia—let me tell you, rather than make up an example, tell you an actual event that happened. The individual was shown a picture of an anchor, and the individual was asked, "Do you know the name of this thing?" "No." "Do you know what's its function is?" "No." "Can you draw it?"

The individual drew an anchor, so clearly this individual was able to identify the shape by vision, but they were unable to name it or tell its function. Now, if you give the person the name, if you say, "Well, that's called an anchor," then the person says, "Oh, yes, an anchor. That's what you use to hold a boat fast, so it won't drift in the water. That's what you use to keep a boat in one place." So when you give them the name, then they can retrieve the function.

This disconnect between the inferior temporal cortex and the language centers for naming is suggestive of another phenomenon that developmental psychologists have long been interested in—the childhood amnesia phenomenon. If you think back to your earliest memories, you really can't remember a whole lot before you have acquired enough language to code things into words, because words is how we store things for the easiest memory retrieval. So that for the first couple of years of life, you have events that have an impact on you, and some of these events are perhaps coded in primitive emotional circuits, but because you don't have language to name these things, you can't retrieve these events even if they're still affecting your behavior.

An example: suppose at the age of a year and one-half you were bitten by a dog, and you were scared and hurt, but because you were too young to have language to code into words this event that happened, you may not have any conscious memory of it. But for the rest of your life you may have a feeling of unease and fear around dogs, especially barking dogs. So the summary statement about this is that we use words to code memories, and we use the name of the object to retrieve that memory, and these people with this particular category of visual form agnosia can't access the word, and if they can't access the word and name the object, they can't retrieve the memory. It's pretty fascinating.

Another category of visual agnosia is called spatial location agnosia. This particular visual perceptual deficit involves the right posterior parietal area of the brain. Now, what is the consequence of right posterior parietal dysfunction? The individual can say, "Yes, I see a red Mustang convertible crossing the parking lot, and it seems to be going about 10 miles per hour," and if you say to them, "Well, where in your visual field is that?" they can't tell you. They don't know if it's in the upper right-hand quadrant or the lower left or the upper left or the lower right. It's pretty hard to conceive of what this must seem like to somebody.

We've known for some time that the posterior parietal lobe is involved in various aspects of non-verbal visual spatial relations. For example, the best known of the adult intelligence tests is called the WAIS, Wexler Adult Intelligence Scale. It has a series of subtests that test different categories of adult memory. I have on occasion used the WAIS in the diagnosis of people who've come to see me because of head injuries and wondering what the consequences of this head injury are.

In general, if somebody has damage to the posterior parietal region of the brain— especially the right hemisphere—they are going to do very poorly on one of the subtests of the WAIS, called the "block design subtest." Some of you may have seen this. What happens is you show the person a design made out of colored blocks. Then you give them a set of colored blocks, and you say, "Reproduce that design."

Now even people of low average intelligence can take these colored blocks and look at the design and look at the colored blocks and make the design. The designs, of course, become more and more complicated until they are unable to accurately match the pattern of the colored blocks. I have, in fact, tested gifted people with IQ's two standard deviations above the average who have right posterior parietal damage, and they can't even do the simplest of the block design tests. So it's been known for some time that the posterior parietal lobe is importantly concerned with non-verbal visual spatial relations—the ability to apprehend spatial sequences of visual events.

So, here is this poor person with apparently enough destruction to the posterior parietal lobe that they're not even able to tell where in the visual field something is located. You'd have to, I guess, see it to believe it, but it is true.

Another highly unusual visual agnosia is called motion agnosia. In motion agnosia the individual is incapable of detecting movement. Their perception of the world is as if it were taken with a time-lapse camera. They see objects appear and disappear, and they don't see them move from one place to another. This is another example of damage to a visual association area. Perhaps the best way to explain what this is like is to share with you the verbal reports—I will summarize them—of a woman who has this motion agnosia.

After she was treated and released from the hospital, the first thing she noticed that was problematic was when she went to cross the street she would look, and the car that she saw would seem very far away so it seemed perfectly safe. She would start crossing the street, and the next thing she knew the car was virtually on top of her, and she would have to leap out of the way. She was unable to detect movement of the car from one location to a closer location. What she ended up doing was, even if there were no cars in sight, she would only cross the street at a traffic light when the light turned red for the traffic and green for her.

After she became more aware of and used to the limitations of her motion agnosia, she was able to use sound to assess the rate of approach of a vehicle, but she could no longer do it with her visual system because she was incapable of detecting movement. Another area where this woman reported a problem was in the filling of a container with liquid, such as pouring a cup of tea or a cup of coffee. We use the rate of filling of the cup, the level of the liquid, as a cue when to stop pouring. So she would look in the cup and it would be empty, and she would start pouring. The next thing she knew the cup was overflowing because she was unable to see the movement of the level of the liquid rise in the cup.

She had a similar problem, for instance, filling a measuring cup at the kitchen sink. If she tried to use a recipe of something that called for two cups of water, she would take the pitcher over there, and the level would start out empty, and the next thing she knew her measuring cup would be overflowing. Here, again, she learned to use auditory cues—because recall that a closed column of air has a resonance frequency, and if she listened to the change in pitch of the sound made by that water—she could tell when the measuring cup was nearing its appropriate level; that's motion agnosia.

Another difficulty that this woman encountered was in following the conversation of people she looked at directly, because their lips didn't seem to move, except they would change shape periodically. So she's was receiving a steady stream of sounds that didn't seem to correlate at all with the lip movements of the speaker. It became so disconcerting to her that she found that the best way to listen to people talking was not to look at their lips. Now, you can perhaps begin to understand how disruptive this was to her.

I've had this experience; maybe you have too. You're at a movie and the sound track is just a little bit out of sync with the visual, so that the person's lip movements are either a little bit too soon or a little bit too late to correlate appropriately with the sound they're making. That's trivial compared to what this woman was dealing with. Just the other night I was watching a movie in a foreign language where the English was dubbed in, and I just keep focusing on the fact that the lip movements don't correspond to the audio. Well, that's just a small taste of what this woman learned to live with, with her motion agnosia.

The last example of how this impacted on her life had to do with her reaction to being in a room with a good number of other people in it, such as a cocktail party, or something of that nature. In this case, people appeared to appear and disappear as they moved around the room. Somebody that she was looking at would suddenly disappear, and they would reappear over here. This was so disconcerting to her that she found it more comfortable to stay out of situations such as that where people were moving about because of this almost magical appearance and disappearance without any in-between movement. Okay. That's an example, then, of motion agnosia.

The last example of visual agnosia that I want to talk about is called prosopagnosia. This is the disorder of human face recognition that I alluded to in Lecture Twenty-Two as being such an important perceptual ability for people that it has a dedicated part of the brain reserved for it. In other words, there is a face recognition area in the brain, and this face recognition area is in the posterior portion of the right inferior temporal lobe. As I alluded to in the earlier lecture, human face recognition is a remarkable perceptual ability on our parts.

When you think about the hundreds of human faces that you can keep separate and identify individually—friends, acquaintances, celebrities, movie stars, sports figures, and what have you—when you consider the similarities between human faces—we all have two eyes, two ears, a nose, a mouth, some of us have hair, some of us don't—but human faces have so much in common that the ability to do this fine-tune discrimination is remarkable, and as I said, no other animal can do it. Even a hawk that can read the advertisement on a book of matches flying over, "Draw my face and win a scholarship to the art institute," they can't tell human faces the way we can. It's a remarkable ability, and it does have a special part of the brain devoted to it.

What happens when somebody experiences prosopagnosia is that they can still identify the individual features of a face. Yes, those are the eyes and that's the nose and that's the mouth and that's the ears and what have you, but they can't identify individual human faces. They cannot identify their loved ones. They cannot identify their own human face. One gentleman suffering from prosopagnosia as a result of focal brain damage reported that every morning he would arise, and go into the bathroom to shave, and he would be shaving the face of a stranger. He didn't recognize his own face in the mirror.

Another individual talked about being at a restaurant, and being highly annoyed by the rude staring of some stranger from the adjoining room that kept looking at him, and the more he looked and the angrier he became, He finally realized he was looking not into an adjoining room but into a mirror, and he was upset by his mirror image staring back at him, because he didn't recognize it as himself.

The experience of prosopagnosia can be—at a very minor level—experienced by all of us in the following way. Take a series of 8x10 in photographs of celebrities, sports stars, your friends, your family, yourself, and turn them upside down, and then try and identify these different individuals. I've done this. It's very, very difficult. When you turn a human face upside down, it still has its basic features—the two eyes and two ears and a nose and a mouth and so on—but it loses some of its "human face quality" You will be hard pressed to accurately identify people that you've known all your life or celebrities that you've known of all your life if you turn the faces upside down. As a matter of fact, when you compare the ability of people with prosopagnosia to recognize upside-down pictures, they are no worse than we are, and it's not that they suddenly are better, it's that we suddenly are worse, because when you turn the face upside down it just takes away the human face quality aspect of it.

The study of prosopagnosia is still leading to unexpected and surprising results. Let me just share one with you. There was a gentleman who suffered damage to the posterior portion of the inferior temporal cortex in the right cerebral hemisphere. He had been a dairy farmer. Now dairy farmers keep their cows long enough to know them—as opposed to beef farmers who fatten them up and sell them to market. So he knew his cows, and he could recognize individual cows by their faces. After he suffered his brain dysfunction, he could no longer recognize the cows by face either. So there are still things to learn about prosopagnosia.

What do the visual agnosias have to tell us in the way of age-related changes? Is the aging process going to produce these kinds of weird visual perceptual aberrations in us? The answer is, again, in the case of normal aging, no. They are not. Because, once again I will remind you that normal aging is accompanied by diffuse brain damage rather than focal brain damage in some specific part of the brain. So we need not worry about this kind of thing happening to us as a consequence simply of normal aging.

The visual agnosias are, indeed, tragic, but they are also serving the function of providing us with some insight into the way that different areas of association cortex cooperate to form our overall visual perceptions.

In our next lecture, Lecture Twenty-Four, which is also our last lecture, I will attempt to achieve two instructional goals. I'll talk about another important perceptual ability, our perception of other people, and then I will provide an overall course summary, and mention some current trends in research on sensation and perception. Thank you.

Lecture Twenty-Four
Perception of Other People/Course Summary

Scope:

In our final lecture, we will first cover some of the dynamics at work in our perception of other people. We will then summarize the overall course content, with mention of some directions in which the field of sensation and perception seems to be going.

Our perception of other people is an active process in which we begin making assumptions about such variables as motives, personality, and intelligence shortly after meeting someone. We will discuss some common perceptual errors that we all have made in our personality assessment of others. The literature also indicates that our perception of other people and their behavior is strongly influenced by their physical attractiveness and by the cultural conditioning we were exposed to during our formative years.

In the remainder of our final lecture, we will revisit the threefold instructional goals for the course: to provide an overview of sensory physiology, to describe the role of the brain in creating perceptions, and to demonstrate how the aging process can affect both sensations and perceptions. The lecture concludes with a survey of current research projects, such as smell and memory, smell and mate selection in humans, aromatherapy, sensory prosthesis, and brain-imaging techniques used to understand perceptual phenomena.

Outline

I. We have two goals in our final lecture.

    A. The first goal is to describe some of the dynamics at work in our perception of other people.

    B. The second goal is to provide an overall course summary, along with some examples of current research directions in the field.

II. People perception is an active process.

    A. We make inferences about people, their motives, their personalities, their goals, and their intentions.

    B. These inferences can lead to the creation of self-fulfilling prophesies in our dealings with other people.

C. These inferences can come from previous information or knowledge we have about people.

D. These inferences also come from the first impressions we acquire when we meet someone.

III. First impressions are of great importance in our perception of other people.

  A. They can actually distort later perceptions of another person, because we become committed to our first impressions.

  B. First impressions once formed can be very difficult to overcome.

  1. We need to avoid being "wedded" to our own first impressions.

  2. If you find that you are the one about whom someone is going to make a first impression, whether during a first date, an initial job interview, or any such situation, you need to make an effort to make a positive first impression.

IV. Three errors in the perception of other people are so common that they have their own names. These are the *halo effect*, the *logical error*, and the *central tendency error*.

  A. The halo effect refers to our tendency to form an overall positive impression of someone based upon knowledge of a single positive trait.

  B. The logical error is the belief that certain traits go together. For instance, knowing someone is polite might predispose us to believe that he or she is also friendly, honest, and intelligent. Con men use this error to their advantage.

  C. The central tendency error causes us to ignore variability and to see people as more consistent than they really are.

V. Although we would prefer to deny it, evidence indicates that our overall perception of someone is influenced by his or her physical attractiveness.

  A. Children react to one another on the basis of physical attractiveness as early as kindergarten.

  B. Elementary school teachers evaluate the same disruptive behavior differently in physically attractive and physically unattractive children.

1. The unattractive child is likely to perceived as a "problem child."
2. The same behavior in an attractive child is more likely to be perceived as an aberration that is uncharacteristic of the child.

C. Physically attractive MBAs have higher salaries than their less attractive counterparts.

VI. Cultural factors also influence our perception of other people. Societies indoctrinate their members from an early age with beliefs, attitudes, preferences, and behaviors. This indoctrination influences the perception of people from other cultures.

A. People who make direct eye contact are perceived as honest, open, direct, and forthright in the United States. Such people are perceived as intrusive, aggressive, and rude in Japan.

B. Different cultures require different amounts of "personal space," that is, the usual and comfortable distance between strangers or casual acquaintances in a conversation.
1. In the United States, such personal space is about three feet.
2. In Sweden, the appropriate personal space distance is four feet.
3. In Arab countries, the usual personal space is less than an arm's length.
4. This difference affects the perception of people with other culturally determined personal space needs.

C. In "high-context" cultures, such as those of the Mediterranean and Middle Eastern regions, body language and nonverbal cues are critical for the accurate interpretation of verbal messages. In "low-context" cultures, such as those of the United States and Britain, the interpretation of spoken words is less dependent on nonverbal cues. Serious misperceptions of meaning can occur as a result of this cultural variable.

VII. The remainder of this lecture will be used to restate the instructional goals for the course and to note some current trends in sensation and perception research.

VIII. The initial instructional goals of the course were threefold.

  A. The first goal was to provide an overview of sensory physiology sufficient to show how our sensory receptors serve as the interface between the physical world and the brain.

   1. Sensory receptors are specialized cells that change electromagnetic, mechanical, chemical, or thermal energy into a form to which the brain is responsive.

   2. Thus, our receptors define our sensory world.

  B. The second goal of the course was to describe how perceptions are created in the brain by integrating basic sense data with our past experiences. Past experiences stored in the brain give meaning to our present sensory experiences.

  C. The third goal was to point to examples of how the aging process can alter both our sensory world and our perceptual world. The aging process influences our perceptual world through changes in personality, life experiences, expectations, wisdom, brain functioning, and the nervous systems.

IX. Current research in the field of sensation and perception suggests that the emphasis has shifted from pure research to applied research. That is, the field is now more concerned with practical, useful applications of knowledge than in the past.

  A. Current research on the sense of smell is a good example of this point.

   1. Investigations into the relationship between the sense of smell and human memory are ongoing.

   2. The relatively new field of evolutionary psychology reports evidence that odor may be involved in human interaction, attraction, and mate selection.

   3. Aromatherapy, long ignored by the scientific community as lacking in scientific merit, is now the subject of scholarly research.

  B. Greater understanding of how our sensory systems operate is leading to improvements in the field of sensory prosthesis, including such devices as cochlear implants and retinal chips.

C. Real-time, high-tech, brain-imaging techniques provide insights into how different parts of the brain cooperate and coordinate in the creation of perceptions.

D. The study of cultural differences in perception takes on considerable practical significance in light of the move toward a global economy.

Suggested Reading:

Lippa, *Introduction to Social Psychology* (2nd ed.), chapter 4.

Questions to Consider:

1. Do you think the halo effect is a universal human trait, or is it more likely to be a cultural phenomenon?

2. Can you devise a standard formula for making a good first impression that would apply to all cultures?

Lecture Twenty-Four—Transcript
Perception of Other People/Course Summary

Hello, and welcome to Lecture Twenty-Four. Lecture Twenty-Four is different from the previous lectures in two ways. First of all, it is our last lecture—metaphorically speaking, the end of the trail.

Another way that it differs is that I have two rather different instructional goals for Lecture Twenty-Four. One of these is to share with you some information about another important human perceptual ability—our ability to perceive other people, which turns out to be perhaps more complicated than you might expect. The other instructional goal for Lecture Twenty-Four is to provide you with a brief overview of the entire course, and then in the time remaining I will share with you some examples of current research in the field of sensation and perception.

As you may recall, in the last lecture, Lecture Twenty-Three, we talked about the visual agnosias—these tragic but fascinating examples of visual dysfunction that come about following focal damage to different regions of visual association cortex, and as I just mentioned, we're about to discuss people perception.

Let me tell you that people perception is an active process. Our perception of other people is in no way similar to our serving as a photographic paper that somebody prints his image on. We are actively involved making inferences. We make inferences about the intentions of people, their motives, their personality, their emotional state, what their goal is in this interaction with us—and these inferences can actually color our perception of what these people do. In other words, sometimes our inferences lead to a self-fulfilling prophecy. We perceive a person as being arrogant, and we treat that person as if he were arrogant, and he in turn acts arrogant, actually as a result of the way we have treated him

Sometimes these inferences that we form about other people are from previous information or previous knowledge that we have about them. For instance—this is hypothetical, of course—if you were to read in the newspaper that Jane Fonda has just adopted a Rwandan orphan—a baby from Rwanda—and you are perhaps a Vietnam veteran who remembers the Hanoi Jane years and has negative feelings toward Jane Fonda, you're going to make the inference that there she is, using a kid to have her name in the paper—how terrible.

On the other hand, if you have positive previous feelings toward Jane Fonda because she comes from an illustrious acting family, and maybe you think that she's a humanitarian, then you're going to say, "What a wonderful thing she's doing." In neither case do you know for sure what her motives are, but your intentions actually create emotions in you. If you have the belief that she has negative goals here, using the child for her own betterment, you'll feel one way; if you think she's acting in a humanitarian fashion, you'll feel the other way, and in neither case do you know for sure.

Another example of our forming impressions and assuming intentions about somebody's motives that we really can't know anything about is if you're in the hallway at work and you see two men walking in front of you, and one leans over and says something to the other, and the other one begins to laugh uproariously. You look closer, and you see that one is the boss and the other is just a worker, and you think to yourself, "There's old so-and-so sucking up to the boss by laughing at his bad jokes." You don't know that that's what happened at all. If you were to look and see that these men were co-workers, you might say, "So-and-so must have just told a funny story. I wish I would have heard it." So our inferences are coloring our perceptions in the absence of any firm data.

Okay now, if you have not had previous experience with somebody—so you don't know anything about these two men, or you don't know anything about Jane Fonda—if we're meeting somebody for the first time, where do these inferences come from? We make inferences based on our first impression of the individual. This is one of the reasons that they say first impressions are so important, because somebody is forming inferences about you based on their first impression of you.

Sometimes these first impressions come about because of some faulty belief that we may have. For instance, suppose that somewhere in your past you developed the belief that people who have a moustache are egotistical. Well then, the first time you meet somebody with a moustache, he is at a disadvantage, because you've already formed the impression that this is an egotistical person.

Your ego involvement in your first impressions, can actually color your interpretation of what people do. Our perceptions can be altered by our first impressions, and by these inferences that we make, and once we make an inference about somebody, it's hard for him or her to overcome it, and it's hard for us to acknowledge we made a mistake.

I think in this instance, I will share a true story with you. When I was 25 years old, somewhere I had picked up the belief that if somebody speaks slowly, they probably think slowly, and if somebody speaks rapidly, they probably think rapidly, so the upshot is that I thought people who spoke rapidly were smarter than people who spoke slowly.

After I earned my Ph.D. I spent a two-year post-doctoral fellowship in a very well equipped laboratory. In fact, this laboratory provided the post-doctoral fellows with two technicians, and we would use these technicians if we ran into an instrumentation problem or an electronics problem or some kind of an experimental design problem or what have you. It turns out that one of these technicians spoke rather slowly, and the other one spoke rapidly. So whenever I encountered a problem, I would seek out the technician who spoke rapidly, and I would tell him my problem, and he'd say, "Yeah, I can fix that," and he would go to work on it. It turns out that on a couple of occasions he didn't understand the nature of the problem as well as I had hoped he would, and I said, "Gee, I must not have explained that properly." I took the blame myself. There were also times when his solution to the problem didn't work out as effectively as I hoped that it would, and I would say to myself, "Gosh, I guess this problem is a trickier problem than I had anticipated." I was so reluctant to change my initial inference that this guy was smarter than the other technician, that I was making excuses for him—I didn't explain it well enough, the problem was too difficult.

Then there came a time when I needed technical help, and this gentleman was out sick or—I don't remember why he wasn't there. So I went to the slow-talking technician, and he seemed to catch on rather rapidly, he repeated back to me what he heard me say as to the nature of the problem, and he said, "Let me think about it." He went off, he came back later, and he said, "I think this is the solution that will work for you." It worked beautifully, and I realized that I had been hurting myself by this faulty impression I had about people's intelligence being related in any way to the speed with which they spoke. This gentleman apparently spoke slowly because he was very thoughtful. So sometimes those first impressions can be detrimental to us.

Let me make two points about first impressions. One, don't be wedded to your first impression because it may be wrong, and the easier it is for you to accept this, the better it will be for you. Two, if you were the person having a first impression made about you, do your best to make a good first impression, because there are some situations where you can't make a second impression. For example, you only have one first date, so make a good first impression. You only have one first job interview with a company, so make that job interview good. You only have a first interview with a condo board or a co-op board if you're applying to buy a condo or a co-op, and there's a screening committee.

I tell all of my students, undergraduate and graduate, when they complete their degree work and go off on the job market, I gently give them advice about the importance of making a good first impression. Some of them are remarkably stubborn, and they say, "No way. I'm not having a haircut and new clothes. If they can't see how wonderful I am as I am, then they don't deserve me." I know one guy who didn't find what he deserved for a number of years until he finally had a haircut and some good clothes.

Now, in addition to the problem of making a first impression that turns out to be incorrect, there are some other common perceptual errors that we make in our judgments of other people. These perceptual errors are so common that they have their own names. Let me talk about some of these perceptual errors.

The first one is called the halo effect. This is our tendency to form an overall positive impression of somebody because we know one positive thing about them. For example, if we know somebody is a good actor, is this any reason to vote for him or her for president or for governor? Yet that sometimes seems to happen. Let me share with you some other instances of people apparently forming overall positive impressions of somebody from a single positive trait, and then being shocked and startled and perhaps even outraged when the person turns out not to be as perfect across the board as they were in the trait that originally attracted you to them.

Take the case of Pete Rose, "Charlie Hustle," in baseball. He'll never be in the Hall of Fame now because he gambled. He gambled on sports. He gambled on baseball. That's not necessarily bad, but the fact that he was such a superb athlete raised people's expectations. They had higher standards for him across the board. That's an example of the halo effect. More recently we have Lance Armstrong, perhaps one of the greatest bicyclists that has ever participated in the sport, and he left his wife and child for Sheryl Crow, and some people were outraged, outraged. Well, Hollywood movie stars do that kind of thing weekly, and nobody says or does anything too much about it, but we had these high expectations of Lance Armstrong because he was such a superb athlete.

Let me share one more example. This one took place about 30 years ago at a well known university that shall be nameless. The selection committee for commencement speakers had the idea that it would be a good thing to invite Roy Rogers, the "King of the Cowboys," "the singing cowboy with the white hat," and Roy Rogers graciously accepted. So he went to commencement, and I'm sure he acquitted himself well. I don't remember exactly what he said, but you could summarize it very quickly, "Howdy folks. I really don't know what I'm doing here, but I wish you well." Just because somebody is the "King of the Cowboys" doesn't necessarily mean that he's the right person for all situations.

Another perceptual error that occurs quite frequently is called the logical error. This is where we make the mistake of assuming that certain personality traits necessarily go together. Let me give you a true example. Social psychologists have studied this and find that many people believe if an individual is polite, that also means that individual is friendly, honest, and intelligent. Now the fact of the matter is that some people who are polite are friendly, intelligent and honest, but some people who are polite aren't. In fact, some con men will use their politeness to lull you into a false sense of security. They will use this logical error to pull a fast one on you. So we need to be careful about assuming that certain personality traits necessarily go together.

The last common perceptual error in the perception of other people is called the central tendency error. This is the tendency we have to overlook the variability in people's behaviors, and see them as more consistent than they really are. I will share another personal example. In 1982 I realized that the income tax forms had become too complicated for me and I started going to a tax preparer. This young man that I hooked up with was about my age and seemed very friendly. He was congenial and he seemed a really honest, straight shooter. If he was unsure about a deduction, or office at home deductions, or employee business expense deductions, whatever, he would look it up because he didn't want to go afoul of the letter of the law. I was impressed with his straightforwardness and his honesty, and over the years we became friendly enough that we discussed things besides income tax. It turns out we were both tennis players, and we agreed to meet and play tennis. The guy made bad line calls. I was appalled. At first I thought it was an accident, or maybe he had a visual impairment, and so once I even said—well meaningly, I said, "You know, if the ball hits the line it's good," and he said, "That ball didn't hit the line." Well, it did. So where I was setting myself up for a big disappointment was in thinking that since this guy was scrupulously honest in preparing incomes taxes, that he might well be scrupulously honest in making line calls in tennis—no.

Another instance of misperceiving the variability in a person's behavior occurred when I was a young married. I lived in a neighborhood with other young married couples, and we would have backyard barbecues and what have you. One of the neighbors was a policeman, but it took a while to find this out because he was very quiet, and he didn't call attention to himself. His young wife who weighed about half what he weighed would boss him around. "Go bring the chair. Do this. Do that." We didn't have a clue what he did for a living, and we were quite surprised to find out he was a policeman. I was even more surprised to see him in action in the city one day in a police episode where I heard him being loud and aggressive and dominant. I couldn't believe it was the same guy. So we need to be aware that people are perhaps not as consistent as we think they are, and not expect too much consistency and be shocked when we don't see it. This inconsistency actually tends to make people a little more interesting than you think they are.

Another dimension that can cause us to err in our perception of other people, believe it or not, is their degree of physical attractiveness. Now, you see, we have all kinds of expressions. We say, "Beauty is only skin deep," or "Don't judge a book by its cover," but the fact of the matter is—and there is a wealth of data to support this—that we do judge people—their behavior and their competence—by their physical attractiveness, and this tendency to judge people by their physical attractiveness starts pretty young.

Observers in kindergarten classes have seen that even at that relatively young age children behave toward and respond toward each other on the basis of physical attractiveness, and elementary school teachers do the same thing. If a physically attractive child and a physically unattractive child engage in the same inappropriate behavior, the physically unattractive child is much more likely to be labeled as a "problem child" by the teacher, whereas for the attractive child, the teacher is likely to say, "This behavior is an aberration, and this is atypical of this child." This tendency to judge people by their physical attractiveness seems to continue for the rest of our lives.

In a fairly recent study at a university with a well known MBA program, some researchers looked through the yearbooks. They had all the pictures of MBA graduates over a rather long period of time, and then they had an independent panel of judges go through these yearbooks and rate the yearbook pictures on the basis of physical attractiveness. So they now had rating, a ranking, from very physically attractive to average to relatively unattractive. Then they sent out a survey to all these MBA graduates, finding out where they were working and what their title was. One of the pieces of information that this survey requested was, "What's your salary?" Then they did a correlation of the ratings of physical attractiveness and the salary, and what they found was that the physically attractive MBAs were on the average making $12,000 a year more than the less physically attractive MBAs. Well, no further discussion of that is needed.

Another factor that can contribute to our perception of other people is cultural differences. Cultures inculcate their members with certain beliefs and attitudes and opinions. What's an appropriate thing to eat? What's an appropriate thing to say? What's an appropriate thing to wear? Cultural conditioning starts so young and it's so pervasive that you think you were born that way, and you think the way your culture does it is the only way to do it. We've talked already about one example of cultural differences that can lead to misperceptions. Let me just review it briefly—direct eye contact. In our culture we tell people, "If you want to make a good impression, look this person right in the eye, because that will tell them that you're not hiding anything, that you're honest and forthright and direct and truthful." In the Japanese culture, of course, they're taught not to make direct eye contact because that is rude and intrusive and overly aggressive. So these two cultures with their different cultural conditioning can come away with misperceptions of each other.

Another cultural factor that can contribute to our perception of other people is the dimension of personal space. Different cultures teach their members that there are different appropriate personal spaces to respect with regard to other people. When you're talking to a casual acquaintance or a stranger, how far away from this person must you be to feel comfortable? Or when you enter an elevator and there is room, how far do you stand from the other people? It seems that everybody has an idea of how far they should stand because in an elevator everybody sorts themselves out so that they're equidistant from everybody else.

Well, this personal space turns out to have a cultural basis. We are taught what the appropriate cultural personal space is with regard to other people. For example, in the United States, personal space from either a stranger or a very, very casual acquaintance for having a conversation is about three feet. In Sweden researchers report that the appropriate personal space distance for a stranger or casual conversation with somebody that you barely know is four feet. In the Arab countries the preferred personal space is less than an arm's length away. In fact, there is an expression in Arabic that you really can't have a meaningful conversation with somebody unless you can feel the breath of the other person on your face.

Now imagine a conversation between a Swede and an Arab. So here they are conversing, and the Swede is backing up because his personal space is four feet, and the Arab is coming forward because his preferred personal space is less than an arm's length away. What are their perceptions of each other? Well, the Arab is thinking, "What a cold, aloof, unfriendly person this is," and, of course, the Swede is thinking, "What a rude, pushy, intrusive person this is." What they are both doing is acting according to their cultural conditioning.

There's another aspect of cultural conditioning that can lead to misperceptions and misunderstandings that can be quite serious. I'm talking now about the difference between coming from a high-context culture and a low-context culture. This has to do with the importance of body language and non-verbals in a spoken conversation. In a high-context culture, the body language and non-verbals are every bit as important as the spoken words in correctly perceiving the intent of this message. In low-context cultures the words stand on their own, and non-verbals and body language are relatively unimportant.

The Mediterranean region and the Middle East have a lot of high-context societies. Examples of low-context societies would be England and the United States. Italy is a high-context society, and I've heard people say that, for instance, an Italian can't talk if he has his hands in his pockets. We can test that right now. Well, that turned out to be true.

Let's talk about a more serious example of high-context and low-context cultures misperceiving each other. Let's go back to January 9, 1991. The government of Iraq sent a delegation to meet with Secretary of State James Baker. The delegation from Iraq included one of Saddam Hussein's half brothers and Tariq Aziz, the Deputy Prime Minister for Iraq. Now, we don't know, of course, what was said, but the United States is a low-context culture, and American diplomats are the lowest of the low context. So we can imagine that Secretary of State Baker invited the people to be seated, offered them coffee or tea, and made sure they were comfortable. When he sat down to discuss business, the message that he delivered was, "Please tell Mr. Hussein that if he does not withdraw his troops from Kuwait, we will launch a military attack against him."

The meeting broke up, and the delegation goes back to Iraq, and Saddam's half brother said, "It was just words. He wasn't angry. He didn't stomp. He didn't pound the table. He didn't point. They won't do anything." In fact, that was a tragic misperception that led, at least in part, to the Persian-Gulf War that resulted in the loss of 100,000 lives.

There are other examples of cultural differences in perception, but I think I need to go on with some of my other instructional objectives for the course, so let's let that suffice.

I promised you a course overview. I had three instructional goals for this course. One, I wanted to expose you to enough sensory physiology that you could understand how our receptors take various forms of physical energy from the world around us—light or sound or chemical senses or touch or whatever—and translate it into a language that the brain understands to send to the brain. That was one of my instructional goals.

Another instructional goal was to give you some insight into how the brain takes this sense data provided by our sensory systems and integrates it with memories from our previous experiences with the same or with similar sense experiences and creates our perceptions for it is our perceptions that form our reality. We behave in the world not according to what is really, really physically out there, but what our perceptions tell us is out there.

My third instructional goal was to share with you ways in which the aging process can actually change our sensory world and our perceptual world. The aging process can change our sensory world because it brings about actual physical changes in the sensory receptors and in their ability to respond accurately to physical stimuli and to the same range of physical stimuli that these receptors responded to when we were younger. The aging process can change our perceptions in that as we age there is a tendency to show personality changes, and personality influences perception. We have a new set of life experiences that can also influence our perception. It's possible that on the way through aging we have acquired some wisdom, and wisdom, for example, also changes our perception.

Let me just interject here. We were talking earlier about how physical attractiveness can influence our perception of other people's behaviors and competence and what have you. The elderly are somewhat less prone to make that error. The older we become the more likely we are to behave as though beauty really is skin deep. This is what I mean by the possibility of acquiring wisdom as we age.

Another age-related change that can influence perception is that our nervous systems are going to undergo certain changes that prevent them from carrying information as rapidly as they did when we were younger, so we're obtaining less precise information from our sensory systems, and we take that into account in our approach to the world. We become more conservative in our approach to the world.

I also had a fourth instructional goal that I never really verbalized. I'll tell you now. I wanted us to have some fun during these 24 lectures, because my personal belief is that teaching and learning are not incompatible with having fun. I know I've had some fun, and I hope that you have too.

Now, in the time remaining let me talk a bit about some current trends in research in the area of sensation and perception. First, a general statement—over my years in the field I have seen a trend where research is becoming more and more practical and useful and applied. There were periods not too long ago when the more esoteric and theoretical your research was, the more prestige you had in the field. But research in sensation and perception is now showing a very practical applied useful orientation, and I think that's really a good thing because discoveries in sensation and perception have the potential to be very useful to people.

Actually, current research on smell is a good example of this applied trend. Several laboratories are continuing to study the relationship between changes in smell sensitivity and memory loss, especially as it accompanies the senile dementias such as Alzheimer's. Remember, at the present time there is a scratch-and-sniff test that is 80% accurate in detecting people who are about to start showing memory loss associated with Alzheimer's disease. Researchers think they can do better, so they are trying to devise tests that measure various aspects of smell sensitivity, which will give a better accuracy rate than 80% in predicting cognitive declines.

The relatively new field of evolutionary psychology is also pursuing studies of the sense of smell. They're interested in the role of smell and the mother-child bonding process. They're interested in smell as it relates to mate selection. They're interested in smell as it relates to other areas of human interaction—again, personal and useful and important information.

The mainstream scientific community is also beginning to recognize that aromatherapy isn't going to go away, and people are going to maintain their interest in it, so it would be a public service to provide people with objectively obtained research data about what aromatherapy can do and cannot do.

In a different area, sensory and perceptual research on prosthetic devices for deaf and blind people is making great strides. For instance, the current generation of cochlear implants for the deaf— by the use of miniaturized speech synthesizers—is providing the real opportunity for the perception of words. Previous cochlear implants simply gave people wearing them some information about the rhythm and cadence of a speaker's voice which aided in lip reading, but now there is actually the possibility of perceiving words by virtue of the new technology.

Research is currently going on regarding retinal chip implants to provide visual experiences to totally blind people. This is very exciting. They're soliciting for subjects across the country now for a project that is going to be under way very quickly.

The interdisciplinary field of cognitive neuroscience is making use of advances in some of these high tech brain imaging techniques to study online phenomena such as automaticity, which we talked about earlier, and to study complex visual perceptions without waiting for some poor soul to suffer a visual agnosia and permit himself or herself to be studied.

Regarding cultural differences in perception, as we move more toward a global economy, people are much more interested in cultural differences in perception to try and head off misunderstandings or behaviors that rub somebody else the wrong way because of their cultural background.

Well, I guess I've about run out of time. I want to tell you that I've enjoyed sharing these 24 lectures with you, and I hope that you have enjoyed them too. Thank you very much.

Glossary

A-delta fibers: Rapidly conducting nerve fibers that carry information from encapsulated end organs in the skin to the central nervous system.

accommodation: The ability of the lens of the eye to alter its focal properties by changing its shape.

active touch: Exploration and identification of objects in the environment through actively touching them.

air conductive hearing: Auditory experiences resulting from sound waves transmitted from the eardrum through the ossicles to the cochlea.

Alzheimer's disease: A form of senile dementia resulting in widespread neural degeneration in the brain, an early sign being memory loss.

anosmia: Inability to perceive odors.

aphasia: A disorder of the associative aspects of language.

arcus senilis: An opaque ring just inside the border between the cornea and the sclerotic coat, usually apparent by the mid- to late 60s.

automaticity: The process by which repetition and practice permits an individual to perform a coordinated sequence of motor movements without conscious thought.

axon: The elongated portion of a neuron that transmits the action potential from the cell body to the terminal end branches.

Ayurvedic medicine: The holistic system of health care that was in use in India 10,000 years ago and is still in use today.

basilar membrane: The flexible membrane located in the cochlea upon which the auditory hair cells are located.

bed spins: A vestibular phenomenon experienced by individuals who drink too much alcohol and lie on their backs in bed.

behaviorism: The school of psychology founded by John B. Watson around 1913 that stated that the subject matter of psychology should be behavior, not the mind.

binocular depth cues: Depth cues that depend on the simultaneous use of both eyes.

blindsight: The ability, following damage to the visual cortex, to point to an object in the visual field with no awareness of seeing it.

blind spot: A small area on each retina where the receptors are pushed aside by the optic nerve leaving the eyeball on its way to the brain.

bone conductive hearing: The perception of sound through vibrations in the temporal bone that are transmitted directly to the cochlea without the involvement of the eardrum and ossicles.

Broca's area: The brain region in the left (usually) frontal lobe necessary for the expression of speech.

C fibers: The small-diameter, slow-conducting nerve fibers that transmit pain information from the free nerve endings to the central nervous system.

cataracts: Clouding of the lens of the eye, usually due to aging.

central tendency error: The perceptual error of seeing people as more consistent than they actually are.

cerebral cortex: The outer mantle of cell bodies that covers the subcortical parts of the brain.

choroid coat: The retinal layer at the back of the eye that absorbs stray light.

cochlea: The bony inner-ear structure that contains the auditory receptors.

conductive hearing loss: Hearing loss caused by interruption or dampening of sound waves before they reach the receptors.

cones: The centrally located visual receptors responsible for detailed color vision in normal levels of illumination.

critical flicker frequency (CFF): The highest rate of visual flicker an individual can perceive before the flicker turns into a steady light.

decibel (dB): A unit of pressure used to measure sound waves.

deep pain: Dull, aching, throbbing pain.

determinism: The basic assumption of science asserting our belief in a lawful universe where cause and effect are in operation.

echolocation: The ability to locate objects in space by emitting high-frequency pulses and using the two ears to sense the location in space from which the object reflects back those pulses.

encapsulated end organs: The general term used to refer to the various types of cutaneous receptors found in the skin.

endorphins: Morphine-like substances produced in the brain that can have analgesic effects.

forebrain: A subcortical brain region involved in emotional reactivity and the expression of the primary drives.

fovea: The central portion of the retina that contains only cones and has the greatest visual acuity.

free nerve endings: The primitive receptors in the skin (and other regions of the body) primarily responsible for pain sensations.

gate-control theory: Melzack and Wall's theory that our perception of pain is determined by the ratio of A-delta to C fibers that a stimulus excites.

Gestalt psychology: An early school of psychology that is best remembered today for its phenomenological approach to perception and perceptual organization.

glaucoma: A medical condition in which increased fluid pressure in the eyeball can damage the retinal elements and the optic nerve.

Golgi organs: Receptors in the tendons that respond to the amount of tension generated by a contracting muscle.

halo effect: The tendency to form an overall positive impression of someone from a single positive trait.

hertz (Hz): A unit of measurement for the number of cycles a sound wave (or any continuous wave) completes in one second.

hindbrain: The primitive portion of the brain that controls vital functions, such as breathing and heart rate.

hippocampus: A forebrain structure known to be involved in the consolidation of short-term memory into long-term memory.

infrared: The portion of the electromagnetic energy spectrum just above the red end of the visible spectrum, invisible to the human eye.

inner ear: The cochlea, semicircular canals, utricle, and saccule.

intra-aural muscles: The two tiny muscles located in the middle ear, known as the stapedius and the tensor tympani muscles.

kinesthetic sense: The sense that responds to the position and motion of our limbs.

Krause end bulbs: One of the encapsulated end organs in the skin, thought to respond to cold.

learned taste aversion: The tendency for humans and other animals to develop an aversion to a taste that is temporally contiguous with feelings of illness, even if the taste is unrelated to the illness.

ligaments: The tough connective tissue that attaches bones together at a joint.

lobes of the brain: The human brain is composed of the frontal, parietal, occipital, and temporal lobes.

logical error: A perceptual error resulting from the faulty belief that certain personality traits (such as politeness and honesty) always go together.

long wavelengths of light: Colors located toward the red end of the visible spectrum.

macular degeneration: Degeneration in the central 5 mm of the retina that surrounds and includes the fovea.

McClintock effect: The phenomenon whereby college coeds who live on the same dormitory floor frequently have menstrual periods that start around the same time.

Meissner corpuscle: An encapsulated end organ in the skin that responds to touch.

midbrain: Subcortical brain region responsible for reflex orientation to sensory stimuli.

middle ear: The air-filled space between the eardrum and cochlea, containing the ossicles and the intra-aural muscles.

monocular depth cues: Depth cues, such as those used by artists in a painting, that can be perceived with one eye.

muscle spindles: Receptors located in muscles that respond to the degree of contraction.

myopia: Nearsightedness; an inability to see distant objects clearly due to a focal error in the eye.

object identification: The higher-order aspect of visual perception requiring the integrity of the visual cortex.

object location: The lower-order aspect of visual perception mediated by neural circuits in the midbrain.

olfactory bulbs: Structures located under the frontal lobes that receive information from the smell receptors.

olfactory epithelium: The area of tissue at the top of the nasal cavity, measuring 2.5 square centimeters, where the smell receptors are located.

olivocochlear bundle: A bundle of nerve fibers going from the central nervous system back to the auditory receptors in the cochlea, thought to be involved in selective attention.

optical instruments of the eye: The cornea and the lens are the optical instruments of the eye.

optic tectum: The midbrain region responsible for reflex orientation to abrupt changes in the visual field.

ossicles: The chain of three tiny bones in the middle ear known as the malleus, incus, and stapes.

otitis media: A middle-ear infection.

otoliths: The tiny calcium carbonate particles found in the utricle and saccule.

otosclerosis: A hereditary condition resulting in partial or complete immobilization of the stapes.

ototoxic drugs: Drugs that can be harmful to auditory and vestibular hair cells.

outer ear: The portion of the auditory system from the ear to the eardrum.

Pacinian corpuscle: One of the encapsulated end organs in the skin, known to be sensitive to pressure and vibrations.

passive touch: The situation in which a person remains passive while tactile stimulation is applied to the skin.

perceptual world: The meaning that a sensory array has for a particular individual as a result of that individual's unique history with that or a similar stimulus array.

perilymph: The liquid having the consistency of blood that fills the cochlea and the semicircular canals.

personal space: In public situations, the distance maintained from another person or persons with which one feels most comfortable.

phenylketonuria: An inherited metabolic disorder that can cause retardation; PKU produces a characteristic odor in those who have it.

phenylthiocarbamide (PTC): A synthetic substance that some people (called *tasters*) can taste and others (called *nontasters*) cannot.

phenylthylamine (PEA): A substance found in chocolate and thought to contribute to chocolate cravings.

pheromones: Odorous chemicals released by some species that produce physiological responses in conspecifics.

phonemes: The smallest distinguishable utterances in a language.

phonemic perceptual maps: Dedicated connections between auditory receptors and cells in the auditory cortex are created in children who repeatedly hear phonemes spoken by caregivers, with each phoneme having a different spatial location in the auditory cortex.

pigment epithelium: The retinal layer containing the blood supply that provides nutrients for the receptors.

placebo effect: The ability of an inert substance to reduce symptoms if the recipient believes in its efficacy.

plasticity: The ability of the brain to compensate for damage.

presbycusis: A progressive loss of hearing for high frequencies as a function of age.

presbyopia: A deficit in near vision resulting from age-related loss of elasticity and accommodation.

prosopagnosia: A form of visual agnosia characterized by an inability to recognize human faces.

pyramidal tracts: The nerve fiber bundles that carry instructions from the motor cortex to the peripheral muscles.

rods: The visual receptors mediating noncolor vision in dim light.

ruffini cylinders: One of the encapsulated end organs in the skin thought to be sensitive to warm stimuli.

saccule: Part of the vestibular system found under the semicircular canals; a protuberance, slightly smaller than the utricle, that responds to changes in the head's orientation.

semicircular canals: The portion of the vestibular system that responds to angular acceleration and deceleration.

sensorineural hearing loss: Hearing loss due to damage or degeneration of receptors and/or auditory nerve fibers.

sensory supporting structures: Structures such as the ossicles or the hairs on the skin that make a stimulus more accessible to the sensory receptors.

sensory suppression: The inability to perceive both of two touch stimuli delivered simultaneously to different body areas.

sensory world: Those portions of the physical environment to which an organism's sensory receptors are responsive.

short wavelengths of light: The blue-violet end of the visible spectrum.

specific gravity: The weight of an object in air divided by the weight of an equal volume of water.

speed of light: The speed of light is 186,000 miles per second.

speed of sound: The speed of sound is approximately 1,110 feet per second in air at normal atmospheric pressures.

stria vascularis: The highly vascularized tissue layer inside the cochlea that appears to act as a DC battery, amplifying the electrical output of the hair cells.

substantia gelatinosa: A nucleus in the dorsal horn of the spinal cord, proposed as the "gate" in the gate-control theory of pain.

superficial pain: "Bright," sharp, surface pain.

"sweet-tooth" phenomenon: Refers to the unlearned preference for the taste of sweet seen in humans and many other species.

sylvian sulcus (or sylvian fissure): The upper boundary of the temporal lobe.

taste bud: A goblet-shaped cluster of cells below the surface of the tongue.

taste papilla: One of the visible bumps on the surface of the tongue, surrounded by moat-like trenches containing the taste buds.

taste receptor: Each of the 10,000 taste buds on the tongue contains a taste receptor.

tectorial membrane: A stiff membrane in the cochlea against which the auditory hair cells rub when vibrations from sound waves are initiated in the basilar membrane.

tendons: Strong bands of connective tissue that attach muscles to bones.

traditional Chinese medicine (TCM): A holistic health care system used in China for more than 5,000 years, which includes acupuncture as a component.

tympanic membrane: The technical term for the eardrum.

ultraviolet: The frequency of electromagnetic energy just below the blue-violet end of the visible spectrum, invisible to the human eye.

utricle: Part of the vestibular system found under the semicircular canals; a protuberance, somewhat larger than the saccule, that responds to changes in the head's orientation.

visible spectrum: That portion of the electromagnetic energy spectrum visible to the human eye, ranging from approximately 400 nm to 700 nm.

visual agnosia: A condition usually caused by brain injury in which different aspects of the visual field are unrecognizable to the individual.

Wernicke's area: A brain region in the upper portion of the left temporal lobe important for speech comprehension.

Biographical Notes

Tiffany Field, Ph.D., University of Massachusetts, 1976, developmental psychology. Founded the Touch Research Institute (TRI) at the University of Miami School of Medicine in 1992, where she remains as director. Dr. Field studies the relationship between touch and health (both physical and psychological health). She is well known for her studies of high-risk infants.

Eleanor Gibson (1910–2002), Ph.D., Yale, 1938, psychology. Studied perceptual development in children and is best known for her work with the *visual cliff*, demonstrating that babies can perceive depth. In 1992, Dr. Gibson became one of only 10 psychologists to be awarded the National Medal of Science.

Harry Harlow (1905–1981), Ph.D., Stanford, 1930, psychology. Best known for his primate work at the University of Wisconsin, where he demonstrated that infant monkeys deprived of tactile stimulation became socially incompetent, showing behaviors similar to autism. Harlow's early studies of what has come to be called "mother love" led to later investigations of the importance of tactile stimulation for human infants.

Herman von Helmholtz (1821–1894), M.D., Medical Institute of Berlin, 1843. Helmholtz had many interests but focused on the role of the sense organs as mediators of experience in the synthesis of knowledge. He published articles on physiological optics and physiological acoustics. He invented the ophthalmoscope and was the first to measure the speed of conduction of nerve impulses. Helmholtz's theories of color vision and auditory frequency analysis turned out to be correct in many respects.

Heinrich Hertz (1857–1894), Ph.D., University of Berlin, 1880, physics, under Hermann von Helmholtz. Professor Hertz was the first person to demonstrate the existence of electromagnetic radiation and the first to produce and broadcast radio waves. The unit of measurement for cycles per second (CPS) was changed to Hertz (Hz) to honor the memory of Dr. Hertz, a physicist who was also an enthusiastic linguist, learning Arabic and Sanskrit.

Martha McClintock (1947–), Ph.D., University of Pennsylvania, 1974, psychology. Currently professor of psychology and director of the Institute for Mind and Biology at the University of Chicago. Best known for her study of menstrual synchronicity among college women living on the same dormitory floor. The existence of human pheromones was first confirmed in Dr. McClintock's laboratory in 1998. Prior to this, pheromones were thought to exist only in the animal world.

Ronald Melzack (1929–), Ph.D., McGill, 1954, psychology. Presently Professor Emeritus at McGill. While a faculty member at MIT in 1959, he began a collaboration with Dr. Patrick Wall that resulted in the gate-control theory of pain. This theory has had a great impact on the field of pain and has resulted in Dr. Melzack receiving numerous international awards for his scholarly contributions.

George Wald (1906–1987), Ph.D., Columbia, 1932, zoology. Nobel laureate in medicine (1967) for his work on physiological and chemical processes in the eye. A pioneer in the measurement of the spectral sensitivity of the cone visual pigments.

John B. Watson (1887–1958), Ph.D., University of Chicago, 1903, psychology. Founded the school of psychology known as behaviorism at Johns Hopkins University in 1913. Watson used the method of Pavlovian conditioning to gain insights into human behavior. He left Johns Hopkins in 1920 to go into advertising and retired in 1945 as vice president of the William Esty Agency.

Carl Wernicke (1848–1905), M.D., University of Breslau, Poland. Dr. Wernicke described the symptoms now referred to as receptive aphasia. These symptoms include loss of comprehension of spoken language, although hearing remains intact. The affected person may retain the ability to speak fluently, although his or her speech has no understandable meaning or syntax. Damage to the brain in the superior portion of the left temporal lobe is responsible for the condition. This part of the brain is now called Wernicke's area.

Max Wertheimer (1880–1943), Ph.D., University of Wurzburg, 1904, psychology. Worked on the fundamentals of Gestalt psychology from 1910 to 1914. A basic idea was that our perceptions have properties not predicted from the sensations comprising them. That is, perceptions do not have a one-to-one correspondence with sensory stimulation. Many known perceptual phenomena can be traced back to the studies of the Gestalt psychologists.

Bibliography

Readings:

Ackerman, D. *A Natural History of the Senses*. New York: Vintage, 1990. This is an absolutely fascinating piece of literature. I regularly recommend it to friends, colleagues, and students.

Backhaus, W. G. K., R. Kliegl, and J. S. Werner, eds. *Color Vision: Perspectives from Different Disciplines*. New York: Walter de Gruyter, 1998. An edited volume that treats the subject of color vision from the perspectives of art, psychology, physiology, genetics, and philosophy.

Bloom, F., A. Lazerson, and L. Hofstadter. *Brain, Mind, and Behavior*. New York: Freeman, 1985. This book takes the stance that the mind is explainable in terms of the interactions among the brain's component parts. Chapter 4 is especially relevant for our purposes.

Bregman, A. S. *Auditory Scene Analysis*. Cambridge: M.I.T. Press, 1990. A challenging but worthwhile experience for those seriously interested in music perception. This long and detailed book provides a summary of the research on the formation of auditory images.

Carlson, N. R. *Physiology of Behavior* (8th ed.). Boston: Allyn and Bacon, 2004. Dr. Carlson does an excellent job of providing current information about sensory psychology.

Colavita, F. B. *Sensory Changes in the Elderly*. Springfield: Charles C. Thomas, 1978. Although published some time ago, this book still contains readable and relevant information.

Corey, D. P., and S. D. Roper, eds. *Sensory Transduction*. New York: Rockefeller University Press, 1992. The contributors to this volume describe original research on the transduction mechanisms used by sensory receptors. Highly technical.

Corso, J. F. *Aging Sensory Systems and Perception*. New York: Prager, 1981. Although out of print, used copies can still be found. Provides practical suggestions for coping with age-related sensory and perceptual changes.

Denes, P. B., and E. N. Pinson. *The Speech Chain* (2nd ed.). New York: Freeman, 1991. This relatively short book will tell you all you want to know (and probably more) about speech production and language comprehension.

Elkins, J. *The Object Stares Back: On the Nature of Seeing.* New York: Harvest Books, 1996. This interesting book takes a nontechnical approach to "looking and seeing." Not only do we capture objects with our gaze, but our gaze is captured by objects.

Ephret, G., and R. Romand, eds. *The Central Auditory System.* New York: Oxford University Press, 1997. This edited book describes in detail the structure and function of the various divisions of the auditory system, from the cochlea to the auditory cortex. The contributors deal primarily with the auditory system of the cat.

Field, T. *Touch Therapy.* New York: Elsevier, 2000. Dr. Field, one of the most prominent researchers in the area of touch therapy, describes the many physical and mental health benefits of massage.

Filshie, Jacqueline, and Adrian White, eds. *Medical Acupuncture: A Western Approach.* Edinburgh, Scotland: Churchill Livingstone, 1998. This edited work includes contributions from Western scientists and from acupuncture practitioners. As might be expected from a Western perspective, the focus is on the analgesic rather than the purported curative properties of acupuncture.

Gazzaniga, M. *The Bisected Brain.* New York: Appleton-Century Crofts, 1970. This book is a classic in the "split brain" area, written by the foremost researcher in the field.

⸻, ed. *The New Cognitive Neurosciences.* Cambridge, MA: MIT Press, 2000. Although this edited volume contains many interesting chapters, your attention is especially directed to the excellent contribution by P. K. Kuhl.

Getchell, B. V., R. L. Doty, L. M. Bartoshuk, and J. B. Snow, eds. *Smell and Taste in Health and Disease.* New York: Raven Press, 1991. This massive work, 55 chapters from 70 contributors, deals exclusively with the senses of taste and smell! The chapters are more or less evenly divided between those dealing with normal functioning and those dealing with gustatory and olfactory disorders.

Gibson, J. J. *The Senses Considered as Perceptual Systems.* Boston: Houghton Mifflin, 1966. Dr. Gibson was an important theorist and a respected researcher in the area of human perception. His book is a classic.

Goldstein, E. B. *Sensation and Perception* (6th ed.). Pacific Grove: Wadsworth, 2002. This is the most popular sensation and perception textbook on the market, read by thousands of college students each semester. If you are going to read a sensation and perception text, this is the one.

Gregory, R. L. *Eye and Brain.* New York: McGraw-Hill, 1966. Although it is more than 40 years old, this book is still an excellent source for the understanding of many visual illusions and other visual phenomena. There is a fifth edition out, but try the old one first.

Jerome, J. *The Elements of Effort.* New York: Simon and Schuster, 1997. If you are or have ever been a runner, you will find this book of interest. The author's description of the role of the Golgi tendon organ in confidence building is unique and creative.

Kruger, L., ed. *Pain and Touch.* San Diego: Academic Press, 1996. This is a rather technical edited volume, describing psychological, neurophysiological, and psychophysical studies of touch and pain.

Laing, D. D., R. L. Doty, and W. Breipohl, eds. *The Human Sense of Smell.* New York: Springer, 1991. This volume contains a wealth of clinical data on human anosmia and other olfactory phenomena. Definitely not light reading.

Leahey, T. H. *A History of Psychology: Main Currents in Psychological Thought* (6th ed.). Upper Saddle River, NJ: Prentice Hall, 2004. If you want to learn more about Gestalt psychology and/or the historical connection between the study of sensory processes and psychology, or about some of the important historical contributors to academic psychology, this book is a fine place to start.

Lippa, Richard A. *Introduction to Social Psychology* (4th ed.). Pacific Grove: Brooks/Cole, 1994. This is a textbook of social psychology. Chapter 4 provides a good overview of the dynamics of people perception.

Mack, A., and I. Rock. *Inattentional Blindness.* Cambridge, MA: MIT Press, 1998. The authors propose and test the hypothesis that attention is necessary for visual perception. Finding supporting results, they expand the hypothesis to include other sense modalities.

Melzack, R., and P. D. Wall. *The Challenge of Pain* (rev. ed.). New York: Penguin Books, 1988. The two best-known pain researchers explore the puzzle of pain, the physiology of pain, and the treatment of pain.

Moore, B. C. J., ed. *Hearing.* San Diego, CA: Academic Press, 1995. This edited volume summarizes virtually all the areas of hearing research. Although the chapters are well written, this work is suggested for highly motivated readers.

Sacks, O. *The Man Who Mistook His Wife for a Hat.* London: Duckworth, 1985. This is an entertaining and informative book by a noted neurologist and writer. The consequences of neurological damage for perceptual processes are skillfully and sensitively described.

Sekuler, R., and R. Blake. *Perception* (4th ed.). Boston: McGraw-Hill Humanities/Social Sciences/Languages, 2002. This book describes recent contributions to the field of perception from cognitive neuroscience.

Shepard, R. N. *Mind Sights.* New York: Freeman, 1990. Dr. Shepard has created original visual illusions and ambiguous figures that he presents and explains. This book is entertaining, interesting, and informative.

Thorne, B. M., and T. Henley. *Connections in the History and Systems of Psychology* (2nd ed.). Boston: Houghton Mifflin, 2001. The authors provide interesting biographical sketches of the important historical figures in psychology.

Wall, P. D., and R. Melzack, eds. *Textbook of Pain* (3rd ed.). London: Churchill Livingstone, 1994. This book, edited by the "fathers" of modern pain research, deals with every conceivable aspect of pain.

Wright, R. D., ed. *Visual Attention.* New York: Oxford University Press, 1998. An edited volume containing chapters contributed by cognitive scientists with an interest in various aspects of visual attention. Some chapters are of general interest, while others are less so, being highly theoretical. The chapter on "change blindness" by O'Regan is especially interesting.

Internet Resources:

"AgingEye Times." This site explores problems facing the aging eye, such as glaucoma, cataract, macular degeneration, and diabetic eye disease. www.agingeye.net.

Chandler, Daniel. "Visual Perception 4." This site examines (among many other things) cultural differences in perception. Have fun! www.aber.ac.uk/media/Modules/MC10220/visper04.html.

"National Eye Institute." U.S. National Institutes of Health. This Web site includes current information about eye health, including eye disease, vision care, research results, funding, and education programs. In addition to a clinical studies database, it provides photos, images, and videos on a number of eye-related topics. www.nei.nih.gov/index.asp.

"Relief of Pain and Suffering." UCLA Louise M. Darling Biomed Library—History and Special Collections. This exhibit covers many aspects of pain, including pain pathways, pain measurement, pain alleviation, phantom limb pain, and the gate-control theory of pain. www.library.ucla.edu/libraries/biomed/his/painexhibit/index.html.

"Sensation and Perception Tutorials." Hanover College Psychology Department. Tutorials on visual phenomena are provided, including motion and depth perception and the Gestalt "laws" of perceptual organization. psych.hanover.edu/krantz/sen_tut.html.

"Serendip." Supported by Bryn Mawr College, the National Science Foundation, and the Howard Hughes Medical Institute. This site provides access to virtually any aspect of sensation and perception, including an online demonstration of the blindsight phenomenon. serendip.brynmawr.edu.